Digital Computer Theory

WILEY SERIES IN ELECTRONIC
ENGINEERING TECHNOLOGY

DIGITAL COMPUTER THEORY

Louis Nashelsky

Assistant Professor, Department of Electrical Technology
Queensborough Community College
of the City University of New York

JOHN WILEY & SONS, INC.

New York / London / Sydney

10 9 8 7

Library of Congress Catalog Card Number: 66–15867
Printed in the United States of America

to Katrin and Kira

Preface

The stimulus for writing this book developed when I first taught a digital computer course at Queensborough Community College. A good textbook with up-to-date coverage, sufficient and clear examples and numerous problems for students was not available. The material presented here is based on what was written and used at the college and improved by the many changes that were shown necessary to make the subject easier to teach. The book should, therefore, be particularly appropriate for classroom use.

The text is divided into three sections, fundamentals, computer circuits, and computer units. The fundamentals section covers basic number systems, computer codes, Boolean algebra, and machine language programming. The computer circuits section presents a detailed study of many modern computer logic circuits and computer blocks. Logic circuits covered are AND, OR, NAND, and NOR gates. The computer blocks include the basic multivibrator circuits—bistable (or flip-flop), monostable (or one-shot), and astable (or clock)—and the Schmitt trigger circuit. The section on computer units covers the memory unit, control unit, arithmetic unit, and input-output unit(s) in separate chapters.

The book contains numerous examples which highlight the important aspects of the chapters to the student. Problems are provided throughout each chapter and at the end of each chapter. This breakdown of problem presentation should allow the instructor to provide suitable problems while he is covering the material of the chapter and then to assign problems relating to the full material of the chapter after it has been completed. (Answers to selected problems are given at the end of the book. The problems for which there are answers are indicated in the text by a line beneath the number.) The text is also supported by many photographs and illustrations which should help the student in understanding digital computer theory and the instructor in presenting it.

There is sufficient material presented in the three sections for curricula in which specific sections of study are more important than others or in which some material has already been covered by a previous course. For example, in a digital computer curriculum in which computer circuits are covered separately, the material in Sections Two and Three is sufficient for another course. If the particular curriculum covers computer units in one course, the material from Chapters 3 through 8, on computer fundamentals and circuits, will provide worthwhile material for a second course. For an advanced high school program only the first section with its coverage of fundamentals may be applicable, but the many examples and problems can be used to good advantage. Another curriculum may need only the material on computer circuits and blocks (Section Two) as the basis for the major part of a course.

In essence, the amount of material provided in the book, and its sequence, is appropriate for a single computer course in a two-year college curriculum but may well be used in many different programs that exist or are developing in schools. The book is divided into sections and chapters that should help the individual instructor find the best grouping for his course or program.

I wish to express my appreciation to the many companies which sent illustrative material for the text. International Business Machines Corporation supplied many of the illustrations and photographs which are used in several chapters (most of them appear in Chapter 12). A number of other fine photographs were supplied by the Burroughs Corporation, Digital Electronics Corporation, General Electric Corporation, and the Minneapolis-Honeywell Corporation.

I should like to pay special thanks to Professor Joseph B. Aidala, head of the Electrical Technology Department at Queensborough Community College, and Professor Leon Katz of the same department for their encouragement and support in the writing of this book. I should also like to thank Mrs. Sylvia Neiman for typing the original manuscript, Mr. Nathan Blumkin for production of the original manuscript used at Queensborough Community College, and Mrs. Ellen Zawel for typing the final copy for publication.

LOUIS NASHELSKY

Bayside, New York
January 1966

Contents

SECTION III.   COMPUTER UNITS

Digital Computer Theory

0001

Introduction

1-1. General

Digital computers have become an important item of study and no doubt will grow in usage and importance. It is, therefore, essential to have an understanding of how the computer is used and how it works. Although calculating machine history can be traced back to the nineteenth century (if not earlier), the modern computer was first considered in the 1930's and actually developed only around 1950. In essence, the modern electronic digital computer has been around for only fifteen years. It seems incredible that in so short a time it could have advanced so far and become so essential a tool in scientific and business operation. There is no doubt that a combination of growth in the technological field and the need for high speed data processors and calculators have spurred development in this very short time.

Because the word "computer" is a general term, it is necessary to describe the various types of computers and specify which types are to be considered in this book. Broadly speaking, there are digital computers and analog computers. These devices are operationally quite different. The digital computer operates in a world of binary ONEs, and ZEROs (the two digits of the binary number system), manipulating these digits at fantastically high rates. Addition time in many modern computers is less than one microsecond (one-millionth of a second) for binary numbers with as many as forty digits. In other words, the computer could do a million additions per second (if it did not have to perform other information handling operations). Being able to perform arithmetic operations so quickly, the digital computer can perform càlculations on large amounts of

1

data in a short length of time.   The analog computer, on the other hand, operates in the "real world," handling electrical signals and mechanical positions which represent the physical problem being considered.   Neither general nor special-purpose analog computers can provide solution rates of much more than a few hundred cycles per second.   However, this slower rate does not necessarily mean that the analog computer is a poorer device.   Were this so, the digital computer would have quickly replaced it.   Actually, each is superior for specific applications.   In fact, in a growing number of fields a combination of analog and digital computer features is used to perform the required operation.   Hybrid computers (the term to describe the resulting functional computer unit device) are of increasing importance in certain types of problems, such as air guidance and navigation.   It is necessary to convert any analog input data into binary form and after computation reconvert the data to analog form for use in most present special-purpose digital computers. A good distinction between analog and digital computers cannot be made until more is understood about at least one of them.

Digital computers fall into two general categories, general-purpose and special-purpose computers.   A general-purpose machine is designed to be programmed to solve a large variety of technical problems.   Within a few minutes it can study some medical problem, do financial bookkeeping, study an engineering design, or play checkers with the operator.   A special-purpose machine is designed around a specific problem and is optimized to do only that type of problem.   As such it is usually smaller, cheaper, and more efficient in performing that specific task.   Two examples are production control of a refinery and guidance control of a missile or plane. Both types of digital computer are basically the same in structure. The distinctions are in specific units used to bring data into the computer and feed information out, and in the flexible steps of operation of the general-purpose as compared to the special-purpose machine.

1–2. Digital Computer System

The basic parts of any digital computer are the input unit, arithmetic unit, control unit, memory unit, and output unit.   Figure 1–1 shows a simplified block diagram indicating the many computer flow paths.   Let us consider a general-purpose machine first; the input units may be paper tape, punched card, magnetic tape, typewriter (specially adapted), or magnetic disk, to list the most common.   The input unit provides data and instructions to the computer.   To change the type of problem being solved only requires feeding a new set of instructions and data to the computer.   Each type of input device is suited to a particular use.   Punched cards may contain individual instructions or data, any one of which can be easily changed.   Each card can be used to represent a specific item or person, for example, the course card given to each student, the phone or electric bill of each customer, the item of purchase from a company, the specific items held in stock by a company, etc.   Punched cards are one of the most useful input devices for such purposes.   However, when large amounts of information are to be handled, punched cards become too slow.   Magnetic tape can provide input data at a faster rate and allows data to be updated and stored back in the same place.   Banking firms, for example, store their records on magnetic tape.   So do insurance companies, which handle the largest amount of data in the business field.   For processing

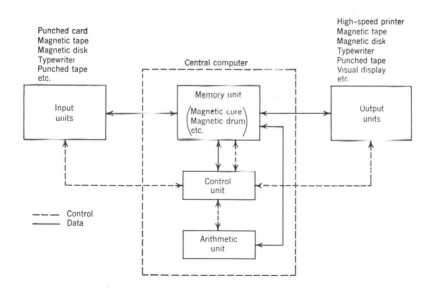

Figure 1–1.   Basic computer units, block diagram.

customers' accounts, the computer calls for the input data from the magnetic tape, performs specified operations, and puts revised data back on the tape. Considering the large number of accounts handled, magnetic tape is an essential feature of the operation. Magnetic disk files are very similar in use to magnetic tape and may be considered the same for this discussion. In the chapter on memory devices, different details of each will be considered. Typewriter input provides an easy means of telling the computer to do an operation or asking it about its various parts. It is not used for large data input but mainly for "quick talk" with the computer. As such, it is very useful. The typewriter is also useful for small programs when little time is needed in communication with the computer (as in debugging or troubleshooting operations). Punched tape can be read fast and requires less equipment and less space for data storage than punched cards. Whereas a magnetic tape can have millions of bits of data, a punched tape can be cut to a specific length (depending on the particular problem) and that piece of tape handled quite easily. A magnetic tape may store many different problems and must be handled carefully to avoid erasing the data. A paper tape may be a few inches or feet and is a permanent record. On the other hand, it cannot be updated (revised) as the magnetic tape can and is less useful in that respect.

In concluding this brief description, it should be clear that with the many types of problems to be solved and with so much data to be handled, many different input devices are needed. Each is best for a specific area of work. In fact, larger computer facilities can handle punched card as well as magnetic tape or disk and typewriter for more flexible and efficient operation.

Once data and instructions are fed into the computer, calculations may be carried out. Generally, the instructions (or program) and data are stored in the computer internal memory which is differentiated from the input device (also a memory) by its speed of operation. The internal memory is designed to handle small amounts of data but at very fast rates. The basic computer speed is often limited by the speed of the internal memory. The most popular internal memory used at present is the magnetic core memory. It can operate at a rate of one million words (data or instruction) per second, which means that it can provide words for computation and accept the answers at the rate of one million operations per second.   The storage capacity, however, has been limited until recently to only a few thousand words.   Computers are now being designed for hundreds of thousands of words of storage. Memory contents may be continually changing, as the computer takes in new data, updates the data, and then reads out the data to make space for more information.

Memory operation is controlled by a main computer unit called the "control unit."   It provides control for all computer operations and is the "heart beat" of the system.   It interprets the instructions in the memory and tells other units where to take data from, where to feed it to, and what operations to perform.   The arithmetic unit performs the addition, subtraction, multiplication, and division operations, and at very high speeds.   The arithmetic section can be operated at higher speeds than the memory if it takes a number of steps to complete an addition while the memory is not being used, thus increasing the operating rate of the system.   The results of arithmetic operations are fed back to the memory, for storage.   It can be read out at a later time to an output unit, which may be a magnetic tape, punched card, typewriter, punched tape, magnetic disk, or high-speed printer.   (Many output devices are also used for input operation.)   The high-speed printer, the fastest permanent visible record of those just mentioned, is essential when large amounts of data are handled.   Specific details of each type of unit are covered in Chapter 12.

The feature of a general-purpose digital computer that is most important in making it a versatile and useful device is its ability to be programmed.   A program is a list of statements telling the computer what operations to perform, in what order, and on what data.   Modern programming languages allow writing these commands in a simplified manner so that the programmer does not have to describe explicitly each step the computer is to perform.   A few instructions may command the computer to perform hundreds of operations. An important point to remember is that if the computer cannot do repeated computations on a large amount of information, it will not be useful.   A calculator can be used to solve a problem quickly once to many significant places.   To do the same problem, varying the numbers used, for thousands of times may not be reasonable on the calculator but is easy work for a computer.

In addition to programming languages, another important

technical achievement that has improved the computer is the use of solid-state components. The first few computers used relays and then vacuum tubes. Relays operate much too slowly, require considerable power, take up large areas, and are not sufficiently reliable. The vacuum tube has too short a lifetime, uses considerable power (operating very hot), and takes up a large amount of space. If we consider that a modern computer requires millions of parts, and malfunctions if even one is bad, the need for reliable components is soon obvious.

The first vacuum-tube computers used thousands of tubes. Any one owning a television set will appreciate the fact that the unit would break down often from tube failure. Moreover, if all the tubes were not replaced after a period of time, the computer would continuously malfunction as one tube after another went bad. With solid-state components—transistors, tunnel diodes, micrologic circuits, etc.—the occurrence of a malfunction because of a breakdown of these components is becoming virtually unknown in modern computers. At present, the auxiliary mechanical equipment—card punchers, card readers, magnetic tape drives, etc.—account for most of the small number of problems that do occur. Because of solid-state components, the computer design has been increased in complexity, allowing much more storage, control, and versatility, without undue taxing of the useful operating time of a computer. The IBM System/360 utilizes the improved reliability and smaller size of micrologic circuits to increase considerably the number of operations done. It has also increased memory size to allow for more computing facility. Figure 1–2 shows both a large computer system (IBM System/360 Model 40) and a small computer (DIGIAC 3080).

A digital computer is designed to perform a specific group of operations. These may include addition of two numbers, subtraction, multiplication, and division. It has a large and fast electronic memory where the numbers (data) to be operated on, the results of the operations, and most essential of all, the instructions, are stored. In addition, the computer is designed to take these stored numbers, compare them to "see" whether they are equal, check their arithmetic sign to "see" whether they are positive or negative, and move data around within the memory. Finally, it can bring in new data and instructions and can feed out data from its memory to provide output of its calculations. Each step or operation of the computer

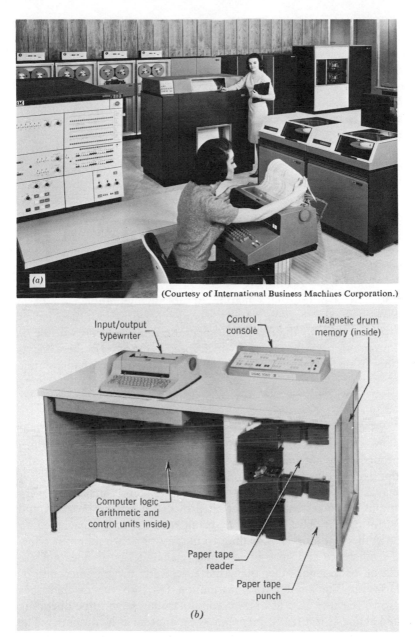

(Courtesy of International Business Machines Corporation.)

Figure 1–2. Typical general-purpose digital computers: (a) IBM System/360 Model 40 data processing system, (b) DIGIAC 3080 computer.

is essentially very simple.   It is the high speed at which it performs these operations that changes the simple nature of each step.   The second aspect of the computer that moves the simple operations to a higher level of performance is the accuracy of the operations.   The accuracy of any step is limited only by the amount of digits used for each number.   In some machines the number length (number of binary digits) is fixed at as many as 64 bits (binary digits).   The precision with such a number (2^{64}) is staggering.   Of course, after many, many operations the final accuracy may be only satisfactory or possibly even poor because of number roundoff throughout the calculations.   The performance can be improved, however, by using a larger number of bits for a word.   In this way the accuracy can always be made as good as desired.   Analog computers are not able to be so manipulated.   The last and most important aspect, which gives the digital computer a dimension completely apart from its simple basic operations, is the program.   The computer cannot solve a differential equation or do an integration as a basic mathematical operation.   It can, though, perform both these calculations using only the few simple operations mentioned by virtue of a program.   It is the program which specifies the order of these operations to enable the final outcome to be something other than a simple answer to a simple operation.   It is the high rate of performing these operations that makes using them to solve large, complex problems possible.

We cannot point out too strongly that of all the things a computer does, and they grow more impressive each day, the real operations occurring are not something mysterious, nor does the machine really think and act by itself.   Technology has not gotten that far yet.   It may surprise some readers, but the computer is essentially very stupid.   It takes each instruction provided it by the program and performs that operation.   If the result were to put the machine into an endless loop of steps leading to no answer, it would never know the difference and go on performing indefinitely.   It does not use reason or thought other than that specifically programmed into it.   However, the amount of information fed into the machine has grown so much that at times a computer may seem to be operating and acting as if it really did create what appears at its outputs.   The people who write programs for the computer really do the thinking and deciding.   The computer only carries out instructions as would a robot. If you keep in mind that the machine can only do the simple steps mentioned, the operation of a computer will not seem mysterious at all and the technique of programming (covered in Chapter 2) will be more easily understood.

Section One

FUNDAMENTALS

0010

Machine language programming

2–1. General

After discussing the computer in general terms in Chapter 1, it would now be meaningful to consider how a problem is solved using a computer. The basic "language" for instructing a computer is called *machine* language. Here the machine is instructed using coded numbers to indicate the operation to be performed and where to take or place the data for that operation. Since the machine is operated by binary digits, the actual commands used are binary. For convenience to the programmer and operator, decimal or octal numbers may be used outside the computer, but these are converted into binary (or binary coded) numbers inside the machine. The control unit of the computer plays a basic part in interpreting the machine instruction and developing the necessary signals to carry out that operational step. It uses the memory and arithmetic units for a large number of operations.

A number of programming examples are shown and discussed to bring out the important features of how the computer is used to solve problems. The main value in considering machine language is that we are discussing computer operations at their basic level. This should help give perspective later on in the book when the different computer units are considered separately. Computer programmers who are more interested in solving problems than in discovering how the computer functions seldom use machine language. The value of higher-level computer languages is discussed after machine language coding.

2–2.   Machine Language Programming

To introduce machine language programming, consider the simple program to solve the equation $Y = 2X + 6$ (Program 2–1).

Program 2–1

Location	Instruction Operation-Address		Remarks
000	10	010	Reset and add 2
001	20	012	Multiply 2 by X
002	14	011	Add 6 to 2X (= Y)
003	30	013	Store Y
004	50	013	Print Y
005	00	–	Stop
010	(2)		Stored value 2
011	(6)		Stored value 6
012	(X)		Stored value X
013	(Y)		Computed value Y

The address on the left indicates which particular memory location we are considering.   Each word in memory is assigned an address which can be used in looking for that word.   This is very much the same as a postman knowing where to deliver mail by the address of the envelope.   There is only one word residing at a particular address in memory to complete the analogy.   The program indicates the sequential order of operations that are to be performed.   This program is stored in memory and the computer, starting at the beginning, performs the operation specified in the first memory location.   The instruction is made up of an operation command which tells the machine *what* to do—and an address (operand), which tells the machine *where* to get the information to perform the operation on.   In addition, it is understood that when the operation is completed, the result remains in an accumulator.   An accumulator is the part of the computer arithmetic section where the results of an arithmetic operation are left at the end of the operation.   In order to do another operation the word in the accumulator must be taken and stored in memory and new data (words) must be put into the accumulator for manipulation.   Thus the machine steps specified are often just those of setting up an operation by loading the accumulator or those of taking data out of the accumulator to allow for further operations.   The arithmetic section operates very quickly, information used in it being fed in from memory and results from it being fed back to memory.   Input data goes first to memory and then to the arithmetic unit as needed.   The answers produced are temporarily stored in memory and read out as required.   Thus the arithmetic unit need not be slowed down by the slower speed of the input/output equipment.

Storage locations (addresses) 010 to 013 are used here to store data for this program.   The data may be stored anywhere in the memory, for it usually takes as much time to reach one location as another.   The program is stored in sequential order.   However, the computer may also be directed by the program to jump around to nonsequential locations for the program.   Jump commands will be considered in more detail in later examples.   Finally, when data is read into the arithmetic unit it is still retained in memory (non-destructive readout).   If a new word is written into a memory location, the old word is lost (or erased).   This is the same as recording a new selection on a magnetic tape recorder.   As the new selection is put on, the old one is erased and only the new one is present after recording.

Starting at location 000, the program tells the computer to reset the adder unit (specifically the accumulator) to zero in case any number was there at the start and then to add the number stored in address 010 to it.   It should be made very clear that the number being placed in the accumulator is *not* 010.   It is whatever number is at present stored in location 010 of the memory.   Thus 2 (stored before the program begins) is added to zero resulting in the sum 2 in the accumulator.   On the next instruction the number previously placed in location 012, X in this case, is multiplied by the number in the accumulator, 2 in this case, resulting in the product 2X in the accumulator.   When we say 2X, we do not mean the algebraic expression as written but the number resulting when the number for X is multiplied by the number 2.   Remember, the computer only performs operations on numbers, resulting in numbers.   The

Table 2–1.   Machine Language Code

Code Form	Operation	Description
00	Stop	Tells machine program is completed.
10	Reset and add	Resets accumulator to zero and adds number stored to operand address.
14	Add	Adds number at operand address to whatever is at present in the accumulator.
15	Subtract	Subtracts number at operand address from whatever is at present in the accumulator.
20	Multiply	Multiplies number at operand address by whatever is at present in the accumulator.
24	Divide	Divides number in accumulator by number at operand address.
30	Store	Stores number in accumulator in operand address.
44	Jump	Tells computer to take next instruction from operand address.
45	Branch if minus	Tells computer to take next instruction from operand address, *if* number now in accumulator is minus (negative); otherwise computer uses the instruction following sequentially as its next.
46	Branch if plus	Tells the computer to take next instruction from operand address *if* number now in accumulator is positive; otherwise the computer takes the instruction following sequentially as its next.
47	Branch if zero	Tells the computer to take next instruction from operand address *if* number now in accumulator is identically zero; otherwise the computer takes the instruction following sequentially as its next.
60	Read	Tells computer to read in new word from input device to operand address.
50	Print	Tells computer to print word stored at operand indicated.

expressions X and Y are just labels attached to these numbers.   The third instruction causes the constant 6, stored in address 011, to be added to 2X leaving the sum $2X+6$ in the accumulator.   Since this equals Y, it is stored in location 013 and on the next instruction the contents of address 013, Y in this case, is printed out.   The final instruction, in location 005, tells the computer that the problem is completed, stopping any further operation of this program.

The operation was indicated in the example just given by the two-digit number (10, 14, 20, etc.) which appears on the left of the instruction word.   For the examples in this book the list of instructions and their coded form given in Table 2-1 will be used.

As a second example consider the program for solving $Y = X^2 + 8X + 12$ (Program 2-2).

Program 2-2

Location	Instruction		Remarks
	Operation-Address		
000	10	020	Reset and add X to accumulator
001	20	020	Multiply X by X
002	30	023	Store X^2
003	10	020	Reset and add X to accumulator
004	20	021	Multiply 8 by X
005	14	022	Add 12 to 8X
006	14	023	Add X^2 to $8X + 12$
007	30	023	Store $Y = X^2 + 8X + 12$
008	50	023	Print Y
009	00	–	Stop
020	(X)		Stored value of X
021	(8)		Stored value of 8
022	(12)		Stored value of 12
023	Temporary storage		Temporary storage location

Locations 020–023 are used to store the constants 8 and 12, the value of X, and any temporary value computed.   On the first step the

computer looks at address 000 for the instruction and is directed to reset and add the number stored in address 020 to the accumulator. Step 2 (at address 001) tells the computer to multiply the value in 020 by the value in the accumulator. Since X is at present in the accumulator and X is the value in address 020, the result of this operation is the product X^2 in the accumulator. Since the accumulator will now be used for a different operation, the intermediate answer X^2 is stored in temporary storage location 023 on the next step. Then the value of X is again added into the accumulator, the accumulator first being reset to clear out X^2. The constant 8 is multiplied by X and 8X is now in the accumulator. The next instruction at address 005 tells the computer to add 12 to the value in the accumulator resulting in $8X + 12$. Finally, the value X^2 previously calculated is added to $8X + 12$, resulting in Y. The computed value of Y is then stored in location 023 (erasing the value X^2 stored previously) and then printed. The last instruction tells the computer to stop scanning the memory for instructions. It is this step that keeps the computer from advancing to location 020 and mistaking the stored number X as an instruction. *The computer is so stupid it would not know whether the value stored is a number or an instruction.* The program leads the computer step by step and should not allow a situation to develop in which a stored number is read as an instruction. In this program the stop instruction is used to keep the computer from continuing to step 020 where data is stored.

So far, we have considered simple programs in which the solution required one cycle of operation and produced a single answer. Obviously, this would not prove to be of tremendous value because we could probably solve the problem faster than we could write the program. To even consider using a computer the problem must require a large number of solutions to a problem. In other words, the computer may do the same problem with many different sets of numbers producing hundreds of thousands of answers. For this case it is more efficient to write a program and have the computer do the tedious calculations. Problems which might take a person a lifetime to complete can be done in minutes by a computer.

Consider the simple example of a computer program (Program 2–3) directing the repeated solution of a problem. The object of the program is to calculate and print out the squares of the numbers from 1 to 100, inclusive. Even with a desk calculator the problem would take a fairly long time to execute. A computer will do it in seconds and, as we shall see, the program is short.

Program 2-3

Location	Instruction Operation-Address		Remarks
000	10	020	Reset and add number in 020
001	14	021	Add 1 to the above
002	30	020	Store in 020
003	20	020	Multiply number by itself
004	30	023	Now store value squared in 023
005	50	023	Print value of square
006	10	020	Reset and add number to accumulator
007	15	022	Subtract 100 from number
008	45	000	Branch if minus to address 000
009	00	–	Stop
020	00000		Stored value (initially zero)
021	00001		Increment each cycle is 1
022	00100		Final value is 100
023	Temporary storage		

The key to the looped or repeated operation is the "branch if minus" statement. The jump or branch command may break the normal sequence of location examined for instructions. The next instruction is taken from either a new place in memory or that following the branch instruction. The table of machine language codes indicates four different jump commands. The first is an unconditional jump (44) which directs the computer to take the next instruction from the address indicated. Thus, 44 216 will always cause the machine to go to location 216 for the next instruction to perform. Assuming this is an arithmetic instruction (or specifically not a branch instruction), the machine will perform that instruction and then take its next instruction from the next location in memory, 217 in this case.

The three conditional branch instructions operate in a similar manner, except that there is an alternate (conditional) operation. The computer looks at either the sign of the number presently in the accumulator or at its value to determine whether to perform the branch instruction or to ignore it.   If, for example, the command is 45 216 and the number now in the accumulator is negative, the next instruction will be taken from location 216.   If, however, the sign is positive, it will ignore the branch and continue to the next sequential instruction following 45 216.   Two directions or two different actions are possible at the time of a branch instruction and only one is carried out.   It is this choice or decision operation which gives the computer the appearance of a "thinking" device.   With many programmed branches, the computer can follow a large variety of alternate procedures, thereby enabling it to solve complicated problems for a variety of conditions.   Let us go back (44) to the program under consideration and see how the branch is used.

Locations 020, 021, and 022 control what value the computation is started at, by how much this value is incremented after each solution, and at what final value to do the last calculation.   At the start of the computation the computer is instructed to reset and add 00000 to the accumulator and then add 00001 to that number. Although we could have started with one right away, we wanted to establish the pattern of incrementing the value in 020 by that in 021 before doing another cycle of computation.   This value is also the number we want to form the square of on this cycle of the computation.   On the first cycle (loop) the value is 00001 (or 1) and the square is formed by multiplying this value by itself (instructions in locations 002 and 003).   The squared value is then stored and printed by instructions in locations 004 and 005, respectively.   The next steps now consider whether to do another loop or end the computation.   After the accumulator is reset the present value is added into the accumulator.   Then the final value is subtracted.   If the final value is larger than the present value, at least one more loop must be executed, and the branch if minus directs that the next instruction is to be taken from address 000.   This instruction, then, tells the computer to go back to the beginning and start again.   Since the program sequence updates the value squared by an increment of 1 at the beginning of a loop, the next number to be squared will be one greater than on the previous loop. This repeated loop continues until the value in the accumulator is zero (or positive) on the branch if minus instruction. This "tells" the computer that it has done enough loops and the program now goes to the next step, which instructs it to stop.

This same program may now be used to calculate the squares of any simple set of numbers by changing the initial, final, and increment value stored in locations 020, 021, and 022. For example, if the initial value stored is 00025, the increment 00005, and the final value 02000, the computer will form the squares of 25, 30, 35, 40, etc., up to and including the square of 2000. Once programs are written it only requires changing specific values to obtain a variety of calculations. This then is a very, very powerful feature of a computer. For example, an insurance company may once program the calculations they must perform on a customer's account. To do the same calculations once, one hundred times, or a million times is easily controlled and, using a computer, it is quickly carried out.

Try the following problems to see whether you understand how the branch if minus is used in looped solutions.

Problem 1–1. Write a program to solve the equation $Y = 3X^2 + 2X + 6$ for values of X from 1 to 50, inclusive. Have the value Y printed out for each computation.

Problem 1–2. Write a program to compute and print out the cubes of the odd numbers from 1 to 61, inclusive.

Problem 1–3. Write a program to compute and print the values of $Y = 3X^3 + 2X$ for all even numbers less than 250.

A relatively difficult problem, but one which will show the basic procedure of decision making is that of determining the largest of three numbers (Program 2–4). Although this program only goes through the operation for one set of three numbers, it could be additionally programmed to read new sets of three numbers and repeat the operation.

Program 2–4 does not easily show the method used to solve the problem. Let us first consider how the problem is analyzed before discussing the way it is programmed. One of the valuable features of programming is the clear understanding that must be obtained before a program can be written. To facilitate this thought process

Program 2–4

Location	Instruction Operation-Address		Remarks
100	10	120	Reset and add X
101	15	121	Subtract Y from X; (X − Y)
102	45	108	If Y > X branch to address 108
103	10	021	X > Y; reset and add X into accumulator
104	15	022	Subtract: X − Z
105	45	113	If Z > X branch to 113
106	50	020	Print X as largest value
107	44	114	Jump to 114
108	10	021	Since Y > X reset and add Y to accumulator
109	15	022	Subtract: Y − Z
110	45	113	If Z > Y branch to 113
111	50	021	Print Y as largest number
112	44	114	Jump to 114
113	50	022	Print Z as largest number
114	00	−	Stop
120	(X)		
121	(Y)		
122	(Z)		

a "flow chart" is often constructed.   Let us only consider how the flow diagram shows the steps required to solve the problem.   Referring to Figure 2–1, the first step is to place X in the accumulator. Next subtract Y from X and transfer the program in one of two directions (one for each possible outcome).   If X is greater than Y, subtract Z from X to see whether X or Z is larger.   Again there are two possible outcomes.   If X is also larger than Z, then X is the largest—print X and stop.   If Z is the largest, print out Z and stop. Had the outcome of the subtraction X–Y resulted in the answer X less than Y, the program would subtract Z from Y (which is larger than X).   If Y is greater than Z, print Y and stop; if Z is greater than Y, print Z and stop.   The flow chart shows how the

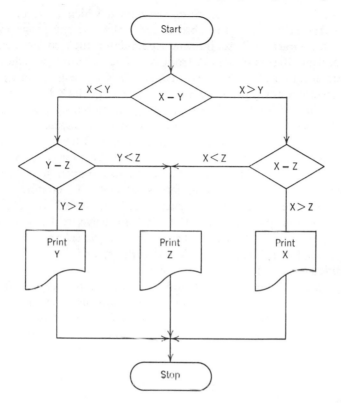

Figure 2–1.   Flow chart for finding largest of three numbers.

problem is solved, as in the discussion just given.   Once the method of solution is determined, the program can be written to accomplish this operation.

Returning to the given machine language program, we find the first instruction resets the accumulator and adds in X.   Then Y is subtracted from X and the sign used to determine where to branch. If Y is larger than X (sign in accumulator negative), the branch if minus command causes the program to look for its next instruction at location 108.   If the sign is plus, the next instruction is taken in sequence.   Since this would result if X is larger than Y, the next instruction (at location 108) resets the accumulator and adds in X. This was necessary because the accumulator contained the difference of X–Y.   Now that it has been determined which of X or Y is larger, the next step is to subtract Z.   Following the program in which X is larger and is set into the accumulator, the next instruction (at location 104) subtracts Z from X.   The program branches to address location 113 if X is less than Z.   If X is greater than Z, the next instruction will print the number stored in 020 (X in this case). A jump instruction then directs the program to the stop command. Had X been largest the program would only have subtracted Y from X, then reset X and subtracted Z, printed X, and finally jumped to the stop instruction to end the operation.   Since, in general, Y or Z could have been larger, the program contains the operations leading to the printing out of Y or Z as largest as well.   To continue, if Y had been larger than X, the instruction at location 102 would cause the program steps stored in 103 to 107, inclusive, to be bypassed. The instruction at 108 causes the value Y to be set into the accumulator.   The subtraction of Y – Z is done, and again a branch condition exists.   If Y is larger than Z, the instruction at 110 allows the program to go on to 111 and Y is printed out as the largest number; instruction 112 unconditionally jumps the program to 114, where a stop instruction is present.   Had Z been greater than Y, the result of instruction 110 would be to take the next instruction from location 113, so that Z is printed as the largest and step 114 then tells the computer to stop.

To go through all the trouble of developing the program just discussed in order to compare three numbers once would have been foolish.   A quick look at the numbers would be enough to see which is greater.   However, if a thousand sets of three numbers each had to be considered, the solution using a computer would then be practical.   Then the written program would have to contain additional commands to cause the procedure to be repeated for each set of values.   This might only require a few additional steps such as a few to read in the new set of X, Y, and Z values and an unconditional jump at the end to return the program to the start.   Either the computer will stop if no more data is available or the program must contain additional steps to count the number of loops and stop after a desired number have been carried out.   The program considered did not handle the cases where any two of the numbers, or all three, are equal.   As an exercise draw some flow charts and write the program for both additional cases.

Let us consider the same problem adding in the few extra steps which will allow it to do the operation for many sets of values. Since the basic procedure in finding the largest is still the same, we can use them as shown in location 100 through 113. Rather than stop at step 114, however, the values of X, Y, and Z will now be updated (a new set of numbers placed in locations 120, 121, and 122, respectively). Since the program reaches location 114 after the largest value has been computed (and printed), it can then read in a new set of values before doing the program again. A test is made to see whether there have been enough computations performed. For example, today there may be 1000 sets to be operated on, whereas next week 2000 may be present. On some machines the fact that no new data are present at the time of a new read command will cause the machine to halt. This is true of punched cards, for example. However, we often are doing this operation as one small part of a larger program and therefore would want the machine to go on to another part of the memory for new program instructions after these computations are completed. A test is therefore necessary at this time. As in a previous example, an initial value, increment, and final value must be stored somewhere in memory so that this test can be performed. A flow chart of the modified problem is shown in Figure 2–2. The additional program steps are given in Program 2–5.

The revised program starts in location 097. New values for X, Y, and Z are placed in locations 120, 121, and 122, respectively. Then the main part of the program is performed and the largest value printed out. The instruction at 114 begins the test procedure. The initial value stored at 123 is placed in the accumulator. It is incremented (by one for this example) and the new value is stored back at location 123. Since no new data was placed in the accumulator, it still has the same value and the next instruction subtracts the final value from the count value. If the count is less than the final, the computer program instructs the next step to be taken from 097, thereby repeating the loop with a new set of values for X, Y, and Z. This will be repeated until the test on step 118 finds a positive value in the accumulator. In this problem a positive value will occur after 1000 computations. It should again be seen that the same program can be run after a new final value is stored and the count can be reset to zero for a different number of sets with

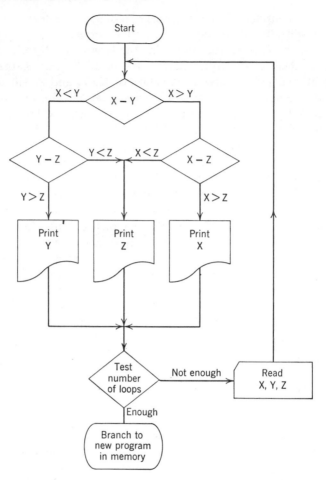

Figure 2–2.   Flow chart for finding largest of three numbers
for repeated sets of X,Y,Z.

very little effort.   That is, the program does not have to be rewritten;
only a new final value must be read in at the start.

When the program is completed and the branch if minus at step
118 is not carried out, the next instruction is performed which moves
the calculations to a different program.   In this way the computer
need never stop operating, for part of the new program may be to

Program 2–5

Location	Instruction Operation-Address		Remark
097	60	120	⎰ Read three new values for X,
098	60	121	⎱ Y, and Z, respectively
099	60	122	
100 ⎫ 113 ⎭	see previous program steps (Program 2–4)		
114	10	123	Place initial value in accumulator
115	14	124	Add increment
116	30	123	Store as present count
117	15	125	Subtract final value
118	45	097	Read a new set of values and repeat loop
119	44	–	Branch to another program stored in the memory
120	(X)		⎰ Storage locations for the set
121	(Y)		⎱ of input numbers
122	(Z)		
123	00000		Initial value (and count)
124	00001		Increment value
125	01000		Final value

read in more programs for later use.   In fact, most large computers are kept operating continuously.   Within a few minutes (or even seconds) it can perform a mathematical study, prepare a large table of data, perform a calculation on the recorded grades for all the students of a school, etc.   Each of these programs contains only a large number of steps like those just described and in terms of the computer are "all the same."   The machine just keeps calculating and calculating with an amazing output of information.

Since the repeated solution to a problem is so important a part of a computer program, let us look at a basic pattern for controlling a looped solution (Figure 2–3).   The initialization steps reset counts to zero and set up proper test values and increment values.   For example, the count value may be reset to zero before starting the

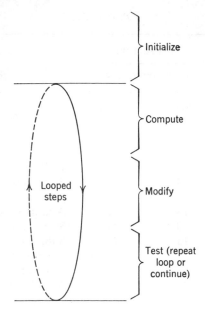

Figure 2–3. Form of program for repeated solution problems.

computation.   When the program is completed, the present count value is left as is.   Before the same procedure can be used again, the count must be reset to zero.   It would therefore be best always to initialize to be sure that the program is set up as desired at the start.   The computation is then carried out (equation solved or comparisons performed).   Although this is the desired operation other steps must be performed for control.   In the modifying steps new data may be read in, present values updated, and any count values incremented by a fixed amount.   A test must now be performed to determine whether enough calculations have been performed.   If there were enough, the test will instruct the computer to go on to a new program (or to halt).   If not, the test will instruct the computer to go to the start of the computation (not initialization) to do another cycle or loop of steps.   An example may help clarify this procedure.   Consider the solution of $Y = X^2$ for 100 values of X (Program 2–6).

Program 2–6

Location	Instruction Operation-Address		Remark
200	10	600 ⎫	⎰ Set count to zero
201	30	300 ⎪ Initialize	⎱
202	60	301 ⎭	Read final value
203	60	302	Read increment value
204	60	250 ⎫	Read new value of X
205	10	250 ⎪	Clear—add value of X
206	20	250 ⎬ Compute	Multiply by X
207	30	251 ⎪	Store X² (= Y)
208	50	250 ⎪	Print X
209	50	251 ⎭	Print Y
210	10	300 ⎫	
211	14	302 ⎬ Modify	
212	30	300 ⎭	
213	15	301 ⎫	
214	46	– ⎬ Test	Exit to new program (if positive)
215	44	204 ⎭	Repeat loop
250		(X)	X storage
251		(Y)	Y storage
300			Count storage
301			Final value
302			Increment value
600		00000	Zero value

The initialization steps reset the count to zero and read in the final value and increment value. These may be different each time the program is used. The program then calculates X^2 and prints X and Y $(= X^2)$ for the compute operation. In the modify steps the increment value is added to the present count and stored as the new count value. If the new count value is less than the final value, the test instructs the program to repeat the loop. If the test for positive (46) is satisfied, the computer branches to a different program in the computer.

Another example is the solution of $Y = 20X^2 + 7X + 6$ for values of X from 0 to 10.   A program to solve for Y is given in Program 2–7.

Program 2–7

Location	Instruction Operation-Address		Remark
000	10	115 ⎫ Initialize ⎰ Reset count to zero	
001	30	100 ⎭	
002	10	100	
003	20	100	
004	20	110	
005	30	101	Store $20X^2$
006	10	100	Form 7X
007	20	111 ⎬ Compute	Form 7X
008	14	112	Add 6
009	14	101	Add $20X^2$
010	30	101	Store Y ($20X^2 + 7X + 6$)
011	50	100	Print X
012	50	101	Print Y
013	10	100	
014	14	113 ⎬ Modify	Increment X by 1
015	30	100	
016	15	114	Subtract final value
017	47	– ⎬ Test	Exit to new program (if zero)
018	44	002	Repeat loop
100		X storage	
101		Y storage	
110		00020	Constant 20
111		00007	Constant 7
112		00006	Constant 6
113		00001	Constant 1
114		00011	Final value
115		00000	Constant 0

The program is simple to follow and should require no detailed explanation.   A few differences with the previous example should, however, be seen. For one, the increment and final values are not read in but are always the same and are stored with the other program constants. This program is not as flexible and cannot be directly used for other final or increment values. A specific change in the constant of the program would be required rather than always having the program look for new values during initialization. Another difference is that the X value and count are the same. Thus when X is incremented it serves as both the new count value for the test and as the new X value on the next loop of the program. Finally, the end value was 11 rather than the indicated last value of 10. This value was necessary because in this program X was updated before the test, and when it was equal to 10 the solution had been done on $X = 9$. To end after the solution with $X = 10$ requires using 11 as the final value, since X was incremented by 1 just before the test. Either of these two methods of setting up looped solutions may be used. It usually depends on the nature of the mathematical computation which is preferred.

Problem 1–4. Write a program for the following problems.
1. Compute $Y = X^3$ for values of X from 0 to 40. Print X and Y for each value of X.
2. Compute $Y = 3X + 17$ for values of X from 2 to 15. Print X and Y for each value of X.
3. Compute $Z = 3Y^2 - 6X + 12$ for X from 1 to 15 and Y of 3. Print X and Z for each value of X.
4. Compute $Z = 3Y^2 - 6X + 12$ for Y from 1 to 15 and X of 3. Print Y and Z for each value of Y.
5. Compute $Z = 3Y^2 - 6X + 12$ for ten sets of X and Y. Print X, Y, and Z for each of the ten sets of data. Each set of data is read in before the computation is done.

Having considered machine language programming, it should be apparent that a long program will be tedious to write and will probably contain mistakes because of the large amount of numbers handled. Because of this, computer users in the middle 1950's developed problem-oriented languages to allow writing the instructions in a form of our everyday language. These languages (FORTRAN, ALGOL, etc.) must, however, be converted into machine language for use in the computer. The job of converting this "Source" program to an "Object" program (in machine language) is called *compilation* and is carried out using the computer. In other words, rather than writing out a machine language program, the program is written in FORTRAN and is compiled into machine language by the computer, thus providing a machine language program without the bother of writing it. In all cases the program that actually operates the computer is in machine language.

Summary

This chapter covered the basic language of programming a digital computer. The instructions to the computer are numbers which are interpreted by the computer into two basic parts, operation code (op code), and instruction address (operand). The computer program directs the machine step by step but branch command may be used to cause repeated use of steps. A number of examples were presented to show what programs are like and how they are used to solve problems.

An essential factor to be gotten from the chapter is that the computer only performs simple operations and that the programmer "solves" the problem. The computer then follows the program stored in memory to effect the solution and put it on paper, display it, put it on tape or disk, etc.

PROBLEMS

1. Write a program to solve the equation $Z = 8X^2 - 7X - 12$ for values of X from 0 to 25, inclusive.

2. Write a program to solve the equation $X = 3Y^3 + 9Y^2 - 7Y + 125$ for values of Y from 10 to 45, inclusive.

3. Write a program to compute and print the integer numbers from 1 to 100.

4. Write a program to compute and print the values of $N = 6M^3 + 3M + 2$ for odd integer values of M from 1 to 50.

5. Write a program to place the largest of three numbers stored in locations 100, 101, 102 in location 200 and the smallest in location 300. Start your program at location 000.

6. Write a program to determine whether a number stored at location 300 is ODD or EVEN. If it is EVEN print the number 0. If it is ODD print the number 1.

7. Write a program to determine whether any two of the numbers stored in locations 100–105 are the same.

8. Write a program to determine whether all the numbers stored in locations 200–210 are the same.

9. Write a program to read ten numbers into locations 100–109 and then ten more numbers into locations 250–259.

10. Write a program to print out the ten consecutive numbers stored in locations 100–109 and then the 10 consecutive numbers in locations 250–259.

0011

Number systems

3–1. General

Those of you who have learned only the decimal number system are
initially surprised and even uncertain when another system is
introduced.   In order to help you along in your reorientation, the
base 10 (decimal) number system will be included in examples.   For
most, operations in the base 10 system may appear simple—they are.
But as rules and operations in other base systems are explained,
reference back to the "usual" number system (decimal) will reveal
that there are some very basic ideas about numbers which have been
learned or understood only intuitively and must now be logically
examined.   Only when these basic operations and laws of numbers
are understood and accepted will the same rules and operations in
other number systems appear simple.   In fact it will be seen that for
the particular uses discussed these other systems are even simpler to
use and understand.

   In examining a number in the decimal system we seldom consider
the actual makeup of the number.   For example, it should be clear
that the number 576 really means 5 hundreds, 7 tens, and 6 units.
The digits of the base 10 system go from 0 (a very important digit)
to 9.   Notice that the number 10 which is called the base of the
decimal system is *not* a basic digit in that system.   It is the result of
the digits 1 and 0, where 10 is specifically 1 ten and 0 units.   Further
examination of the number system reveals that the important concept
of position of a number can be formalized.   The position referred
to is the very important concept (growing out of the use of zero as a
digit) which makes 061 mean 0 hundreds, 6 tens, and 1 unit; and
610 mean 6 hundreds, 1 ten, and 0 units.   Thus the *position* of the

digits in the base 10 system determines the magnitude of the number read.   This concept may seem simple, but the Greeks, with all their brilliant contributions to basic mathematical science, used a numerical system which had to rely on new symbols for larger and larger numbers, thus losing out on the enormous benefits of the arithmetic manipulation possible in the positional number system.

When the number 623 is read, it of course means 6 hundreds, 2 tens, and 3 units.   It also may be read as follows:

$$623 = 6 \times 10^2 + 2 \times 10^1 + 3 \times 10^0$$
$$= 6 \text{ hundreds} + 2 \text{ tens} + 3 \text{ units}$$

where
$$10^2 \text{ is 10 squared or } 100$$
$$10^1 \text{ is } 10$$
$$10^0 \text{ is 1 (by definition)}$$

From this examination of the number it can be seen how the idea of a base of 10 applies.   The base of a number system is the number which, raised to the zero power, is the lowest position value, raised to the first power is the second position value, raised to the second power is the third position value, etc.

A general description of any number system is

$$N = d_n R^n + \cdots + d_3 R^3 + d_2 R^2 + d_1 R^1 + d_0 R^0$$

where N is the number, d_n the digit in that position, and R the radix or base of the system and the subscript or power number gives the positional value.

For example, 1257 in the decimal system may be written
$$1257 = 1 \times 10^3 + 2 \times 10^2 + 5 \times 10^1 + 7 \times 10^0$$
$$N = d_3 R^3 + d_2 R^2 + d_1 R^1 + d_0 R^0$$

3–2.   Binary Number System

Were we to continue discussing only the decimal system, all this generalization would have little significance.   Let us now apply the definition given to the lowest useful base system, which is quickly found to be the base of 2 (binary).   Note that the binary system has digits 0 and 1 only (again the radix is not a basic digit but is made of grouping basic digits).   From this it is also seen that the base 0 system does not exist and the base 1 system has only the digit 0 (not a very interesting system).   This brings us again to base 2 as the lowest useful base. The following tabular comparison provides a start in the examination of base 2 numbers.

$$10^0 = 1 \quad = \text{units}$$
$$10^1 = 10 \quad = \text{tens}$$
$$10^2 = 100 \quad = \text{hundreds}$$
$$10^3 = 1000 = \text{thousands}$$
$$\text{etc.}$$

$$2^0 = 1 = \text{units}$$
$$2^1 = 2 = \text{twos}$$
$$2^2 = 4 = \text{fours}$$
$$2^3 = 8 = \text{eights}$$
$$\text{etc.}$$

A binary number is made up of only the basic digits 0 and 1 so that the general definition simplifies to

$$N = \cdots + 8d_3 + 4d_2 + 2d_1 + d_0$$

where d_3, d_2, d_1, d_0 are either 0 or 1. For example, binary 1011 is $1 \times 2^3 + 0 \times 2^2 + 1 \times 2^1 + 1 \times 2^0 = N = 8 + 0 + 2 + 1 = 11$, where 8, 0, 2, 1, and 11 are terms of the familiar decimal system. Table 3–1 lists the numbers 0–9 (decimal) in both base systems.

Table 3–1

Decimal	Binary
0	0
1	1 (1×2^0)
2	10 $(1 \times 2^1 + 0 \times 2^0)$
3	11 $(1 \times 2^1 + 1 \times 2^0)$
4	100 $(1 \times 2^2 + 0 \times 2^1 + 0 \times 2^0)$
5	101 $(1 \times 2^2 + 0 \times 2^1 + 1 \times 2^0)$
6	110 $(1 \times 2^2 + 1 \times 2^1 + 0 \times 2^0)$
7	111 $(1 \times 2^2 + 1 \times 2^1 + 1 \times 2^0)$
8	1000 $(1 \times 2^3 + 0 \times 2^2 + 0 \times 2^1 + 0 \times 2^0)$
9	1001 $(1 \times 2^3 + 0 \times 2^2 + 0 \times 2^1 + 1 \times 2^0)$

It is obvious that the binary system is wasteful of space needing four digits to specify a number that only requires one digit in decimal. The large use of binary (mainly in computers) comes from the simplicity of the basic digits 0 and 1. Since there are only two they can be represented on a computer by a switch being ON (1) or OFF (0), an indicator light being ON (1) or OFF (0), a vacuum tube fully conducting (1) or fully OFF (0), a transistor ON (1) or OFF (0), a voltage being present (1) or zero volts (0), etc. The use of binary by computers will be more fully discussed in later chapters.   At present the binary system and the arithmetic operations with it will be considered.   Study the following two examples and then try the similar problems below.

Example 3–1.   Read the following binary number and write its decimal equivalent—101101.

$$\begin{aligned}
Solution: N &= 1 \times 2^5 + 0 \times 2^4 + 1 \times 2^3 + 1 \times 2^2 + \\
&\quad 0 \times 2^1 + 1 \times 2^0 \\
&= 1 \times 32 + 0 \times 16 + 1 \times 8 + 1 \times 4 + \\
&\quad 0 \times 2 + 1 \times 1 \\
&= 32 + 8 + 4 + 1 \\
&= 45 \text{ (decimal)}
\end{aligned}$$

Example 3–2.   Repeat Example 3–1 for the binary number 1101100.

$$\begin{aligned}
Solution: N &= 1 \times 2^6 + 1 \times 2^5 + 0 \times 2^4 + 1 \times 2^3 + 1 \times 2^2 + \\
&\quad 0 \times 2^1 + 0 \times 2^0 \\
&= 1 \times 64 + 1 \times 32 + 0 \times 16 + 1 \times 8 + 1 \times 4 + \\
&\quad 0 \times 2 + 0 \times 1 \\
&= 64 + 32 + 8 + 4 \\
&= 108 \text{ (decimal)}
\end{aligned}$$

Problem 3–1.   Convert the given binary number to its decimal equivalent.

1. 1101101   2. 10111   3. 01011
4. 1101   5. 111011101

Converting a binary number to a decimal now seems simple enough.   How about converting a decimal number to a binary? What is the binary number for 2576 (decimal)?   This problem is not as straightforward, is it?   It can be, though, if the following method is used.   The conversion of $(26)_{10}$—which is read as 26 in base 10—is as follows.

$$
\begin{array}{lllll}
 & & \text{quotient} & \text{remainder} & \\
\frac{26}{2} &=& 13 &+\; 0 & \text{———————— LSD} \\
\frac{13}{2} &=& 6 &+\; 1 & \\
\frac{6}{2} &=& 3 &+\; 0 & \\
\frac{3}{2} &=& 1 &+\; 1 & \\
\frac{1}{2} &=& 0 &+\; 1 & \text{——— MSD} \longrightarrow 11010
\end{array}
$$

Read last remainder as most significant digit (MSD) and first remainder as least significant digit (LSD).   Answer: $(26)_{10} = (11010)_2$. To check our answer let us convert back to the decimal:

$$N = 1 \times 2^4 + 1 \times 2^3 + 0 \times 2^2 + 1 \times 2^1 +$$
$$0 \times 2^0 = 16 + 8 + 2 = (26)_{10}$$

The continuous division by 2, keeping track of the remainder, allows a simple method of conversion.   It will be seen later that conversion of the decimal system to any number system requires division by the base of that number system, keeping track of the remainder, and reading the answer from the last remainder back. See the following two additional examples of decimal to binary conversion and then try the few problems.

Example 3–3.   Convert the following decimal number to binary $(35)_{10}$.

$$\begin{array}{ccccc}
 & \text{quotient} & & \text{remainder} & \\
\frac{35}{2} & = & 17 & + & 1 \\
\frac{17}{2} & = & 8 & + & 1 \\
\frac{8}{2} & = & 4 & + & 0 \\
\frac{4}{2} & = & 2 & + & 0 \\
\frac{2}{2} & = & 1 & + & 0 \\
\frac{1}{2} & = & 0 & + & 1 \longrightarrow 100011
\end{array}$$

Answer: $(35)_{10} = (100011)_2$.

Check: $N = 1 \times 2^5 + 0 \times 2^4 + 0 \times 2^3 + 0 \times 2^2 +$
$$1 \times 2^1 + 1 \times 2^0$$
$$= 32 + 2 + 1$$
$$= (35)_{10}$$

Example 3–4.   Convert $(353)_{10}$ to binary.

$$\text{quotient} \quad \text{remainder}$$

Solution: $\frac{353}{2}$ = 176 + 1 ─────────────────┐

$\frac{176}{2}$ = 88 + 0

$\frac{88}{2}$ = 44 + 0

$\frac{44}{2}$ = 22 + 0

$\frac{22}{2}$ = 11 + 0

$\frac{11}{2}$ = 5 + 1

$\frac{5}{2}$ = 2 + 1

$\frac{2}{2}$ = 1 + 0

$\frac{1}{2}$ = 0 + 1 ──────→ 101100001

Answer: $(353)_{10} = (101100001)_2$.

Problem 3–2.
1. $(37)_{10} = (?)_2$ 2. $(49)_{10} = (?)_2$ 3. $(85)_{10} = (?)_2$
4. $(100)_{10} = (?)_2$ 5. $(557)_{10} = (?)_2$

Fractional Binary Numbers.   Having considered the integer (whole) numbers of the binary system, we can turn our attention to fractional numbers.   In decimal the number 0.5176 is read 5 tenths, 1 hundredth, 7 thousandths, and 6 ten-thousands.   Notice that the first position was tenths.   A fractional number may be written in general as

$$N = d_1 \times R^{-1} + d_2 \times R^{-2} + d_3 \times R^{-3} + \cdots + d_n \times R^{-n}$$

Example 3–5.   0.725 is $N = 7 \times 10^{-1} + 2 \times 10^{-2} + 5 \times 10^{-3}$
$$N = d_1 \times R^{-1} + d_2 \times R^{-2} + d_3 \times R^{-3}$$

In binary a fractional number 0.1011 is read as

$$1 \times 2^{-1} + 0 \times 2^{-2} + 1 \times 2^{-3} + 1 \times 2^{-4}$$

where $2^{-1} = \dfrac{1}{2^1} = 0.5$, $2^{-2} = \dfrac{1}{2^2} = 0.25$, $2^{-3} = \dfrac{1}{2^3} = 0.125$

and $$2^{-4} = \dfrac{1}{2^4} = 0.0625.$$

Therefore $(0.1101)_2 = (0.5 + 0.125 + 0.0625)_{10}$
$$= (0.6875)_{10}$$

Here are two more examples.

Example 3–6. Convert $(0.101101)_2$ to decimal.

Solution: $(0.101101)_2 = 1 \times 2^{-1} + 0 \times 2^{-2} + 1 \times 2^{-3} +$
$$1 \times 2^{-4} + 0 \times 2^{-5} + 1 \times 2^{-6}$$
$$= 0.5 + 0.125 + 0.0625 + 0.015625$$
$$= (0.703125)_{10}$$

Example 3–7. Convert $(0.10001)_2$ to decimal.

Solution: $(0.10001)_2 = 1 \times 2^{-1} + 0 \times 2^{-2} + 0 \times 2^{-3} +$
$$0 \times 2^{-4} + 1 \times 2^{-5}$$
$$= 0.5 + 0.03125$$
$$= (0.53125)_{10}$$

Problem 3–3. Convert the given binary fractional number to a decimal.

1. 0.11011   2. 0.01010   3. 0.00101
4. 0.11101   5. 0.01110

Converting fractional binary numbers to decimal seems straightforward enough. How about converting 0.57251 to binary? It appears to be quite a formidable problem, but it is not. You merely use the following method.

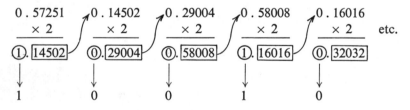

The answer is read as $(0.10010\cdots)_2$.
As a check $(0.10010)_2 = 1 \times 2^{-1} + 0 \times 2^{-2} + 0 \times 2^{-3} +$
$$1 \times 2^{-4}$$
$$= 0.5 + 0.0625$$
$$= (0.5625)_{10}$$

It can be seen that these two numbers are not exactly the same. If the number of places of the binary number is carried out further to the right, the value approaches closer and closer to the given decimal number.   Only if the decimal number is a fraction such as $\frac{1}{2}$, $\frac{1}{8}$, $\frac{1}{16}$, etc., or an exact combination of these will there be a finite length fraction.   There is no difficulty if the binary equivalent of the decimal fraction is not finite for we can always carry out the conversion to the desired accuracy (or number of significant places) required.   Here are two examples, one of which ends and one that does not.

Example 3–8.   Convert $(0.65625)_{10}$ to binary.

$$
\begin{array}{ccccc}
0.65625 & 0.31250 & 0.62500 & 0.25000 & 0.50000 \\
\times 2 & \times 2 & \times 2 & \times 2 & \times 2 \\
\hline
①.31250 & ⓪.62500 & ①.25000 & ⓪.50000 & ①.00000 \\
\downarrow & \downarrow & \downarrow & \downarrow & \downarrow \\
1 & 0 & 1 & 0 & 1
\end{array}
$$

Answer: 0.10101

Check: $(0.10101)_2 = 1 \times 2^{-1} + 0 \times 2^{-2} + 1 \times 2^{-3} +$
$\qquad\qquad\qquad 0 \times 2^{-4} + 1 \times 2^{-5}$
$\qquad\qquad = 0.5 + 0.125 + 0.03125$
$\qquad\qquad = (0.65625)_{10}$

Example 3–9.   Convert $(0.8176)_{10}$ to binary.
Solution:

$$
\begin{array}{cccccc}
0.8176 & 0.6352 & 0.2704 & 0.5408 & 0.0816 & 0.1632 \\
\times 2 & \times 2 & \times 2 & \times 2 & \times 2 & \times 2 \quad \text{etc.}\\
\hline
1.6352 & 1.2704 & 0.5408 & 1.0816 & 0.1632 & 0.3264 \\
\downarrow & \downarrow & \downarrow & \downarrow & \downarrow & \downarrow \\
1 & 1 & 0 & 1 & 0 & 0
\end{array}
$$

Answer: $(0.110100\cdots)_2$

Check: $(0.110100)_2 = 1 \times 2^{-1} + 1 \times 2^{-2} + 0 \times 2^{-3} +$
$\qquad\qquad\qquad 1 \times 2^{-4} + 0 \times 2^{-5} + 0 \times 2^{-6}$
$\qquad\qquad = 0.5 + 0.25 + 0.0625$
$\qquad\qquad = 0.8125$

This answer may not be accurate enough, requiring the conversion to be carried out to more places.   For the illustrative example it will do.

Try the following problem converting from decimal to binary for fractional numbers.   Carry the answer to eight places if it does not end sooner.

Problem 3–4.

1. $(0.7257)_{10}$ 2. $(0.2501)_{10}$ 3. $(0.001876)_{10}$
4. $(0.9765)_{10}$ 5. $(0.734375)_{10}$

Converting a number made up of an integer and a fractional part from binary to decimal is straightforward. For example, $(11010.10110)_2$ gives

$$N = 1 \times 2^4 + 1 \times 2^3 + 0 \times 2^2 + 1 \times 2^1 + 0 \times 2^0 + 1 \times 2^{-1} +$$
$$0 \times 2^{-2} + 1 \times 2^{-3} + 1 \times 2^{-4} + 0 \times 2^{-5}$$
$$= 16 + 8 + 2 + 0.5 + 0.125 + 0.0625$$
$$= (26.6875)_{10}$$

Two more examples follow.

Example 3–10.   Convert from binary to decimal 10110.1101.

Solution: $(10110.1101)_2 = 1 \times 2^4 + 0 \times 2^3 + 1 \times 2^2 +$
$$1 \times 2^1 + 0 \times 2^0 + 1 \times 2^{-1} +$$
$$1 \times 2^{-2} + 0 \times 2^{-3} + 1 \times 2^{-4}$$
$$= 16 + 4 + 2 + 0.5 + 0.25 + 0.0625$$
$$= (22.8125)_{10}$$

Example 3–11. $(101101.110001)_2 = (?)_{10}$

Solution: $(101101.110001)_2 = 1 \times 2^5 + 0 \times 2^4 + 1 \times 2^3 +$
$$1 \times 2^2 + 0 \times 2^1 + 1 \times 2^0 +$$
$$1 \times 2^{-1} + 1 \times 2^{-2} + 0 \times 2^{-3} +$$
$$0 \times 2^{-4} + 0 \times 2^{-5} + 1 \times 2^{-6}$$
$$= 32 + 8 + 4 + 1 + 0.5 + 0.25 +$$
$$0.015625$$
$$= (45.765625)_{10}$$

Problem 3-5. Convert the following numbers from binary to decimal.

1. $(10111.011)_2$ 2. $(1011.101)_2$ 3. $(11011.111)_2$
4. $(110.0111)_2$ 5. $(111011.001101)_2$

Now convert $(274.1875)_{10}$ to binary. This can be done piecemeal using the repeated division by 2, reading the remainder for integer digits, and the repeated multiplication by 2, using the units integer as the binary value. Follow this example and then try the next problem.

Example 3-12.

$$\frac{274}{2} = 137 + 0$$
$$\frac{137}{2} = 68 + 1$$
$$\frac{68}{2} = 34 + 0$$
$$\frac{34}{2} = 17 + 0$$
$$\frac{17}{2} = 8 + 1$$
$$\frac{8}{2} = 4 + 0$$
$$\frac{4}{2} = 2 + 0$$
$$\frac{2}{2} = 1 + 0$$
$$\frac{1}{2} = 0 + 1 \longrightarrow 100010010$$

Read as $(100010010)_2$.

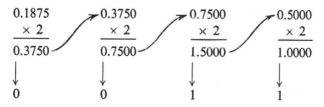

0.1875	0.3750	0.7500	0.5000
× 2	× 2	× 2	× 2
0.3750	0.7500	1.5000	1.0000
0	0	1	1

Read as 0.0011.

Answer: $(274.1875)_{10} = (100010010.0011)_2$

Problem 3–6.

1. $(27.75)_{10} = (?)_2$ 2. $(37.875)_{10} = (?)_2$
3. $(521.1875)_{10} = (?)_2$ 4. $(259.498)_{10} = (?)_2$
5. $(32.32)_{10} = (?)_2$

3–3. Octal and Other Number Systems

Having practiced conversion to and from binary you should now be able to apply the concept to other base systems.   The following two examples outline how the basic rules are applied.

Example 3–13.   Convert (124) base 5 to decimal.
Solution: Base 5 can be outlined in the following table.

base 5		decimal	
5^1	5^0	10^1	10^0
0	0	0	0
0	1	0	1
0	2	0	2
0	3	0	3
0	4	0	4
1	0	0	5
1	1	0	6
1	2	0	7
1	3	0	8
1	4	0	9
2	0	1	0
etc.		etc.	

$$(124)_5 = 1 \times 5^2 + 2 \times 5^1 + 4 \times 5^0$$
$$= 25 + 10 + 4 \ (5^0 = 1, \text{ remember})$$
$$= (39)_{10}$$

Example 3–14.   Convert (376) octal to decimal.

Solution: Base 8 can be outlined as follows:

$$8^0 = 1$$
$$8^1 = 8$$
$$8^2 = 64$$

base 8 (octal)		decimal	
8^1	8^0	10^1	10^0
0	0	0	0
0	1	0	1
0	2	0	2
0	3	0	3
0	4	0	4
0	5	0	5
0	6	0	6
0	7	0	7
1	0	0	8
1	1	0	9
1	2	1	0
	etc.		etc.

$$(376)_8 = 3 \times 8^2 + 7 \times 8^1 + 6 \times 8^0$$
$$= 192 + 56 + 6$$
$$= (254)_{10}$$

Try the following problem to see whether you have the procedure clearly in mind.

Problem 3–7.

1. $(376)_8 = (?)_{10}$
2. $(256)_n = (?)_{10}$
3. $(143)_5 = (?)_{10}$
4. $(1212)_3 = (?)_{10}$
5. $(666)_7 = (?)_{10}$

Conversion from decimal to any other base can be carried out using the repeated division for the integer portion and repeated multiplication for the fractional. For octal follow this next example.

Example 3–15. $(127)_{10} = (?)_8$

Solution: $\frac{127}{8} = 15 + 7$
$\frac{15}{8} = 1 + 7$
$\frac{1}{8} = 0 + 1 \longrightarrow 177$

Read as $(177)_8$

Check: $(177)_8 = 1 \times 8^2 + 7 \times 8^1 + 7 \times 8^0$
$$= 64 + 56 + 7$$
$$= (127)_{10}$$

Problem 3–8.

1. $(139)_{10} = (?)_8$ 2. $(2137)_{10} = (?)_8$
3. $(12)_{10} = (?)_8$ 4. $(675)_{10} = (?)_5$
5. $(95)_{10} = (?)_3$

As octal numbers have practical importance in computers, conversion from octal to binary should be possible. In fact, the simplicity of this conversion (and back) is what makes octal numbers so useful. First try the conversion using the basic technique as before. Here is an example.

Example 3–16.   Convert $(275)_8$ into binary.

$$\frac{275}{2} = 136 + 1$$
$$\frac{136}{2} = 57 + 0$$
$$\frac{57}{2} = 27 + 1$$
$$\frac{27}{2} = 13 + 1$$
$$\frac{13}{2} = 5 + 1$$
$$\frac{5}{2} = 2 + 1$$
$$\frac{2}{2} = 1 + 0$$
$$\frac{1}{2} = 0 + 1 \longrightarrow 10111101$$

Read as $(10111101)_2$.

By now you should be exclaiming that the example is all wrong, the divisions are incorrect, and even though the answer is correct (have you checked it?) the whole process looks phoney. None of this is true and the method is entirely correct, as is the answer. What you have probably failed to consider is that the division was carried out using octal numbers. For example, 2 into 275 means 2 into 2 = 1, 2 into 7 = 3 with a remainder of 1 and 2 into 15 is really 2 base 8 into 15 base 8 [where $(15)_8$ is 13 base 10] and equals 6 base 8 with a remainder of 1. As was indicated before, there is a simple method of conversion—and this is obviously not it.   See how simple the same conversion can be done.

$$(275)_8 = \quad \underbrace{010} \qquad \underbrace{111} \qquad \underbrace{101}$$

$$\qquad\qquad \downarrow \qquad\qquad \downarrow \qquad\qquad \downarrow$$

2 in binary   7 in binary   5 in binary
010 111 101 answer in binary

Look back to see that this is the same answer obtained by division. The procedure is to write a three-place binary number for each octal number.   Since base 8 has integers from 0 to 7 and a three-place binary number can handle numbers from 0 to 7, they match nicely. See how easily the following two conversions are done.

$$(3576)_8 = (011\ 101\ 111\ 110)_2$$
$$= (011101111110)_2$$
$$(2412)_8 = (010\ 100\ 001\ 010)_2$$
$$= (010100001010)_2$$

Can this conversion be done?

$$(3978)_8 = (?)_2$$

No!   This number is not an octal number—octal numbers only go as high as 7, then they require more places.   Problem 3–9 provides practice in conversion from octal to binary.

Problem 3–9.

1. $(261)_8 = (?)_2$ 2. $(372)_8 = (?)_2$
3. $(42176)_8 = (?)_2$ 4. $(25)_8 = (?)_2$
5. $(1376)_8 = (?)_2$

Converting from binary to octal is just as easy to do.   Here are two examples and a problem to try.

Example 3–17. $(101110110)_2 = (?)_8$
   Solution: $(101\ 110\ 110)_2 = (5\ 6\ 6)_8$
Example 3–18. $(1011011110)_2 = (?)_8$
   Solution: This problem requires an additional amount of care only in reading the number properly.   Digits should be grouped in three's (number of places) starting from the *right.*

1 011 011 110   which is   001 011 011 110

This converts to $(1\ 3\ 3\ 6)_8$.   Had you read the number 101 101 111 0, you would have been wrong.   You must be careful not to make such mistakes.

Problem 3–10.

1. $(101111110)_2 = (?)_8$ 2. $(101101)_2 = (?)_8$
3. $(11101110)_2 = (?)_8$ 4. $(101101111)_2 = (?)_8$
5. $(11101)_2 = (?)_8$

When a binary number is read its length tends to make it hard to recognize. For example, read 10111101110111. If this same number were read in octal, you would find it easier. It would read $(27567)_8$. Some computers print the answers out in octal. Operations in the computer have been carried out in binary and when the answer is printed, the computer provides the result in octal, so that the human operator will find it easier to read. Of course it would be easier to print out the answer in the familiar decimal system. However, this requires that the computer "convert" from the internal binary "language" to the external decimal, which takes time and requires special circuits. Many computers do provide this facility, some use the quicker conversion to octal, and a few just read out in binary. The choice depends mainly on the user, and the conversion operation can usually be added on when desired as either a programmed conversion or additional circuitry.

3–4. Binary Arithmetic

Having considered the binary number system used by the computer, it will now be possible to see how basic arithmetic operations are performed. These, of course, include adding, subtracting, multiplying, and dividing. The operations are the same as in decimal, but because of the simplicity of binary numbers some modifications can be used which further simplify the operations. The basic four operations, as done with "pencil and paper," will be studied. Actual computer implementation will be deferred until the discussion of the computer arithmetic unit so that the qualification of practical circuitry can be considered in the choice of the "best" scheme to implement the function.

Binary Addition.   Binary addition can be learned from the following addition table (Table 3–2).   It should be obvious that it is much simpler than the decimal addition table.

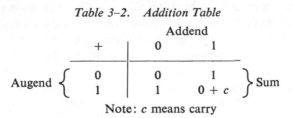

Table 3–2.   Addition Table

Note: c means carry

As the table shows, there are only four combinations to "memorize." In the decimal system you may recall that you had to "memorize" 100 combinations (many of which repeated).   The addition of $0 + 0$, $1 + 0$, $0 + 1$ is obvious.   The addition of $1 + 1$, which we know is 2, in binary must be written using two places.   The largest digit possible in any position in binary is 1, just as the largest decimal digit in any position is 9.   Thus $1 + 1$ is 0 and a carry. The carry, of course, is added into the next higher place.   Some addition examples are given next, followed by a few problems, for practice.

Example 3–19.
$$\begin{array}{r} 001101 \\ + 100101 \\ \hline 110010 \end{array} \qquad \left(\begin{array}{r} 13 \\ +37 \\ \hline 50 \end{array} \right)_{10}$$

Example 3–20.
$$\begin{array}{r} 1011011 \\ + 1011010 \\ \hline 10110101 \end{array} \qquad \left(\begin{array}{r} 91 \\ +90 \\ \hline 181 \end{array} \right)_{10}$$

Example 3–21.
$$\begin{array}{r} 110111011 \\ + 100111011 \\ \hline 1011110110 \end{array} \qquad \left(\begin{array}{r} 443 \\ +315 \\ \hline 758 \end{array} \right)_{10}$$

Problem 3–11.   Add the following.

1. $\begin{array}{r} 01101 \\ + 10101 \end{array}$ 2. $\begin{array}{r} 11011 \\ + 10110 \end{array}$ 3. $\begin{array}{r} 1100011 \\ + 1011011 \end{array}$

4. $\begin{array}{r} 1001101111 \\ + 1011100110 \end{array}$ 5. $\begin{array}{r} 101010101 \\ + 111111111 \end{array}$

Binary Subtraction. Binary subtraction is again the same operation as in decimal. But you may find the operation more difficult than the addition. This will be either because you find subtraction itself harder (as most do) or because you cannot subtract well with decimal numbers and are even more confused with binary. This fact comes from firsthand classroom experience, and it is suggested that you clear up subtraction in decimal so that binary operation (which should be simpler) is understood. As a guide, consider that some have been taught to subtract by borrowing and adding, and some by borrowing and reducing. Both methods are valid, but do not confuse the two. A simple subtraction is indicated below in decimal.

$$
\begin{array}{r}
1572 \\
-964 \\
\hline
608
\end{array}
\quad
\begin{array}{l}
\text{(minuend)} \\
\text{(subtrahend)} \\
\text{(difference)}
\end{array}
$$

The terms in subtraction are defined as minuend (1572), subtrahend (964), and difference (608). Review the subtraction table (Table 3–3), the few examples, and "try your luck" with Problem 3–12 using binary numbers.

Table 3–3.   Subtraction Table

	Minuend	
−	**0**	**1**
Subtrahend { 0	0	1
1	1 + b	0

Difference

Note: b means borrow

Example 3–22.

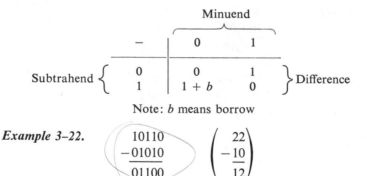

$$
\begin{array}{r}
10110 \\
-01010 \\
\hline
01100
\end{array}
\qquad
\left(
\begin{array}{r}
22 \\
-10 \\
\hline
12
\end{array}
\right)_{10}
$$

Example 3–23.

$$
\begin{array}{r}
11011001 \\
-10101011 \\
\hline
00101110
\end{array}
\qquad
\left(
\begin{array}{r}
217 \\
-171 \\
\hline
46
\end{array}
\right)_{10}
$$

Try this example yourself (without looking at the answer). Is it so easy?

The way to become proficient at subtracting binary numbers is the same as with decimal—practice. Try the following as a start.

Problem 3–12.

1. 110101
    − 101010

2. 1101101
    − 0011110

3. 10111010
    − 01111011

4. 11011101
    − 10111110

5. 10101010
    − 01010101

One way to help simplify the subtraction is to read the numbers in groups. This is sometimes helpful. Here is one example in which it is an aid.

Example 3–24.

100110011101		1001	1001	1101
− 010101110010	→	− 0101	0111	0010

	1001	1001	1101
	0101	0111	0010
	0100	0010	1011

Answer: 010000101011.

Another technique that works well with subtraction is the use of complements. The use of complements in the decimal system could be shown, but because the main value comes in its use in the binary system, and to avoid any chance of confusion, only the binary system will be used. First, a few definitions. A TWO's complement of a number (N) of n binary places is defined as $2^n - N$. A ONE's complement of a number N of n binary places is defined as $(2^n - N) - 1$. The ONE's complement is *one* less than the TWO's complement, or the TWO's complement is *one* greater than the ONE's complement. Here are a few examples.

Example 3–25. Find the TWO's complement of $N = 101101$.

$$N = 45 \qquad n = 6 \text{ (6 places)}$$
$$2^n = 2^6 = 64$$
$$2^n - N = 64 - 45 = 19 = 010011$$

In binary operation,

$$N = 101101$$
$$2^n = 2^6 = 1000000$$
$$2^n - N = \begin{array}{r} 1000000 \\ -101101 \\ \hline 0010011 \end{array}$$

The ONE's complement is then $\begin{array}{r} 010011 \\ -1 \\ \hline 010010 \end{array}$

We started by saying that the use of complements would simplify subtraction, and so far all you have seen is that the procedure involved is as difficult as subtraction. Let us clear up the situation. Obtaining the ONE's complement of a number (binary of course) is really just rote operation. In Example 3–25 the number N was 101101 and its ONE's complement came out to be 010010. Looking at these two carefully we see that every term in N is exactly opposite ($0 \rightarrow 1$, $1 \rightarrow 0$) in the ONE's complement. This is not just coincidence. It is always true, and it is this relation which makes the use of complements easy. Follow the next example of getting ONE's and TWO's complements of a number N.

Example 3–26. $N = 0110110101$
  ONE's complement $= 1001001010$
  TWO's complement $= 1001001011$ (ONE's complement $+$ 1)

Problem 3–13. Find the ONE's and TWO's complement for the following binary numbers.
  1. 0110101   2. 011110111   3. 110110111

Now that getting complements is so easy, what of it. First, let us see how complements can be used to implement a subtraction and then how it is done practically. A subtraction may be obtained by *adding* the minuend to the TWO's complement of the subtrahend.

Example 3–27.

$$\begin{array}{r} 1011011 \quad N_1 \\ -0101110 \quad N_2 \\ \hline 0101101 \end{array} \quad \Rightarrow \quad \begin{array}{r} 1011011 \quad N_1 \\ +1010010 \quad (2^n - N_2) \\ \hline \text{disregard} \rightarrow (1)0101101 \end{array} \quad \left(\begin{array}{r} 91 \\ -46 \\ \hline 45 \end{array} \right)_{10}$$

Notice that the two numbers to be subtracted each had the same number of places, the correct answer using complements was of this same length, and the extra ONE to the left is disregarded.

Example 3–28.

$$
\begin{array}{c}
11011011 \\
-\ 10111 \\
\hline
11000100
\end{array}
\Rightarrow
\begin{array}{c}
11011011 \\
-\ 00010111 \\
\hline
\end{array}
\Rightarrow
\begin{array}{c}
11011011 \\
+\ 11101001 \\
\hline
1\ 11000100
\end{array}
\left(
\begin{array}{c}
219 \\
-23 \\
\hline
196
\end{array}
\right)_{10}
$$

Again the number had to be written using the same number of places for each (000 was added before the subtrahend) and the answer read with the same number of places, the extra ONE to the left being disregarded. Since the use of complements often involves the ONE's complement, let us consider that next.

The ONE's complement is used because it is easily implemented in a computer. It only requires changing all ONEs to ZEROs and all ZEROs to ONEs in the subtrahend. This specific operation is called "complementing" a number, and the term "complement" refers here to the ONE's complement only. When the TWO's complement is discussed it will be called specifically the TWO's complement. As the correct answer is obtained mathematically from using the TWO's complement and the implementation is done with the ONE's, all that is required is that the answer be increased by ONE. Since it is possible to subtract a smaller or larger number, the exact operation is best explained with the following examples.

Example 3–29.

$$
\begin{array}{c}
1110111 \\
-\ 0101101 \\
\hline
\end{array}
\Rightarrow
\begin{array}{c}
1110111 \\
+\ 1010010 \\
\hline
(1)1001001 \\
\!\!\longrightarrow\!1 \quad \text{add 1} \\
\hline
1001010
\end{array}
\left(
\begin{array}{c}
119 \\
-45 \\
\hline
74
\end{array}
\right)_{10}
$$

Since the extra *ONE* is present and a *ONE* must be added to obtain the answer, the procedure is mechanized with the addition of the extra *ONE* in the lowest-order position, called an "end-around carry." This is always done when using the ONE's complement. If no extra *ONE* appears, no end-around carry is performed. Instead the answer is recognized as being a negative number (and in

ONE's complement form).   The number may be read by complementing and putting a minus sign in front when this condition occurs.   Here is an example.

Example 3-30.

$$
\begin{array}{r}
1011101 \\
-1101100 \\
\end{array}
\Rightarrow
\begin{array}{r}
1011101 \\
+0010011 \\
\hline
1110000 \\
\end{array}
\quad
\left(
\begin{array}{r}
93 \\
-108 \\
\hline
-15 \\
\end{array}
\right)_{10}
$$

Answer: -0001111.

There was no extra *ONE*, therefore no end-around carry was needed.   The answer was read by complementing and putting a minus sign in front.

Try these next two examples and the problem.

Example 3-31.

$$
\begin{array}{r}
10111011 \\
-01100110 \\
\end{array}
\Rightarrow
\begin{array}{r}
10111011 \\
+10011001 \\
\hline
(1)01010100 \\
\end{array}
\quad
\left(
\begin{array}{r}
187 \\
-102 \\
\hline
85 \\
\end{array}
\right)_{10}
$$

$\llcorner\!\!\longrightarrow 1$ end-around carry

01010101 *Answer*

Example 3-32.

$$
\begin{array}{r}
101110100111 \\
-110110110111 \\
\end{array}
\Rightarrow
\begin{array}{r}
101110100111 \\
+001001001000 \\
\hline
110111101111 \\
\end{array}
\quad
\left(
\begin{array}{r}
2983 \\
-3511 \\
\hline
-528 \\
\end{array}
\right)_{10}
$$

no extra one—answer is negative

Answer: -001000010000

Problem 3-14.   Subtract using complements.

1. $\begin{array}{r} 110111 \\ -101101 \end{array}$ 2. $\begin{array}{r} 110101 \\ 101101 \end{array}$ 3. $\begin{array}{r} 1101101 \\ -1110000 \end{array}$

4. $\begin{array}{r} 1011101 \\ -1001111 \end{array}$ 5. $\begin{array}{r} 10111101 \\ -11000011 \end{array}$

In review, *subtraction* of binary numbers may be implemented by *adding* the complement of the subtrahend (ONE's complement is understood). A more complicated subtraction is replaced by addition to obtain the same difference.

Binary Multiplication. Multiplication in the binary number system is probably easier than in any other number system. This should be apparent when you consider that a multiplier digit can only be a ZERO or a ONE. Thus the partial product formed is either zero or exactly the multiplicand. An example will show this very nicely.

Example 3–33.

$$
\begin{array}{l}
110101 \text{ — multiplicand} \\
\underline{\times\, 111} \text{ — multiplier} \\
110101 \\
110101 \\
\underline{110101} \\
101110011 \text{ — product}
\end{array}
\qquad
\left(
\begin{array}{r}
53 \\
\times 7 \\
\hline
371
\end{array}
\right)_{10}
$$

In a computer the multiplication operation is performed by repeated additions, in much the same manner as the addition of all partial products to obtain the full product. Details of this procedure are covered when implementation of the operation is considered. The formation of partial products is quite easy. The addition of these may be more difficult, however, since each addition of two ONE's creates a carry. A little practice will help in learning to perform the operation properly. Example 3–34 is given with a large number of carries to impress the reader with how the carries must be handled, after which the few problems should be tried.

Example 3–34. Perform the following binary multiplication.

$$
\begin{array}{l}
110110111 \\
\underline{\times\, 1010111} \\
110110111 \\
110110111 \\
110110111 \\
000000000 \\
110110111 \\
000000000 \\
\underline{110110111} \\
1001010100110001
\end{array}
\qquad
\left(
\begin{array}{r}
439 \\
\times 87 \\
\hline
38193
\end{array}
\right)_{10}
$$

An easy way to add the numbers is to *count* the number of ONE's (and carries) in the column.   If it is even the sum is a ZERO and if odd a ONE.   Then count the pairs of ONE's to determine how many ONE's to carry to the next higher position.   This procedure is more automatic and easier to follow (and should lead to fewer errors). Try the addition this way to see whether you find it easier.

Problem 3–15.   Perform the indicated multiplications.

1.   1011   2.   1001   3.   111
    × 110   × 1011   × 100

4.   1101   5. 1001111
    × 101   × 11101

Binary Division.   As with multiplication, the reader will soon find that binary division is simple to perform.   This, again, is due to the fact that you can divide into a part of a number only once or not at all.   No other quotient terms than ONE or ZERO are possible. Consider the following example.

Example 3–35.

$$
\begin{array}{r}
1100 \quad \text{(quotient)} \\
110 \overline{)\ 1001000} \quad \text{(dividend)} \\
-110 \\ \hline
00110 \\
-110 \\ \hline
0000000
\end{array}
\qquad
\left(6\ \overline{)\ 72}^{\,12}\right)_{10}
$$

(divisor)   110

Try to divide the dividend by the divisor using the same number of places as the divisor (110 into 100) in this example.   If it does divide in at all, try using a larger dividend (110 into 1001).   If it does go in, it can only go in once, so the first quotient term is a ONE. The division procedure continues similar to decimal division.   Try the following problem for practice.

Problem 3–16.   Perform the following binary divisions.

1. 101 $\overline{)\ 11001}$ 2. 011 $\overline{)\ 10010}$
3. 1001 $\overline{)\ 1010001}$ 4. 1010 $\overline{)\ 1100100}$
5. 1101 $\overline{)\ 100111}$

Summary

The binary number system was introduced, and conversion of both integer and fractional parts from binary to decimal and decimal to binary was covered.   Proficiency using the binary number system is essential when dealing with the basic operations in a digital computer, since these all are done in binary or a binary-coded form.

The octal number system is also important to know since machine language in a number of computers is presented in octal form.   That is, the op codes and operands are typed as octal numbers, and "straight" machine output is in octal form.   As mentioned before, decimal input and output is possible as a programmed conversion for such a machine.

The use of complements to subtract binary numbers is important since it is carried out that way in a number of computers.   Although the subtraction was shown mainly as an addition of the ONE's complement and the use of an end-around carry, TWO's complement operation is also very popular in computers.   The TWO's complement may be obtained directly by using special computer circuits and then added to the minuend to effect the subtraction.

Binary multiplication and division are shown as done with pencil and paper.   The computer actually performs these operations as repeated additions and repeated subtractions, respectively.   These operations will be covered later in Chapter 10 when the arithmetic unit is discussed.

PROBLEMS

1. Convert the following integer binary numbers into decimal.
(a) 110111   (b) 111000   (c) 010101
(d) 101010   (e) 1111110

2. Convert the following decimal numbers into binary.
(a) 25   (b) 67   (c) 99   (d) 135   (e) 276

3. Convert the following fractional binary numbers into decimal.
(a) 0.1010   (b) 0.11   (c) 0.001
(d) 0.011   (e) 0.11001

4. Convert the following fractional decimal numbers into binary.
(a) 0.8750   (b) 0.0930   (c) 0.370
(d) 0.53125   (e) 0.4375

5. Convert the following octal and decimal numbers.
(a) $(45)_8 = (?)_{10}$ (b) $(63)_{10} = (?)_8$
(c) $(125.3)_8 = (?)_{10}$ (d) $(119)_{10} = (?)_8$
(e) $(625.5)_{10} = (?)_8$

6. Convert the following binary and octal numbers.
(a) $(1101101)_2 = (?)_8$ (b) $(372)_8 = (?)_2$
(c) $(101110.111)_2 = (?)_8$ (d) $(2753)_8 = (?)_2$
(e) $(25.57)_8 = (?)_2$

7. Perform the following additions in the indicated base system *only*.

(a) $\left(\begin{array}{r} 111011 \\ +110 \\ \hline \end{array}\right)_2$

(b) $\left(\begin{array}{r} 111110111 \\ +111001 \\ \hline \end{array}\right)_2$

(c) $\left(\begin{array}{r} 365 \\ +23 \\ \hline \end{array}\right)_8$

(d) $\left(\begin{array}{r} 2732 \\ +1265 \\ \hline \end{array}\right)_8$

(e) $\left(\begin{array}{r} 10111 \\ 11011 \\ 10111 \\ \hline \end{array}\right)_2$

8. Perform the following subtractions in the indicated base system *only*.

(a) $\left(\begin{array}{r} 11001 \\ -110 \\ \hline \end{array}\right)_2$

(b) $\left(\begin{array}{r} 5372 \\ -2561 \\ \hline \end{array}\right)_8$

(c) $\left(\begin{array}{r} 375 \\ -127 \\ \hline \end{array}\right)_8$

(d) $\left(\begin{array}{r} 11101101 \\ -01001111 \\ \hline \end{array}\right)_2$

(e) $\left(\begin{array}{r} 11011011110 \\ -10100111001 \\ \hline \end{array}\right)_2$

9. Perform the following multiplications or divisions in the indicated base system *only*.

(a) $\left(\begin{array}{r} 1011 \\ \times 11 \\ \hline \end{array}\right)_2$

(b) $\left(\begin{array}{r} 2325 \\ \times 23 \\ \hline \end{array}\right)_8$

(c) $\left(\begin{array}{r} 110 \\ \times 11011 \\ \hline \end{array}\right)_2$

(d) $(1010\ \overline{\smash{\big)}\,1100100}\ )_2$

(e) $(24\ \overline{\smash{\big)}\,740}\ )_8$

10. Perform the following base two subtractions by addition of

complements.   List the ONE's and TWO's complements for each of
the given numbers.

(a)   1011
      − 0011

(b)   10101
      − 01100

(c)   101010
      − 010111

(d)   100001
      − 11110

(e)   1011011101100
      − 1100101101111

0100

Codes

Coding of information is a means of specifying characters (numeric or alphabetic, for example) using other symbols. Codes have been used for security reasons, so that others will not be able to read the message. In computers, however, codes provide a means of specifying these characters using only the 1 and 0 binary symbols available. In addition, the choice among the numerous binary codes depends on the function or use they are to serve. Some codes are suitable when arithmetic operations are being performed. Others are good because they are highly efficient—giving more information using fewer bits (a bit is a binary digit, 1 or 0). Of continuing importance are the codes that allow for error detection or correction—codes that enable the computer to determine whether a character which was coded and transmitted is received correctly and, if there is an error, to correct it. As coding itself is a detailed subject, only some of the more familiar codes are considered here.

4–1. Binary-Coded Decimal

A basic code to consider is called "Binary-coded decimal," or BCD. It uses the binary number system to specify the decimal numbers 0–9. Since BCD numbers are written using 1's and 0's it is a code. Table 4–1 specifies the code characters.

Notice that the code requires using a four-place (four bit) binary character to specify the one-digit decimal character. Obviously this code is much less efficient than the decimal system, but it has the advantage that it is in the 1, 0 language of the computer and may

Table 4-1.   BCD Code

Decimal	Binary-Coded Decimal
0	0000
1	0001
2	0010
3	0011
4	0100
5	0101
6	0110
7	0111
8	1000
9	1001

thus be used in a computer.   A few examples of how numbers are written with this code are

Decimal	BCD
22	0010 0010
35	0011 0101
671	0110 0111 0001
2579	0010 0101 0111 1001

As you see, each decimal number requires its four-bit binary-coded equivalent.   BCD code requires more positions to specify a number than the decimal system.   However, it is in binary notation and therefore extremely useful.   Another point to recognize is that the position within the four bits of a number is important (as in any number system).   The weighting of a position can be specified and is sometimes used to describe this coded form.   The weight of the first (right-most) position is 2^0, or 1, the second 2^1, or 2, the third 2^2, or 4, and the fourth 2^3, or 8.   Reading from left to right the weighting is 8-4-2-1, and the code is called an 8-4-2-1 code.

To help you to see clearly that this code (8-4-2-1) is not the same as binary numbers, consider the following.   Ten in binary is 1010. Ten in binary-coded decimal is 0001 0000.   Sixteen in binary is 10000.   In 8-4-2-1 (BCD) code it is 0001 0110.   See the difference? Actually, any confusion between the two is that the first nine numbers in BCD and binary are exactly the same.   After that they are completely different.   Try the next problem for practice.

Problem 4–1. Write the following decimal numbers in BCD code.

1. 275   2. 362   3. 9256   4. 100   5. 2790

The main value of BCD coding is similar to that of octal numbers —it can be recognized and read easily by people. For example, compare binary and BCD by reading numbers in each form.

Decimal	Binary	BCD
141	10001101	0001 0100 0001
2179	100010000011	0010 0001 0111 1001

When it comes to using this coded form in arithmetic operations, however, additional difficulties are involved. See what happens when adding 8 and 7 in both forms (binary and BCD).

Decimal	Binary	BCD	
8	1000	1000	
+ 7	+0111	+0111	
15	1111	1111	←—— not an acceptable character in BCD (15 is 0001 0101)

Special adders are needed to operate with the BCD code.   Where the recognition property is desired and arithmetic manipulation is important, a modified code may be used.

4–2.   Excess-Three Code

Excess-three code, a modified form of BCD, is shown in Table 4–2 for the decimal numbers 0–9.

If you compare BCD and excess-three carefully, it will become clear what the difference is and how excess-three is derived. As the name implies, each coded character in the excess-three code is three larger than in BCD. Thus six, or 0110, is written 1001, which is nine. It is only nine in BCD, though.   In excess-three code 1001

Table 4–2.   Excess-Three Code

Decimal	BCD	Excess-Three
0	0000	0011
1	0001	0100
2	0010	0101
3	0011	0110
4	0100	0111
5	0101	1000
6	0110	1001
7	0111	1010
8	1000	1011
9	1001	1100

is *six*! Do not make the mistake of forgetting the excess *three*. Here are a few examples of the code.

Decimal	Excess-Three
2	0101
25	0101 1000
629	1001 0101 1100
3271	0110 0101 1010 0100

An example of how excess-three helps in the arithmetic operation is

```
  3            0110
 +9            1100
 ‾‾            ‾‾‾‾
 12      1     0010
     Add 0011  0011
         ‾‾‾‾  ‾‾‾‾
         0100  0101
```

Read 0100 0101 or 12 (in excess-three).

There are a few special rules to follow in the addition (as the adding of 3 to each number in the example just given), but these steps are automatic in a computer and easy to implement, making excess-three more desirable for arithmetic operations.   Recognition is poorer because you reduce each by three in your mind as you read, but it is still easier than straight binary for large numbers.   Try the following problem in writing excess-three code.

Problem 4–2.   Write the following numbers in excess-three code.
   1. 279   2. 301   3. 2176   4. 1568   5. 21769

Recall that BCD is a weighted code; excess-three is not.   A bit in the second position (2^1) of BCD means 2.   In excess-three a bit present in any position does not indicate the addition of a numerical value to the number.   For example, in BCD 0100 is 4.   Adding the 2^1 bit adds 2, making the number 0110—two greater.   In excess-three 0111 is 4 and 6 is 1001—no systematic numerical change.

4–3.   Biquinary Code

Another weighted code which is interesting to consider is called a "biquinary code."   "Bi" meaning "two" and "quinary" meaning "five," the code is seen to be of seven bits where 2 and 5 are considered separate parts of the whole.   Since the code is weighted, Table 4–3 lists the coded forms of 0 to 9 and the weighting of each bit position.

Table 4–3

Decimal	Biquinary	
	5 0	4 3 2 1 0
0	0 1	0 0 0 0 1
1	0 1	0 0 0 1 0
2	0 1	0 0 1 0 0
3	0 1	0 1 0 0 0
4	0 1	1 0 0 0 0
5	1 0	0 0 0 0 1
6	1 0	0 0 0 1 0
7	1 0	0 0 1 0 0
8	1 0	0 1 0 0 0
9	1 0	1 0 0 0 0

Here we see that it takes seven bits to specify a decimal number (compare this to four bits in BCD or excess-three).   Biquinary has as its important feature the built-in provision of indicating when there is an error in the code word.   Where information is transmitted from place to place, as from computer unit to unit, through space from air to ground, from ground station to ground station, etc., a code which allows checks to determine whether an error occurred in transmission is very desirable. Looking carefully at the biquinary code listing in Table 4–2, you should observe the following. Each word has only two 1's. Thus if any extra 1's appeared in the answer, it would be obvious that something was wrong and that the word should not be accepted. If only one 1 was received, again an error would be obvious. In addition, recognition and acceptance of a word as being correct requires that there be one and only one 1 in the first two bits to the left and one and only one 1 in the next five. Because it is easy to implement a circuit which will check for one 1 out of two bits and another to check for one 1 out of five bits, the checking feature is easily established.

Example 4–2. See whether you can determine any errors in the following set of biquinary code words.

		Biquinary	Decimal
(a)		01 10001	4
(b)		01 10010	5
(c)		10 10101	6
(d)		11 00010	6
(e)	01 01000	01 00010	31
(f)	10 10000	10 10000	99
(g)		01 00001	0

Examples (a)–(d) are incorrect whereas (e)–(g) are correct.

Problem 4–3. Write the following numbers in biquinary code.

1. 56   2. 731   3. 68   4. 732   5. 509

4–4. Parity in Codes

Error detection and/or correction is a growing area of study and application in digital data transmission. A very popular means of detecting an error is the use of parity bits. Some punched paper tapes, for example, have parity detection coding to improve the accuracy of reading from the tape into a computer or vice-versa. Parity can be either odd or even, and the addition of a parity bit (binary 1 or 0) will make the total number of 1's in a code character either an odd number or an even number.   For illustrative purposes the BCD code will be modified by the addition of a parity bit.   This bit will be added to the right of the 2^0 position.   In an even parity scheme the added parity bit will make the total number of ONE's *even*, and in an odd parity scheme it will be selected to make the total number of ONE's *odd*.   When a code word is received it is checked for parity (even or odd being previously chosen) and is accepted as correct if it passes the test.   Table 4–4 lists the BCD code, BCD with even parity and BCD with odd parity.   Observe that the parity bit is opposite for the different parity types.

Table 4–4.   Parity in BCD Code

Decimal	BCD Code	BCD with Odd Parity			BCD with Even Parity		
0	0000	0000	1	or 00001	0000	0	or 00000
1	0001	0001	0	or 00010	0001	1	or 00011
2	0010	0010	0	or 00100	0010	1	or 00101
3	0011	0011	1	or 00111	0011	0	or 00110
4	0100	0100	0	or 01000	0100	1	or 01001
5	0101	0101	1	or 01011	0101	0	or 01010
6	0110	0110	1	or 01101	0110	0	or 01100
7	0111	0111	0	or 01110	0111	1	or 01111
8	1000	1000	0	or 10000	1000	1	or 10001
9	1001	1001	1	or 10011	1001	0	or 10010

Example 4–3.   See whether you can determine an error (or not) in the following parity-coded BCD words.

	word	parity bit	parity type
(a)	1001	0	odd parity
(b)	1000	0	odd parity
(c)	0001	0	even parity
(d)	1010	0	even parity
(e)	0110	1	odd parity

Examples (a) and (c) are incorrect and (b) and (e) are correct. Example (d) is incorrect only because it is not a BCD code character. The parity bit is, however, correct for even parity.   Parity is used elsewhere than in BCD codes.   If a set of miscellaneous words are sent with parity added, the parity bit is similarly chosen.

Example 4–4. See if you can determine whether an error is present in the following.

	word	parity bit	parity type
(a)	0110111101	1	even parity
(b)	1101110100	0	odd parity
(c)	1110111011	0	odd parity
(d)	1011011100	0	even parity
(e)	1010111010	1	odd parity

Examples (b) and (c) are incorrect; (a), (d), and (e) are correct. Getting back to BCD coding, here are a few correct examples.

(f) decimal 57 is   0101 1   0111 0   with odd parity

(g) decimal 79 is   0111 1   1001 0   with even parity

Problem 4–4. Write the correct coded form using BCD with the indicated parity.

1. Decimal 95 with even parity
2. Decimal 7986 with odd parity
3. Decimal 605 with odd parity
4. Decimal 71 with even parity
5. Decimal 6094 with odd parity

4–5. Gray Code

Gray code is used largely with optical or mechanical shaft position encoders.   It is a nonweighted code whose main feature is that only a single bit changes between each successive word.   It is used on a type of code wheel which has successive positions around the circumference indicated by a new word; the Gray code allows ambiguity of only one place.   This feature will be expanded on in the discussion of input equipment (Chapter 12).   For the present, the code itself is our main consideration.

Because there are a large number of codes of, say, ten bits per word that can be formed where only one bit at a time changes, the selection of one particular code—called "Gray"—is of interest. The code form on the input piece of equipment is important in improving reading accuracy and simplifying construction problems. Its use in the computer presents great difficulties because of its nonweighted feature, however.   Thus the code would best be used if it were now (in the computer) converted to a weighted code—the best one being straight binary. Gray code is a particular code which is useful because of its one-bit-change external feature and the simplicity of converting it to binary form.

A listing of straight binary and the Gray code equivalent is given for decimal numbers 0–12 in Table 4–5. There is a Gray code for every possible binary number, so that the listing is only illustrative.

Table 4–5.   Gray Code for Decimals 0–12

Decimal	Binary	Gray Code
0	0000	0000
1	0001	0001
2	0010	0011
3	0011	0010
4	0100	0110
5	0101	0111
6	0110	0101
7	0111	0100
8	1000	1100
9	1001	1101
10	1010	1111
11	1011	1110
12	1100	1010

Notice how only one bit changes between any two successive words in Gray code. This is not true in binary. In going from decimal 7 to 8, the binary changes all four bits, whereas the Gray code only changes one. In going from decimal 9 to 10, the binary changes from 1001 to 1010, where the 2^0 bit goes from a 1 to a 0 and the 2^1 goes from a 0 to a 1—two changes. In Gray the change of 1101 to 1111 has the 2^1 bit changing from 0 to 1—one change only. Since there are clearly defined rules for converting from Gray to binary or from binary to Gray, a description of these, with examples, will be considered next.

In converting the Gray-coded word into binary code, the conversion must begin with the most significant bit (MSB) first. In binary the least significant bit (LSB) is the 2^0 bit and the MSB is the one of highest weight position (with four bits the 2^3).   A binary number and its Gray code equivalent is

                   MSB
     Gray   1   0 1 1 0 1 0 1 1 1 0 0 1
     Binary   1   1 0 1 1 0 0 1 0 1 1 1 0

where the MSB is on the left.   To convert, repeat in the binary the same bit as in Gray until and including the first 1.   In this example we start with a 1, which is then repeated as the first binary bit (MSB first).   Repeat the same binary bit as long as the next Gray bits are 0 (one position in this example).   For every following 1 (after the first) in the Gray code word, *change* the bit in the binary word from what preceded *in the binary* word.   The second Gray 1 signifies changing the binary bit.   Since it was a 1 on the preceding, it gets changed to a 0.   Continuing the rules, the next Gray 1 means change the binary bit preceding (0) to 1.   The following Gray 0 means leave the binary bit preceding alone—repeat the 1 again for the binary.   This procedure continues for the rest of the word.   Although a description is cumbersome, a few examples should help make the procedure clear.

Follow the next three examples closely and then try converting from Gray to binary in the given problems.

Example 4–5.
                    leave
                    binary change
                    alone binary

     Gray   0 1 0 1 1 0 0 1 1 1 1 0 1 0 1
     Binary   0 1 1 0 1 1 1 0 1 0 1 1 0 0 1

            first 1

Example 4–6.
                    change
                    pre-
              repeat ceding
              first binary   leave
              one   bit   binary as
                            it was

     Gray   1 1 1 1 0 0 0 1 0 1 0 1 1 1 0 0 1 0 1
     Binary 1 0 1 0 0 0 0 1 1 0 0 1 0 1 1 1 0 0 1

Perhaps some arrows will help impress the few rules.

Example 4–7.
     Gray   1 0 1 0 1 1 0 0 1 1 1 0 0 0 1 1 1 1 0 0 0 0 1
     Binary 1 1 0 0 1 0 0 0 1 0 1 1 1 1 0 1 0 1 1 1 1 1 0

If a 1 appears in the Gray word it causes the preceding binary bit to change (from whatever it was); a 0 leaves the binary as it *was*.

Problem 4–5. Convert the following Gray-coded words to binary form.

1. 1 0 0 1 1 1 0 1 0 1 1 0 1
2. 1 0 1 0 1 0 1 0 1 0 1 0
3. 0 1 1 1 0 1 1 1 0 1 1 1 1 0
4. 1 0 0 1 1 0 0 0 1 1 1 0 0 0 0 1 1 1 1
5. 1 1 1 1 1 1 1 1 1 1 1 1 1

The procedure for converting a binary word into Gray form is somewhat easier to state.   The rule is to compare each pair of succeeding bits (starting from the MSB).   If they are the same, write a 0 for the Gray word.   If they are different, write a 1 for the Gray code word.   Compare the first bit to zero to start.

Example 4–8.

Binary 0 1 1 0 1 0 1 1 1 1 0 1 1 0 0 1 0 1 0

Gray   0 1 0 1 1 1 0 0 0 1 1 0 1 0 1 1 1 1

Example 4–9.

Binary 0 1 1 1 0 1 0 1 0 1 0 1 1 1 1 1

Gray   0 1 0 0 1 1 1 1 1 1 1 0 0 0 0

Note: ⌣ means add two bits, modulo two (no carry), and put result on bottom as Gray bit.

Problem 4–6.   Convert the given binary number into Gray code.

1. 0 1 1 0 1 0 1 1 1 1 0 1 1 1 0 1 1
2. 1 0 0 0 1 1 1 1 0 1 1 0 1 0 1 1 0
3. 1 0 1 0 0 1 0 1 1 0 1 0 0 1
4. 1 1 1 1 1 1 1 1 1 1
5. 0 0 1 0 1 0 1 1 1 0 1 1 1

4–6.   ASCII Input/Output Code

When alphabetic letters, decimal numbers, special characters, or commands are used with a computer, they must be coded in binary. A four-bit code is needed to represent the decimal digits (as does BCD).   To handle these plus the twenty-six alphabetic letters plus some special characters, a code of at least six bits is required ($2^6 = 64$ combinations).   A standardized code which is being widely accepted by industry is the ASCII code—American Standards Code for Information Interchange. The code is an eight-bit code and allows representation of both lower-case and upper-case alphabetic characters (e.g., *, +, =) and over thirty command or control operations (e.g., start of message, end of message, carriage return, line feed).

Table 4–6 lists the ASCII code for the decimal digits, alphabetic characters, and a few special characters. The ASCII numbering convention calls for a sequence from left to right, so that bit position 7 is the high-order position. The same code representation may be used with punched paper tape, magnetic tape, magnetic disk, high-speed printers, some teletype equipment, etc. Examples of these are provided in the section on input/output units (Chapter 12).

The eight-level code is used to represent characters in the input and output pieces of equipment. Once in the computer they may be handled more conveniently for different operations. For example, the decimal digits need not be carried in the computer as an eight-bit word. The 4321 bits were purposely chosen as the BCD code form for the digits 0–9. By stripping off the 76X5 bits the computer need save only four bits of BCD form to represent decimal digits. If the standard word length is eight bits as indicated, the computer can handle decimal digits internally by grouping two four-bit BCD digits in a single word. Consider Example 4–10.

Example 4–10. Packing of two ASCII digits into one eight-bit word.

The number 29 represented as 0 1 0 1 0 0 1 0 0 1 0 1 1 0 0 1 in the input/output units can be regrouped in the computer as follows,

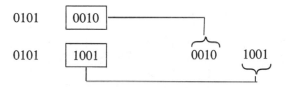

which is an eight-bit word of two decimal digits.

Computer designs have recently started calling a group of bits which may represent a word or a few characters by the descriptive term "byte." For example, IBM's System/360 uses eight-bit bytes. Data is handled by byte rather than by bit within the computer system. The eight-bit byte could be used to represent a single ASCII character as it comes into the computer or two decimal digits

Table 4–6. ASCII Code (partial listing)

Character	7	6	5	X	4	3	2	1	Character	7	6	5	X	4	3	2	1
0	0	1	0	1	0	0	0	0	@	1	0	1	0	0	0	0	0
1	0	1	0	1	0	0	0	1	A	1	0	1	0	0	0	0	1
2	0	1	0	1	0	0	1	0	B	1	0	1	0	0	0	1	0
3	0	1	0	1	0	0	1	1	C	1	0	1	0	0	0	1	1
4	0	1	0	1	0	1	0	0	D	1	0	1	0	0	1	0	0
5	0	1	0	1	0	1	0	1	E	1	0	1	0	0	1	0	1
6	0	1	0	1	0	1	1	0	F	1	0	1	0	0	1	1	0
7	0	1	0	1	0	1	1	1	G	1	0	1	0	0	1	1	1
8	0	1	0	1	1	0	0	0	H	1	0	1	0	1	0	0	0
9	0	1	0	1	1	0	0	1	I	1	0	1	0	1	0	0	1
:	0	1	0	1	1	0	1	0	J	1	0	1	0	1	0	1	0
;	0	1	0	1	1	0	1	1	K	1	0	1	0	1	0	1	1
<	0	1	0	1	1	1	0	0	L	1	0	1	0	1	1	0	0
=	0	1	0	1	1	1	0	1	M	1	0	1	0	1	1	0	1
>	0	1	0	1	1	1	1	0	N	1	0	1	0	1	1	1	0
?	0	1	0	1	1	1	1	1	O	1	0	1	0	1	1	1	1
blank	0	1	0	0	0	0	0	0	P	1	0	1	1	0	0	0	0
!	0	1	0	0	0	0	0	1	Q	1	0	1	1	0	0	0	1
"	0	1	0	0	0	0	1	0	R	1	0	1	1	0	0	1	0
#	0	1	0	0	0	0	1	1	S	1	0	1	1	0	0	1	1
$	0	1	0	0	0	1	0	0	T	1	0	1	1	0	1	0	0
%	0	1	0	0	0	1	0	1	U	1	0	1	1	0	1	0	1
&	0	1	0	0	0	1	1	0	V	1	0	1	1	0	1	1	0
'	0	1	0	0	0	1	1	1	W	1	0	1	1	0	1	1	1
(	0	1	0	0	1	0	0	0	X	1	0	1	1	1	0	0	0
)	0	1	0	0	1	0	0	1	Y	1	0	1	1	1	0	0	1
*	0	1	0	0	1	0	1	0	Z	1	0	1	1	1	0	1	0
+	0	1	0	0	1	0	1	1	[	1	0	1	1	1	0	1	1
,	0	1	0	0	1	1	0	0	\	1	0	1	1	1	1	0	0
−	0	1	0	0	1	1	0	1	]	1	0	1	1	1	1	0	1
.	0	1	0	0	1	1	1	0	↑	1	0	1	1	1	1	1	0
/	0	1	0	0	1	1	1	1	←	1	0	1	1	1	1	1	1

in arithmetic operations.   Words may now represent a fixed number of bytes.

Practice using the ASCII code in the following problems.

Problem 4–7.   Use the ASCII code to represent the following.
1. 86   2. 293   3. HELLO
4. DIGITAL   5. DIGIT No. 3
Problem 4–8.   Regroup the following ASCII code characters into
two four-bit digits per byte and write the decimal equivalent.
1. 01010100   01010101   2. 01010011   01010110
3. 01011001   01010010   4. 01010001   01011000
5. 01010111   01010000

Summary

A number of very popular codes were presented in this chapter.
Each code has different good features and the codes are generally
used in different areas.   The most popular code is BCD, which is
used to represent the decimal digits 0–9.   It is read more easily than
straight binary.   It is not as easily used in arithmetic calculations.
Where these are important a modified form, called "excess-three,"
is used (but this code form is not as recognizable as BCD).

To allow checking for errors when transmitting binary data the
biquinary code form may be used or a parity bit may be included
with the coded character.   Many other codes are used, and the
choice is dependent on the extent that data must be reliable, on
how much extra information can be sent, and on how much extra
equipment is necessary to carry out the checking operation.

Gray code is used primarily to represent data on a code wheel
(discussed in Chapter 12).   Since the code must have one form on
the code wheel or disk and is best handled as straight binary in the
computer, conversion from Gray to binary and binary to Gray is
necessary.

Finally, the ASCII code for representing the many characters and
commands of input/output equipment was presented.   Some more
examples with this code will be given in Chapter 12.

PROBLEMS

1. Write the binary-coded decimal (BCD) form of $(2573)_{10}$.
2. Write the BCD form of the base ten numbers from 10 to 16.
3. Write the BCD form of $(39287)_{10}$.

 4. Write the decimal number 2718 in excess-three code form.
 5. Write the biquinary code form of $(6259)_{10}$.
 6. Write the biquinary code form of the BCD number 1001 1000 0101.
 7. Convert the binary number 1101101101 into Gray code.
 8. Convert the Gray code number 110110101 into binary.
 9. Write $(3572)_{10}$ in BCD with EVEN parity.
 10. Write $(2598)_{10}$ in excess-three with ODD parity.
 11. Write 27 using ASCII code.
 12. Write A + B = C using ASCII code.

0101

Boolean algebra

5–1. Boolean Algebra Fundamentals

Boolean algebra is the mathematical technique used when consider-ing problems of a logical nature.   In 1847, an English mathematician, George Boole, developed the basic laws and rules for a mathematics which could be applied to problems of deductive logic.   Until 1938 these techniques remained in the mathematical field.   At this time a very good scientist, Claude Shannon, seeing the useful features of such an algebra, adapted it for analyzing multicontact networks such as those considered in telephone work.   (He worked for Bell Laboratories.)   With the development of computers the use of Boolean algebra in the electronics field increased to where it is now mainly used by engineers to aid them in logic design.

Originally, Boolean algebra described propositions whose out-come could be either true or false.   Shannon used it to define a network of contacts which could be opened or closed.   In computer work it is used in addition to describe circuits whose state can be either 1 or 0.   The logical 1 of 0 can be those of the binary number system.   They can also be identified with an open or closed condi-tion or a true or false condition—these being binary in nature. Since the mathematics involves only two-valued variables and since the possible condition of any unknown in a problem can be specified as either 0 or 1, Boolean algebra will turn out to be quite simplified compared to regular algebra, where the variables are continuous.

Let us first consider some of the basic rules, operations, and identities of this algebra.   When considering operations with the numbers 0 and 1, two such operations must be clearly defined.   In particular, the OR operation is similar to addition and the AND operation to multiplication. The reasons for these newly defined operations will become clear as they are used in practical applications. The OR operation can be specified by considering all combinations of OR'ing two variables.

$$0 + 0 = 0$$
$$0 + 1 = 1$$
$$1 + 0 = 1$$
$$1 + 1 = 1$$

Note: " + " means "OR."

Notice that only the last operation $1 + 1 = 1$ is not straight addition. It is read 1 OR 1 equals 1. The turning on of a single light bulb by two people throwing switches in an interconnecting system can demonstrate an OR function. Referring to the combinations listed, if both people leave their switch OFF (0) the light remains OFF (0). If one turns his switch ON (1) and the light goes ON (1), OR if the other throws his switch ON causing the light to go ON, the OR function describes the operation. Finally, if both switches are turned ON and the light goes ON, the OR'ing of these switches still only results in the light going ON (1)—this is described by the statement 1 OR 1 equals 1. Thus a function whose outcomes for the combinations of conditions are those shown is called an OR function.

A circuit which can be used to provide the OR operation will contain parallel switches. If letters designate the different switches, the circuit will look like Figure 5–1.

The Boolean OR function can be used to describe the switching network in the box of Figure 5–1: A + B = output to light bulb.

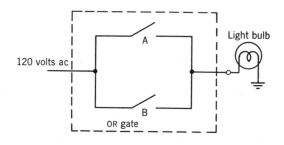

Figure 5–1. OR gate.

Switch A being closed is defined as the state 1 and open as the state 0. A 1 to the light bulb means the light goes ON (1), whereas a 0 to the light bulb leaves it OFF (0).   If either A or B is closed (1), the output is 1.   If both A and B are closed, the output is still 1.   Only when both switches are open (0) is the light bulb OFF (0).   The OR function describes all these possible combinations and the circuit in the box is an OR gate.

We should be aware of another basic interconnection for the two switches and the light bulb, namely, a series connection of the switches to the light bulb (Figure 5–2).   This arrangement is descriptive of an AND operation which resembles multiplication.   All four possible combinations of 0 and 1 for the AND operation are

$$0 \cdot 0 = 0$$
$$0 \cdot 1 = 0$$
$$1 \cdot 0 = 0$$
$$1 \cdot 1 = 1$$

The dot is used to indicate the AND operation.   When letters are used (in general cases) the dot is sometimes even omitted.   Let us examine the switch-lamp circuit of Figure 5–2 and check to see how it describes the AND function.

When switch A is closed (1) but B open (0), the light is OFF (0). Switch B closed but A open gives the same result, and so does having both A and B open.   Only when A and B are both closed does the light bulb go ON.   In the OR operation the light bulb also went ON when both switches were closed.   However, in the OR operation it also went ON when either switch was closed; in the AND operation it only goes ON when both switches are closed and not any other time.   To specify either function (AND or OR) uniquely, all combinations must satisfy the function.

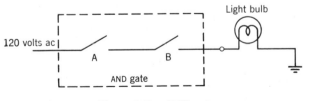

Figure 5–2.   AND gate.

Using these basic functions we can now specify some basic identities.

$$A + 0 = A$$
$$A \cdot 0 = 0$$
$$A + 1 = 1$$
$$A \cdot 1 = A$$
$$A + A = A$$
$$A \cdot A = A$$

To check the validity of these statements we need only see whether they hold true for all possible conditions.   Since the variable A can only be 0 or 1 the checking is quite simple.   For $A + 0 = A$

$$\underline{A + 0 = A}$$
$$0 + 0 = 0$$
$$1 + 0 = 1$$

all combinations of A give valid statements.

For $\underline{A \cdot 0 = 0}$

$$1 \cdot 0 = 0$$
$$0 \cdot 0 = 0$$

all combinations are true

The method used to check these last two statements tests the truth of the statement.

If we check the remaining statements, we find they are all valid.

$\underline{A + 1 = 1}$	$\underline{A \cdot 1 = A}$	$\underline{A + A = A}$	$\underline{A \cdot A = A}$
$0 + 1 = 1$	$0 \cdot 1 = 0$	$1 + 1 = 1$	$1 \cdot 1 = 1$
$1 + 1 = 1$	$1 \cdot 1 = 1$	$0 + 0 = 0$	$0 \cdot 0 = 0$

Continuing our study of this different algebra, we find that it satisfies some of the basic laws of ordinary algebra.   These are

Commutative law $A + B = B + A$
$$A \cdot B = B \cdot A$$
Associative law $A + (B + C) = (A + B) + C$
$$A(B \cdot C) = (A \cdot B) \cdot C$$
Distributive law $A \cdot (B + C) = A \cdot B + A \cdot C$

A truth table is used to test *all* possible combinations of the variables and their outcomes, in a systematic manner.   When the truth table is applied, the different expressions being compared are "solved" for each input combination, on each line of the table.   If we examine the value resulting for each input combination, we can conclude that the two terms being compared are equal, *if and only if* they have the *same* value for every input combination.   One good way to be sure that you have included all combinations in the table would be to write the binary numbers in order, down the table (as in the examples).   You can also check to see that you have included a sufficient number of combinations by seeing that for two variables there are four (2^2) combinations, for three variables there are eight (2^3) combinations, for four variables there are sixteen (2^4) combinations, etc.   Generalizing, for n variables there are 2^n combinations to consider.

Let us see how a truth table is used to verify the algebraic laws (see Figure 5–3).   Since the combinations for A + (B + C) are the same as those for (A + B) + C for *all possible conditions*, the two functions are identical.   Compare (A + B) with (A + B) + C below in the same table.   They differ only once, but that is sufficient to make them different.   A · (B · C) is identical to (A · B) · C because it has the same value for every possible combination of the variables.

A truth table test of the distributive law shows that it too is valid in Boolean algebra (see Figure 5–3c).   For every combination of A, B, and C the statement A · (B + C) is the same as AB + AC.

A	B	(A + B)	(B + A)	
0	0	0	0	
0	1	1	1	(A + B) = (B + A)
1	0	1	1	
1	1	1	1	

A	B	A · B	B · A	
0	0	0	0	
0	1	0	0	A · B = B · A
1	0	0	0	
1	1	1	1	

Figure 5–3a.   Truth tables for commutative law (two variables).

A	B	C	(B + C)	A + (B + C)	(A + B)	(A + B) + C
0	0	0	0	0	0	0
0	0	1	1	1	0	1
0	1	0	1	1	1	1
0	1	1	1	1	1	1
1	0	0	0	1	1	1
1	0	1	1	1	1	1
1	1	0	1	1	1	1
1	1	1	1	1	1	1

$$A + (B + C) = (A + B) + C$$

A	B	C	(B · C)	A · (B · C)	(A · B)	(A · B) · C
0	0	0	0	0	0	0
0	0	1	0	0	0	0
0	1	0	0	0	0	0
0	1	1	1	0	0	0
1	0	0	0	0	0	0
1	0	1	0	0	0	0
1	1	0	0	0	1	0
1	1	1	1	1	1	1

$$A \cdot (B \cdot C) = (A \cdot B) \cdot C$$

Figure 5–3b.   Truth tables for associative law (three variables).

A	B	C	(B+C)	A·(B+C)	(A·B)	(A·C)	(A·B)+(A·C)
0	0	0	0	0	0	0	0
0	0	1	1	0	0	0	0
0	1	0	1	0	0	0	0
0	1	1	1	0	0	0	0
1	0	0	0	0	0	0	0
1	0	1	1	1	0	1	1
1	1	0	1	1	1	0	1
1	1	1	1	1	1	1	1

$$A \cdot (B + C) = (A \cdot B) + (A \cdot C)$$

Figure 5–3c.   Truth table for distributive law.

A Boolean variable can take on one of any two values—H and L, T and F, 0 and 1, etc.   Consider a variable A and its negation NOT

A, or symbolically, $\bar{A}$ or A'.   The bar over a letter or the prime after it is used to denote the negation function.   Some simple applications of this function are

$$A + A' = 1$$
$$A \cdot A' = 0$$
$$(A')' = A$$

Checking the validity of these identities with a simple truth table we find they are all valid.

$A + A' = 1$	$A \cdot A' = 0$	$(A')' = A$
$0 + 1 = 1$	$0 \cdot 1 = 0$	$1 = 1$
$1 + 0 = 1$	$1 \cdot 0 = 0$	$0 = 0$

One special relationship resulting from the NOT function is called De Morgan's theorem.

$$\text{NOR} \quad (A + B)' = A'B'$$
$$\text{or}$$
$$\text{NAND} \quad (A \cdot B)' = A' + B'$$

Check these statements yourself using a truth table.   The theorem indicates that when a multivariable expression is negated, each term is negated and each operation (AND, OR) is reversed.   A few examples will suffice to show how the theorem is applied.

Example 5-1.   Negate $A + BC$.
  Solution: $(A + [B \cdot C])' = A' \cdot (B \cdot C)'$
$$= A' \cdot [B' + C']$$
$$= A'B' + A'C'$$
Example 5-2.   Negate $AB + C'D'$.
  Solution: $(AB + C'D')' = (AB)' \, (C'D')'$
$$= (A' + B') \cdot (C + D)$$
$$= A'C + B'C + A'D + B'D$$
$$= C(A' + B') + D(A' + B')$$
Example 5-3.   Negate $A'B'C' + A + B + C$.
  Solution: $(A'B'C' + A + B + C)' = (A'B'C')' \cdot A' \cdot B' \cdot C'$
$$= (AA') \, B'C' + (BB') \, A'C' + (CC') \, A'B'$$
$$= 0 \cdot B'C' + 0 \cdot A'C' + 0 \cdot A'B'$$
$$= 0 + 0 + 0$$
$$= 0$$

The last example also illustrates the simplification or reduction of a Boolean expression by applying the identities defined. It is this operation—manipulation of terms, reduction of expression—which makes Boolean algebra so useful to a logical designer. A number of examples are provided to indicate the general procedure. Follow these carefully before trying the numerous problems.

Example 5–4. Simplify $(AB + C)A$.

  Solution: $(AB + C)A = A \cdot AB + A \cdot C$
  $$= (A \cdot A) B + A \cdot C$$
  $$= A \cdot B + A \cdot C$$
  $$= A(B + C)$$

Example 5–5. Simplify $A + A'B$.

  Solution: Although the statement appears simple, it can be further simplified.

$$A + A'B = A(B + B') + A'B$$

Multiplication of A by $B + B'$ does not change the expression since $B + B' = 1$. Expanding,

$$A(B + B') + A'B = AB + AB' + A'B$$

Adding an additional AB to the expression again, it is valid since

$$AB + AB = AB$$
$$AB + AB' + A'B = AB + AB + AB' + A'B$$

Regrouping,

$$= A(B + B') + (A + A')B$$
$$= A(1) + (1)B$$
$$= A + B$$

To restate the result, $A + A'B = A + B$. Prove that this is true by checking with a truth table.

Since the reduction is not straightforward but the result is quite useful, the relation should be memorized so that it can be used to simplify terms in more complicated problems. Recognition of this form $(A + A'B)$ in a problem will sometimes help in simplifying.

Example 5–6. Simplify $A'B + AB + A'B'$.

  Solution: $A'B + AB + A'B' = A'(B + B') + AB$
  $$= A'(1) + AB = A' + AB$$
  $$= A' + B \text{ (using rule in}$$
  $$\text{Example 5–5).}$$

Example 5-7.   Simplify $(AB' + A'B)'$.

Solution: $(AB' + A'B)' = (AB')'(A'B)'$
$$= (A' + B)(A + B')$$
$$= A'A + A'B' + BA + BB'$$
$$= 0 + A'B' + AB + 0$$
$$= AB + A'B'$$

Problem 5-1.   Simplify the following expressions.

1. $AB + BC$
2. $AB' + BC + C'A$
3. $A'(BC + AB + BA')$
4. $ABC + CAB + AB + A$
5. $(A' + AB)(A' + B)$
6. $XY + YZ + Z'Y$
7. $[(X + Y)' + (X + Z)']Z$
8. $(XYZ + WX')'$
9. $UVW + XVW + YVW$
10. $BC + AD + ABCD + CDA + A'$

Problem 5-2.   Use the truth table to determine whether the following expressions are identical.

1. $XY + X'Y + X'Y' = X' + Y$
2. $ABC + AC + BC = A + B + C$
3. $(X'Y + Y'X)' + XY = (XY' + Y'X)'$
4. $ABD + A'B'D + AB'D' = A(B'D' + BD)$
5. $(AND)(DAN) + AN(AD) = AND$

5-2. Relay Logic

When the OR function was introduced, a parallel arrangement of switches was used to illustrate the practical OR circuit. A series arrangement of switches illustrated a practical AND circuit. Complex circuits made of series, parallel, and series-parallel switch connections found largely in telephone operation are also used in other practical forms in computers. Considering first the switch as a gating element, we can see how Boolean operations can be used to simplify circuits. Let us define a closed circuit as a 1 (electrical signal is passed) and an open circuit as a 0 (electrical signal blocked). A switching circuit can be described by a Boolean equation. Consider the following examples. (Note the new symbol used for relay contacts.)

Example 5–8. Write the Boolean expression for the circuit given in Figure 5–4.

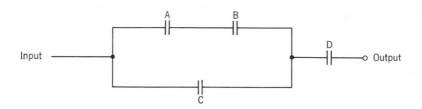

Figure 5–4. Relay circuit for Example 5–8.

Solution: $(AB + C)D$ = Output.

Example 5–9. Write and simplify the Boolean equation of the circuit given in Figure 5–5.

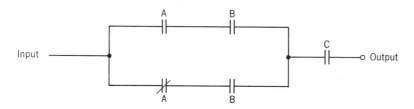

Figure 5–5. Relay circuit for Example 5–9.

Solution: $\text{Output} = (A\,B + A'B) \cdot C$
$$= (A + A') \cdot B \cdot C$$
$$= (1) \cdot B \cdot C$$
$$= B \cdot C$$

Notice that the letter B is used to represent more than one contact pair. This indicates that both switches are operated identically as, for example, multiple contacts on a relay. When the relay is energized all switches of the relay are operated, even though they may be used to interconnect many different circuits or parts of circuits. As simplified, the circuit could be replaced by only two switches B, C. Referring to the circuit diagram, it should now be clear that when A is open, A' is closed and the path is completed through B and C. If A is closed, A' is open and there is also a path through B and C.   In other words, it does not matter what state A is in; only the states of B and C matter.   The simplified expression indicates this operation.   Although you may be skeptical about so simple a case requiring Boolean techniques to improve the circuit, you must appreciate the complex operation of switches in both telephone switching operation and logic circuit use and the large number of connections in a system.   Boolean algebra has proved not only useful but essential in designing and simplifying telephone and computer circuits.

Problem 5–3.   Write and simplify the output expression for the given circuits (see Figure 5–6).

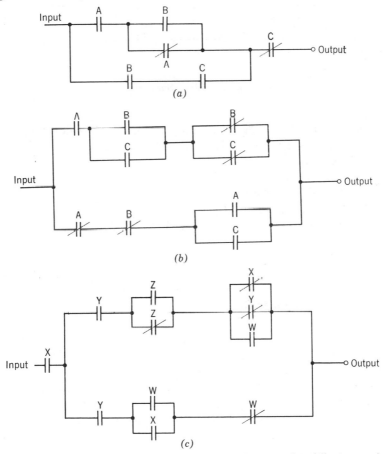

Figure 5–6.   Relay circuits for Problem 5–3.   (*Continued on following page*)

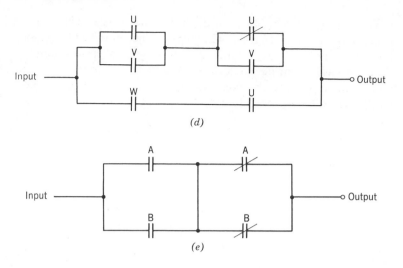

(d)

(e)

Figure 5–6.   (*Continued*)

Problem 5–4.   Draw the circuit diagram of the following Boolean expressions.   Do not simplify the expressions.
   1. WX + WZ + XY + X′Y′
   2. XUV + WX + U′V + X′
   3. AB + CD + (AB)(C + D)
   4. (AM + FM)(DC + AC)
   5. UV + U + V + X′Y′ + X′ + Y′

5–3. Electronic Logic Gates

Electronic gating as used primarily in computers employs transistors, diodes, and other solid-state components to perform the AND and OR function, the NOT, or negation, operation or combinations of these.   A symbol specifies the type of gate, and the interconnection of these gates provides basic operations in a computer.   Although other symbols are shown in the literature, the

ASA standard will be used in this book (see Figure 5–7); in addition, a circle termination indicates an output, straight lines indicate an input, and signal flow on diagrams is from top of page to bottom or left to right, unless an arrow specifies otherwise.

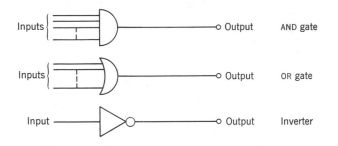

Figure 5–7.   Electronic gate symbols.

The inverter provides the NOT function.   A 1 applied to the input results in a 0 at the output and vice versa.   As before, these blocks when interconnected can be described by a Boolean equation.   They can also be used to provide a circuit which will operate to implement a Boolean expression.

Example 5–10.   Write and simplify the Boolean expression defined by the block diagram in Figure 5–8.

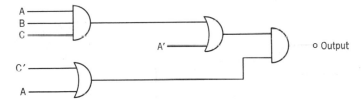

Figure 5–8.   Logic diagram for Example 5–10.

Solution: $(A \cdot B \cdot C + A')(A + C') = $ Output
$AABC + AA' + ABCC' + A'C' = $ Output
$ABC + 0 + AB(0) + A'C' = $ Output
$ABC + A'C' = $ Output

Example 5–11.   Draw the circuit diagram for the Boolean expression AB + AC + A′C′ + B′C′.

Solution: See Figure 5–9.

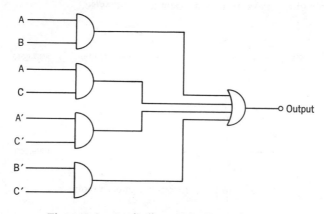

Figure 5–9.   Logic diagram for Example 5–11.

Problem 5–5.   Write and simplify the Boolean (logical) expressions for the block diagrams of Figure 5–10.

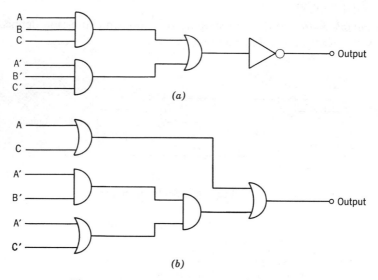

Figure 5–10.   Logic diagrams for Problem 5–5.

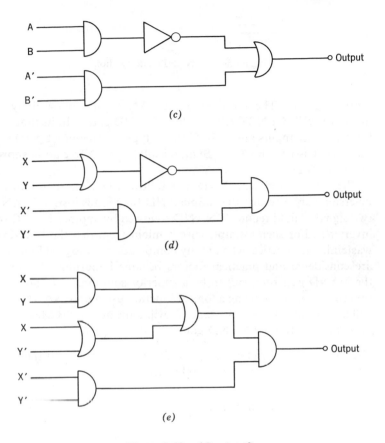

Figure 5-10.   (*Continued*)

Problem 5-6.   Draw the logical diagrams for the given equations. Do not simplify.

1. (AB + CD) C′
2. (A′B′ + CD)(AB + C)
3. (XY + Z)′(X′Y′Z′)
4. WUV + W′U′V′ + (UV + WX)
5. (X + Y)′ + (X + Z) · (UY) · (X + Z)

NAND/NOR gates.   Besides the three basic gates (AND, OR, INVERTER), two practical combinations of these have become

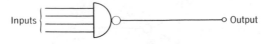

Figure 5–11. NAND gate symbol.

more popular. The grouping of an AND gate followed by an inverter is called a NOT AND gate or NAND gate. In its practical form the gate inputs are A, B, C (for a typical three-input gate) and the output is $(A \cdot B \cdot C)'$. Symbolically, a NAND gate is shown in Figure 5–11.

The symbol used is an AND gate followed by a circle to indicate inversion. Notice that the simple AND function is lost. To AND two signals would require a NAND followed by another NAND (or inverter). For such a simple case it might seem that the NAND is wasteful. In practice, when many combinations of logical functions are considered and practical factors become important, the use of the NAND gate turns out to be a superior solution. For now, the procedures of synthesizing a logical function using only NAND gates will be considered. A few examples will indicate the basic technique of working with only NAND gates.

Example 5–12.   Develop the block diagram to implement the given logical equation using *only* NAND gates.

(a) XYZ

   Solution: See Figure 5–12*a*.

Figure 5–12*a*.   NAND gate logic diagram for XYZ.

(b) X + Y + Z

   Solution: See Figure 5–12*b*.

Figure 5–12*b*.   NAND gate logic diagrams for X + Y + Z.

By De Morgan's theorem $(X'Y'Z')' = X + Y + Z$. The use of De Morgan's theorem will prove a most valuable tool in using the NAND gate.

(c) $XY' + X'Z$

Solution: First let us rework the equation into NAND form.

$$(XY' + X'Z) = [(XY')' \cdot (X'Z)']'$$

Notice that the right-hand expression is made up of AND terms inverted. This form can now be implemented directly with NAND gates, as in Figure 5–12c.

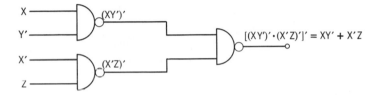

Figure 5–12c.   NAND gate logic diagram for $XY' + X'Z$.

(d) $XYZ + Y'Z' + YZ'$

Solution: Let us formalize the technique of Example 5–12c. First, write the given expression with a double negation. This does not change the expression since $(A')'$ is still A.

$$[(XYZ + Y'Z' + YZ')']'$$

Next, use the inner NOT sign and De Morgan's theorem to rework the expression.

$$[(XYZ)' \cdot (Y'Z')' \cdot (YZ')']'$$

Notice that starting with an expression containing OR'd terms the use of these two steps has converted the form to that suitable for NAND implementation (see Figure 5–12d). The final logical equation can be reduced even further.

$$
\begin{aligned}
XYZ + Y'Z' + YZ' &= XYZ + Z'(Y' + Y). \\
&= XYZ + Z'(1) \\
&= XYZ + Z' \\
&= XY + Z' \quad \text{(using } AB + B' = A + B' \text{ rule)}
\end{aligned}
$$

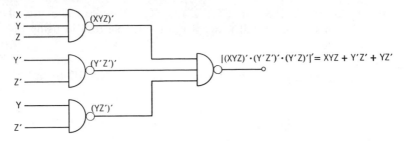

Figure 5–12*d*.   NAND gate logic diagram for $XYZ + Y''Z' + YZ'$.

To develop this last expression in NAND form

$$XY + Z' = [(XY + Z')']'$$
$$= [(XY)' \cdot (Z')']'$$
$$= [(XY)' \cdot Z]'$$

This can be implemented with the logic diagram of Figure 5–12*e*.

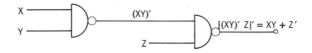

Figure 5–12*e*.   NAND gate logic diagram for $XY + Z'$.

(e) $(XY' + Z)(X'Z + Y')(XY' + Z')$

Solution: To be able to bring this expression into the proper form for NAND gate use, it will first be expanded into the form in which the interconnecting terms are OR'd.

$$\doteq (XY' + Z)(XX'Y'Z + X'ZZ' + Y'XY' + Y'Z')$$
$$= (XY' + Z)(0 + 0 + XY' + Y'Z')$$
$$= XY' + XY'Z' + XY'Z + Y'ZZ'$$
$$= XY' + XY'Z' + XY'Z$$
$$= XY' (1 + Z' + Z)$$
$$= XY'$$

See Figure 5–12*f*.

(f) $(XY + U)(W + XZ)(UV + Y)$

  Solution: Expanding first,

Figure 5–12*f*.   NAND gate logic diagram for XY′.

$(XY + U)(W + XZ)(UV + Y) =$

$\qquad\qquad (XY + U)(UVW + YW + UVXZ + XYZ)$

$= UVWXY + UVW + XYW + UYW +$

$\qquad\qquad UVXYZ + UVXZ + XYZ + UXYZ$

$= UVW(XY + 1) + XYW + UYW +$

$\qquad\qquad XYZ(UV + 1) + UVXZ + UXYZ$

$= UVW + XYW + UYW + XYZ(1 + U) + UVXZ$

$= UVW + XYW + UYW + XYZ + UVXZ$

Applying the double negation and De Morgan's theorem

$= [(UVW + XYW + UYW + XYZ + UVXZ)']'$

$= [(UVW)' \cdot (XYW)' \cdot (UYW)' \cdot (XYZ)' \cdot (UVXZ)']'$

See Figure 5–12*g*.

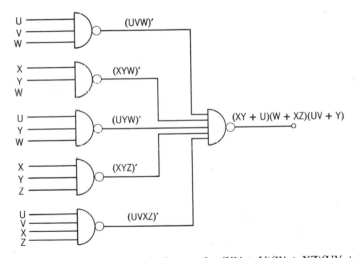

Figure 5–12*g*.   NAND gate logic diagram for $(XY + U)(W + XZ)(UV + Y)$.

A gate made of an OR followed by an inverter is called a NOT OR gate or NOR gate. Implementing a logical equation using only

NOR gates requires a similar treatment to using NAND gates. Again, a few examples will illustrate the method best.   The symbol used for the NOR gate is an OR gate followed by a circle.

Example 5–13.   Develop the block diagram to implement the given logical equation using *only* NOR gates.

(a) X + Y + Z

Solution: See Figure 5–13*a*.

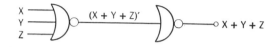

Figure 5–13*a*.   NOR gate logic diagram for X + Y + Z.

(b) XYZ

Solution: See Figure 5–13*b*.

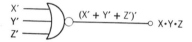

Figure 5–13*b*.   NOR gate logic diagram for X·Y·Z.

(c) (X + Y′)(W + Z)

Solution: $(X + Y') (W + Z) = [[(X + Y')(W + Z)]']'$
$= [(X + Y')' + (W + Z)']'$

See Figure 5–13*c*.

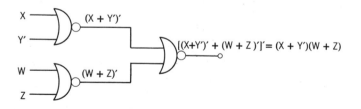

Figure 5–13*c*.   NOR gate logic diagram for (X + Y′)(W + Z).

Notice that for the NOR gate implementation the logical equation was first put into the form of AND terms.   This was double-negated, the inner negation, by De Morgan's theorem giving negated OR terms, the OR terms being all negated by the outside NOT function.

(d) $(X + Y + Z)(U + V)$

Solution: $(X + Y + Z)(U + V) = [[(X + Y + Z)(U + V)]']'$
$$= [(X + Y + Z)' + (U + V)']'$$

See Figure 5–13*d*.

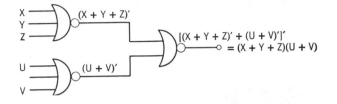

Figure 5–13*d*. NOR gate logic diagram for $(X + Y + Z)(U + V)$.

(e) $(XYZ) + (UV)$

Solution: $XYZ + UV = [(XYZ + UV)']'$
$$= [(XYZ)' \cdot (UV)']'$$
$$= [(X' + Y' + Z')(U' + V')]'$$
$$= (X'U' + Y'U' + Z'U' + X'V' +$$
$$Y'V' | Z'V')'$$

See Figure 5–13*e*. The preceding function could have been developed more simply as follows.

$$XYZ + UV = (X' + Y' + Z')' + (U' + V')'$$
$$= [[(X' + Y' + Z') + (U' + V')]']'$$

See Figure 5–13*f*.

The first method of this example is straightforward but does not necessarily lead to the simplest solution. Practice with NAND or NOR functions will provide the best basis for "seeing" what the simplest solution may be. Much work has been done to develop theorems and methods to lead to the simplest solution or prove that it is the simplest. Because these techniques are complex themselves, they will not be used here for the routine work.

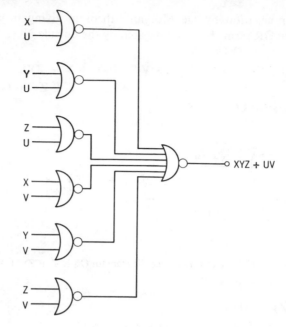

Figure 5–13*e*.   NOR gate logic diagram for XYZ + UV.

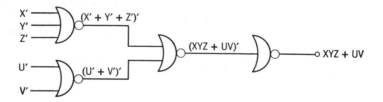

Figure 5–13*f*.   NOR gate logic diagram XYZ + UV.

Problem 5–7.   Develop the simplest block diagram to implement the logic equations given using *only* NAND gates.

1. X′ + Y + Z′
2. XY + XZ + YZ′
3. AC + BD + B′C + A′B
4. (XYZ)(XW)(YW)
5. (AB + C)(DE + F)

Problem 5-8. Develop the simplest block diagram to implement the logic equations given using *only* NOR gates.
1. X'Y'Z'
2. (XY)(XZ) + YZ
3. X'Y'Z + XYZ + YZ'
4. (WX + YZ)(UV + WZ)
5. (XY + U) + (UV + X)

5-4. Karnaugh Map

A Karnaugh map provides a method for simplifying Boolean expressions in a systematic manner. Although the technique may be used for any number of variables, it is seldom used for more than six, and we will consider four variables maximum. Although the map may appear similar to a truth table in principle, in application it is quite different. The map is made of boxes (or areas), each representing a unique combination of the variables. For one variable only two boxes are needed (A and A'). Two variables

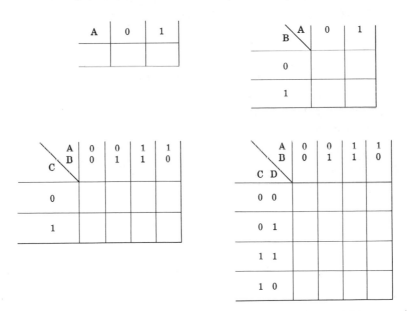

Figure 5-14. Karnaugh maps for one, two, three, and four variables.

result in four combinations (2^2) and four boxes. Each box represents one of the unique combinations AB, AB′, A′B, A′B′. For
three variables there are 2^3, or eight boxes, and for four variables 2^4,
or sixteen, boxes. The form of the map for these four cases is
shown in Figure 5–14.

For three and four variables the map was made so that there was
overlap of each variable to produce all the combinations required.
In use a 1 is placed in a box when that combination appears in the
given expression. The simplification comes about in reading the
expression out of the map by grouping terms in the simplest and
most complete way.

Example 5–14.   Map the following Boolean expressions.
(a) AB + A′B′
   Solution: See Figure 5–15a.

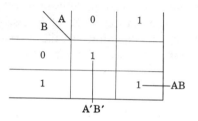

Figure 5–15a.   Karnaugh map for AB + A′B′.

(b) ABC + A′B′C′ + ABC′ + AB′C + A′BC
   Solution: See Figure 5–15b.

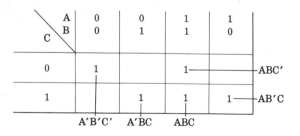

Figure 5–15b.   Karnaugh map for ABC + A′B′C′ + ABC′ + AB′C + A′BC.

(c) ABCD + A'BCD + AB'CD + ABCD'
Solution: See Figure 5–15c.

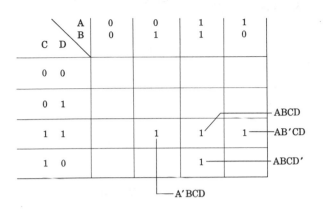

Figure 5–15c. Karnaugh map for ABCD + A'BCD + AB'CD + ABCD'.

(d) AB + A'C
Solution: See Figure 5–15d.

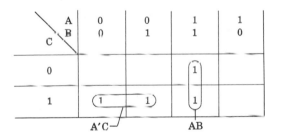

Figure 5–15d. Karnaugh map for AB + A'C.

Here we see that it requires two 1's to define a two-variable term in a three-variable map.   One box defined a unique three-variable term.   Two boxes may define a unique two-variable term and four boxes may define a unique one-variable term in this diagram.   The condition *may* is important because although all two-variable terms may be mapped in two boxes, in this map not all pairing of two 1's will define a two-variable expression.   The two 1's must be adjacent to be combined.

(e) B + AC + A'C'

Solution: See Figure 5–15e.

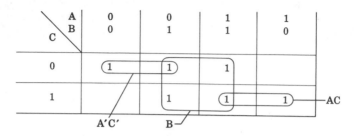

Figure 5–15e.   Karnaugh map for B + AC + A'C'.

The important point to see in this example is that a 1 may be part of more than one term in the expression.   When this occurs it is sometimes simpler to regroup the 1 with another set of 1's than it was entered with to reduce the overall expression.

(f) An example of this simplification can be seen in mapping AB + AC + AB'C' and regrouping when reading out.

Solution: See Figure 5–15f.

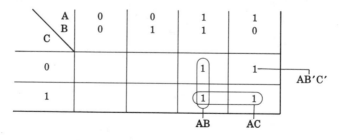

Figure 5–15f.   Karnaugh map for AB + AC + AB'C'.

Reading all four 1's as one term, the map may be read as the logical expression A.   Thus, AB + AC + AB'C' = A.   Although the reduction may not be apparent from the original expression, the map clearly shows the simplification exists. The simplification can be shown algebraically, but in this case the map was easier to use. Reducing algebraically,

$$AB + AC + AB'C' = A(B + C + B'C')$$
$$= A(B + C + C') \quad [B + B'C' = B + C']$$
$$= A(B + 1) \quad [C + C' = 1]$$
$$= A \quad [B + 1 = 1]$$

(g) Simplify the given expression using a Karnaugh map: XY + XZY + X'Y + XZY'.

Solution: See Figure 5–15g.

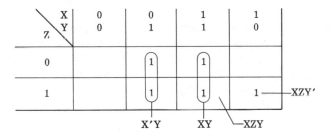

Figure 5–15g. Karnaugh map for XY + XZY + X'Y + XZY'.

To simplify, regroup the map.
The simplified expression is
$$XY + XZY + X'Y + X'ZY' = Y + XZ.$$

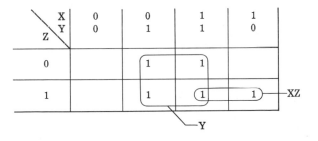

Figure 5–15h. Karnaugh map for Y + XZ.

(h) When the 1's fall in adjacent boxes they may be grouped together. Outer boxes may also be grouped together, as B'C in Figure 5–15*i*.

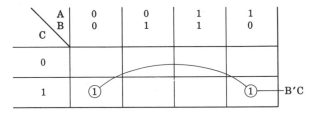

Figure 5–15*i*.   Karnaugh map for B'C.

(i) Alternate 1's, however, cannot possibly be grouped together. For example, the map of Figure 5–15*j* is made of four unique terms, each requiring three variables to define the box.   No other grouping is possible except this.   The logical expression ABC' + AB'C + A'BC + A'B'C' is mapped in Figure 5–15*j*.

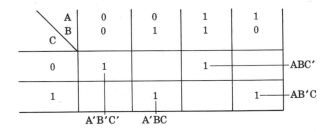

Figure 5–15*j*.   Karnaugh map for ABC' + AB'C + A'BC + A'B'C'.

(j) With four-variable maps the grouping for one term requires eight boxes, two terms require four boxes, three terms require two boxes, and four terms require one box.

Map ABC'D' + AB'D + A'C.

Solution: See Figure 5–15*k*.

As with many new techniques practice will serve to help clarify the process.

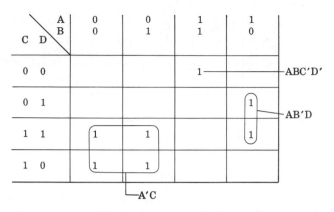

Figure 5–15*k*. Karnaugh map for ABC′D′ + AB′D + A′C.

Problem 5–9. Draw a Karnaugh map for each of the following logical expressions. Write a simplified expression wherever possible from the map.

1. AB + BC + AC
2. ABC + A′B′C′ + BC′ + B′C
3. XY + X′Z + Y′Z′
4. WXYZ + W′X′YZ′ + WYZ′ + YX
5. UVX + UVX′ + U′X + UV′
6. AB + B′C + A′B′
7. AC + AC′B + BC + B′C′
8. A + CD + AC′D + A′C′D′
9. XY + YZ + XZ + X′Y′
10. UV + UX + XV + U′X′

A similar method used to simplify Boolean functions is the Veitch diagram. A three-variable map is shown in Figure 5–16.

In the three-variable Veitch diagram the variables A and B change by more than one bit from one box to the next. Although the map appears to be the same as the Karnaugh map, there are differences in how effective each can be in simplifying a problem using systematic techniques. Having studied one we will pass over the second as it offers no new material. The Karnaugh map will be used exclusively in examples to come because it makes simplifications easier to "see."

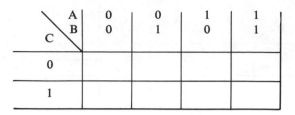

C \ A	0	0	1	1
\ B	0	1	0	1
0				
1				

Figure 5–16.   Veitch diagram for three variables.

5–5. Application of Logic Techniques

To point out how all the techniques of the present chapter are applied in practical problems, we will consider a detailed analysis of binary arithmetic adders and subtractors.   In order to develop a circuit which will provide the correct binary sum of two numbers, first work out the truth table.   An adder which only adds two inputs is called a half-adder, for to add a number fully also requires adding any carry from a lower-order summation.   A full-adder must have

A (Input 1)	B (Input 2)	S (Sum)	C (Carry out)
0	0	0	0
0	1	1	0
1	0	1	0
1	1	0	1

Figure 5–17.   Truth table for half-adder.

three inputs, two for the numbers being added and one for the possible carry.   The truth table for the half-adder is shown in Figure 5–17.

For $A = 0$, $B = 1$ and $A = 1$, $B = 0$ the SUM is $0 + 1 = 1 + 0 = 1$.

For $A = 0$, $B = 0$ the SUM is $0 + 0 = 0$.

For $A = 1$, $B = 1$ the SUM is $1 + 1 = 0$ (carry a ONE)

so that   SUM = 0   and   CARRY = 1.
The SUM is 1 when A = 0 or A' = 1 and B = 1 OR when A = 1
and B = 0 or B' = 1.

The expression S = A'B + AB' says the same but in equation
form.   Also, C = AB defines when the carry out is a 1.   A logical
circuit that provides the defined half-adder functions is shown in
Figure 5–18.

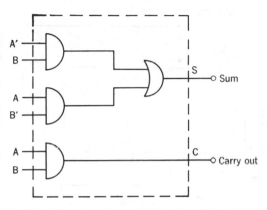

Figure 5–18.   Logic diagram for half-adder.

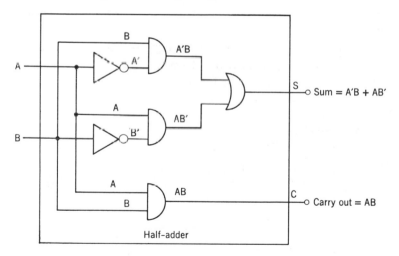

Figure 5–19.   Logic diagram for half-adder (no inverted inputs available).

To provide a circuit that has only two inputs (A and B) and two
outputs (sum and carry out) will require two additional inverters
(see Figure 5–19).

Although the above two half-adder logic circuits are correct, they are not the simplest (least components) possible. If we use S = (AB)′ (A + B) to implement the sum function, we obtain a simpler half-adder logic circuit. Use either a truth table, map, or expand the function to see that it is the same as S = A′B + AB′. Notice also that the carry expression C = AB is developed as part of the sum expression and need not be developed separately. A simpler logic circuit is shown in Figure 5–20.

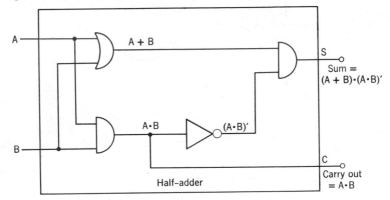

Figure 5–20. Simplified logic diagram for half-adder (inverted inputs not needed).

Another way of implementing the half-adder is to use NOR gates only. A circuit which provides the sum and carry-out signals using only NOR gates is shown in Figure 5–21. Such a circuit would be

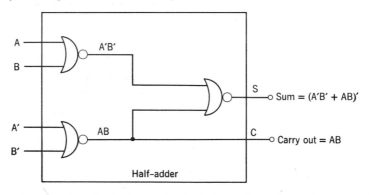

Figure 5–21. Logic diagram for half-adder using only NOR gates.

used in a system that has only NOR gates for all the logic operations.

A frequently encountered circuit is the Exclusive-OR gate which
can differentiate when two inputs are identical or different. As a
comparator circuit it provides a 1 output when the input terms are
different and a 0 output when they are the same. Use the truth
table of Figure 5–22 to develop the circuit.

A	B	Output Different
0	0	0
0	1	1
1	0	1
1	1	0

Figure 5–22.   Truth table for comparator circuit (Exclusive-OR).

The expression for the output being different is output different =
A′B + AB′ and the circuit to implement this function is shown in
Figure 5–23.   A closer look at the expression and the circuit reveals

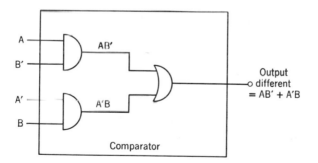

Figure 5–23.   Logic diagram of comparator (Exclusive–OR).

that this is the identical form of the sum part of a half-adder.

A full-adder requires three inputs—A, B, and the previous carry
called a carry in. By putting the problem into a truth table (see

A (Input 1)	B (Input 2)	C (Carry In)	S (Sum)	C_o (Carry Out)
0	0	0	0	0
0	0	1	1	0
0	1	0	1	0
0	1	1	0	1
1	0	0	1	0
1	0	1	0	1
1	1	0	0	1
1	1	1	1	1

Figure 5-24. Truth table for full-adder.

Figure 5-24) we can find the expression for the sum and carry out.

The expression for the sum is

$$S = A'BC_i' + AB'C_i' + A'B'C_i + ABC_i.$$

A Karnaugh map could now be used to try to simplify the sum expression (see Figure 5-25). Reading the numbers directly from

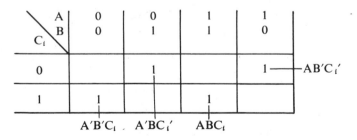

Figure 5-25. Karnaugh map for full-adder sum,
$S = A'BC_i' + AB'C_i' + A'B'C_i + ABC_i.$

the truth table onto the map is straightforward.   Reading in order (ABC), we have

A	B	C_i
0	1	0
1	0	0
0	0	1
1	1	1

From the map it is quickly evident that no easy simplification is possible, the best being

$$S = C_i' (A'B + AB') + C_i (A'B' + AB).$$

For the carry out, reading in order (ABC), we have

A	B	C_i
1	1	0
0	1	1
1	1	1
1	0	1

which maps into Figure 5–26.   Here we see that a simplification is

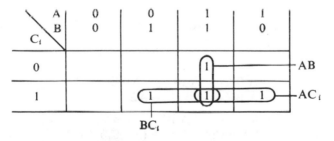

Figure 5–26.   Karnaugh map for carry out of full-adder,
$C_o = AB + AC_i + BC_i.$

quite possible because adjacent 1's occur.   One possible expression is

$$C_o = AB + BC_i + AC_i$$
$$C_o = AB + C_i (A + B)$$

Implementing the full-adder circuit results in the diagram shown in Figure 5–27.

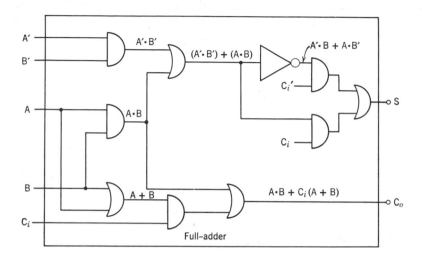

Figure 5–27.   Full-adder logic diagram.

If the diagram seems complicated, it is only because all the lines are drawn in. The circuit would look clearer if the letter were carried along in place of crossing lines. Another possibility for obtaining the same function is to use NAND gates or NOR gates to provide the sum and carry-out signals. Rewriting the S and C_o expressions, we will use the double negation and De Morgan's theorem to provide the suitable form for NAND gates.

$$S = A'B'C_i + A'BC_i' + AB'C_i' + ABC_i$$
$$C_o = A'BC_i + AB'C_i + ABC_i' + ABC_i$$

$$S = [(A'B'C_i + A'BC_i' + AB'C_i' + ABC)']'$$
$$S = [(A'B'C_i)' (A'BC_i')' (AB'C_i')' (ABC_i)']'$$
proper NAND form

$$C_o = [(A'BC_i + AB'C_i + ABC_i' + ABC_i)']'$$
$$C_o = [(A'BC_i)' (AB'C_i)' (ABC_i')' (ABC_i)']'$$
proper NAND form

If C_o were reduced using a map technique (as before), the simplified expression $C_o = C_i(A + B) + AB$ put into proper NAND form would be $C_o = [(AB)' \ (AC_i)' \ (BC_i)']'$, which would require one less NAND gate. However, in forming the SUM the same term $(ABC)'$ is formed as needed for the C_o expression. A look at the two Karnaugh maps shows that this is the only term for which there are similar 1's in each map position. One possible circuit to provide the full-adder function is shown in Figure 5–28.

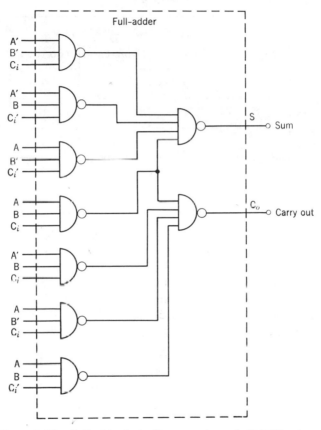

Figure 5–28.   Full-adder logic diagram using only NAND gates.

Try implementing the full-adder using only NOR gates as an exercise.

When doing subtraction of binary numbers the lower most numbers (2^0 position) require only a half subtraction. Any higher-order position, however, requires full subtraction, as a borrow from a lower-order operation may be present. In designing a circuit which will provide the proper difference and borrow outputs, a truth table is first used to consider all possible cases and the resultant Boolean equation is then simplified or reworked into a desirable form using map techniques when they are helpful. A half-subtractor truth table for X − Y is that of Figure 5–29.

X (Input 1)	Y (Input 2)	D (Difference)	B (Borrow)
0	0	0	0
0	1	1	1
1	0	1	0
1	1	0	0

Figure 5–29.   Truth table for half-subtractor (X − Y).

From the truth table we see that the difference is 1 when $X = 1$ and $Y = 0$ ($Y' = 1$) OR when $X = 0$ ($X' = 1$), and $Y = 1$. In equation form this reads $D = XY' + X'Y$. The borrow is 1 when $X = 0$ ($X' = 1$) and $Y = 1$ giving $B = X'Y$ (the same term as one of the terms in the difference expression). Using AND, OR, and INVERTER gates to build a half-subtractor circuit (see Figure 5–30) would give $D = XY' + X'Y$; $B = X'Y$.

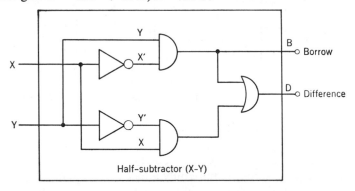

Figure 5–30.   Logic diagram for half-subtractor (X − Y).

A full-subtractor has the two inputs to be subtracted (X − Y) and the borrow from the previous order subtraction. First let us develop the truth table for the full-subtraction operation (Figure 5–31).

X (Input 1)	Y (Input 2)	B_i (Borrow In)	D (Difference)	B_o (Borrow Out)
0	0	0	0	0
0	0	1	1	1
0	1	0	1	1
0	1	1	0	1
1	0	0	1	0
1	0	1	0	0
1	1	0	0	0
1	1	1	1	1

Figure 5–31.   Truth table for full-subtractor [(X − Y) − B_i].

Writing the logical equations for the difference and borrow out from the truth table gives

$$D = XY'B_i' + X'YB_i' + X'Y'B_i + XYB_i$$
$$B_o = X'YB_i' + X'Y'B_i + XYB_i + X'YB_i$$

To simplify these functions and compare them a Karnaugh map for each is shown in Figure 5–32.

Again, the difference map indicates that no simplification is possible whereas the borrow-out function may be regrouped into a simpler expression. However, it can also be seen that there are three common boxes between the two maps. As an exercise the NOR circuit for the full-subtractor will be developed here and the reader can try a NAND gate implementation separately. Neglecting the

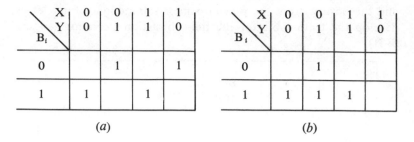

Figure 5–32.   Karnaugh map for full-subtractor $[(X - Y) - B_i]$: (*a*) Difference (D), (*b*) Borrow out (B$_o$).

inversion necessary to obtain the primed (negated) functions for drawing simplification the entire subtraction can be implemented with seven NOR gates (see Figure 5–33).   To develop the expression

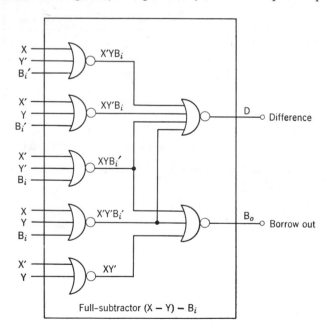

Figure 5–33.   Logic diagram for full-subtractor $(X - Y) - B_i$, using NOR gates only.

for the NOR gate circuit read off the ONE for D'.

$$D' = X'Y'B_i' + XYB_i' + X'YB_i + XY'B_i$$
$$D = (X'Y'B_i' + XYB_i' + X'YB_i + XY'B_i)' \quad \text{NOR form}$$

Similarly, for the borrow out, we can obtain,

$$B_o' = X'Y'B_i' + XYB_i' + XY'$$
$$B_o = (X'Y'B_i' + XYB_i' + XY')'$$

Summary

Boolean algebra is introduced and then applied to practical problems. The AND, OR, INVERTER, NOR, and NAND functions are used. It is important to be able to "read" logic diagrams or prepare them from a Boolean equation. Using rules of operation logic equations can be reworked into either a more suitable form or a simplified form. One very important theorem used in Boolean algebra is De Morgan's theorem which states that

$$(X + Y)' = X' \cdot Y'$$

or that

$$(X \cdot Y)' = (X' + Y')$$

To facilitate better reduction and operation on Boolean expressions the technique of mapping—using Karnaugh maps in the examples shown is introduced.

In order to tie the material presented together, a number of very popular (and important) circuits were designed. These included the half- and full-adder, half- and full-subtractor, and the Exclusive-OR circuit.

PROBLEMS

1. Simplify the following Boolean equation $(A + A'B)(A + B')$.

2. Draw the logic diagram to implement the Boolean equation $AB' + (AB) \cdot (A + B)$.

3. Simplify the Boolean equation $UV + VW + UW + VW'$.

4. Simplify the Boolean equation $A'BC + ABC' + ABC + A'B$.

5. Use only NOR logic circuits to implement the Boolean equation $(AB' + A'B)C$.

6. Use only NAND logic circuits to implement the Boolean equation $(A'B' + AB)C + (A'B + C')D$.

7. Draw the Karnaugh map for $ABC + BC' + AC + BC$.

8. Draw the Karnaugh for $XY + Z + XYZ + Z'Y$. Using the map read off a simplified expression for that given.

<u>**9.**</u> Write a logical equation from the following Karnaugh map.

U V	X 0 Y 0	0 1	1 1	1 0
0 0	1			1
0 1	1			1
1 1				
1 0	1			1

10. Develop the logic diagram for a full-subtractor using only NAND gate logic.

Section Two

COMPUTER CIRCUITS
AND BLOCKS

0110

Computer logic gates

The field of computer circuits is constantly changing and growing at a very quick rate. Initially, computer circuitry (or logic circuits) was ingeniously made using relays and switches. The first computers built had little or no memory and operated from a wired or fixed program only. When the memory feature was added, making it possible to store programs, the entire concept of computer utilization changed. Relays soon left the mainstream of computer circuits because they were slow, large, and had poor mechanical reliability. Vacuum tubes (triodes and diodes) came into use for a short time. They too have been quickly replaced because of the size factor, power used (heater power alone is considerable for a computer with a few thousand tubes), and reliability. Solid-state components now entered the computer field (and many other fields) and quickly took complete control. Switching transistors, switching diodes, tunnel diodes, field-effect transistors, zener diodes, silicon-controlled rectifiers, unijunction transistors, power transistors, etc., all have the advantages of the solid-state device—small size, no heater power (and no warm-up time), and high reliability. Initially, these components proved themselves very useful to the military because of weight (size) and power for use in sea and aerospace operation. Once accepted and used, the initial high cost was overcome, and because of their high reliability these components have been universally accepted in the civilian consumer market. Figure 6–1a shows some practical computer circuits as built on printed circuit connector boards. Circuits similar to those to be studied in this chapter are shown.

In the past few years a further advance in solid-state electronics has again changed the character of computer circuits. Integrated circuits containing complete gates or even groups of gates have been

119

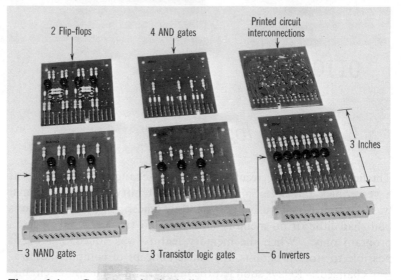

Figure 6–1a. Computer circuits built on printed circuit boards (courtesy of Digital Electronics, Westbury, N.Y.).

made in a single manufacturing process.   The general designation for these new "components" is microelectronics (see Figure 6–1b). They are of a few orders of magnitude smaller (as a whole) and have very good reliability.   Although cost is now a deterrent to large-scale use, it is being quickly reduced, and newer computer systems on the market are now using microelectronic circuits.   At present a few different types of microelectronic circuits are available, and research to develop better circuits results in continual changes in the circuit configuration and basic components used.   Integrated circuits are made on silicon waffers which are diffused, etched, and inter-connected all in one piece (or process), similar to the technique of manufacturing transistors.   External handling is at a minimum, most processing being automatic, so that reliability is very high.   Cost, however, is still high, so that other modifications are considered in circuit techniques.   Hybrid circuits use separately manufactured pieces to make up the circuit, but all of these are made in an inte-grated package of similarly small size.

With all this past change and continuing development in the field of computer circuitry, there are still at least half a dozen basic circuits

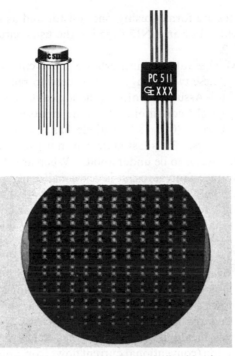

Figure 6–1b.   Computer circuits built with microelectronics (integrated) components.

that are used most often, and there is a fairly well-standardized form
for each of these.   Not surprisingly, the complexity of the circuits
has grown with time, so that a discussion starting with the simpler
circuits is also historically developmental.   Because semiconductors
(solid-state) devices are very popular and would be encountered in
practice, they will be used to describe these typical building blocks.
Computer OR gates and AND gates are made of diode and resistor
combinations, with the diode as the gating or logic element.   Inverter circuits require an active device, the transistor in this case, to
negate or complement or invert the signal.   Finally, a NAND gate
or NOR gate made of a combination of diodes, resistors, and transistors with the diode again the logic element and the transistor the
inverting component is covered.

6–1. Diode AND, OR Gates

Diode gates are formed using one resistor and as many diodes as inputs needed.   For an AND function the usual circuit used is that of Figure 6–2.

The two voltage values of importance in this circuit are 0 volts and + 10 volts.   These two voltages can be used to represent the logical states 0 and 1.   Assume 0 volts as the logical 0 condition and + 10 volts as the logical 1 condition.   If all the inputs are at 0 volts (0) the output is at 0 volts (0).   If any diode has 0 volts at its input the output is at 0 volts.   This last statement must be clear if the operation of diode gates is to be understood.   When any diode is forward-biased the voltage drop across it is very small (only a few tenths of a volt).   Since this voltage is so different from + 10 volts it is easily distinguished.   Ideally, or for convenience, we can consider the drop across the diode as 0 volts, so that when we say the output is also 0 volts, we mean that it is close enough to zero to approximate the diode drop as ideal.

A review of a diode characteristic might be helpful at this point. First, let us look at a typical diode characteristic for the forward-bias condition shown in Figure 6–3.   As the current through the diode changes by a large amount, the voltage across the diode hardly changes.   This means that the diode has a low resistance in the forward direction (conventional current flows from anode to cathode).

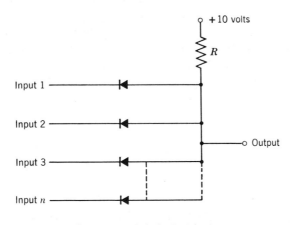

Figure 6–2. Diode AND gate.

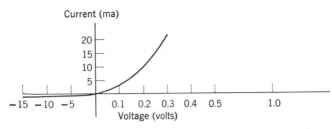

Figure 6–3.   Diode characteristic.

In the reverse direction only the small, minority current flows and the voltage changes by a large amount with only a slight change in current.   This means that in the reverse direction the diode has a high resistance.   In order to forward-bias a diode the anode voltage must be made more positive than the cathode.

A single-input diode gate performs no logic since the output follows the input, but it will still demonstrate the electrical operation of the circuit (see Figure 6–4a).   When the input is at 0 volts (0) the ⏋10 volt supply voltage forward biases the diode through a resistor connected to the anode side of the diode.   The diode is forward-biased with a few tenths of a volt across it.   Current through the diode is limited by the resistor to less than $10/R$ ma (where R is in kilohms).   The output voltage taken from the anode to ground is nearly 0 volts.

With no current flowing through the diode, none flows through the resistor so that there is no voltage drop across it (see Figure 6–4b).

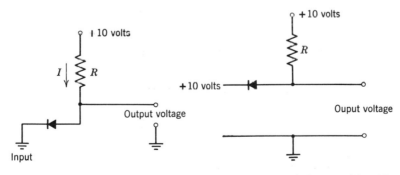

Figure 6–4a.   Output for diode gate with 0-volt input.

Figure 6–4b.   Diode gate with + 10-volt input.

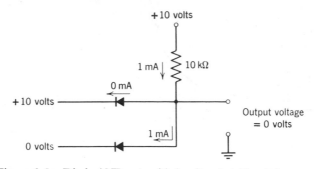

Figure 6–5.   Diode AND gate with 0-volt and +10-volt inputs.

The output voltage (voltage from anode to ground) is +10 volts, the same as the input voltage.

Now let us consider a gate which can perform logical operations, namely, a diode gate with two or more inputs (see Figure 6–5). If both inputs are ground the output is nearly 0 volts. If either diode alone is at ground potential and the other at +10 volts, the diode with its input at ground remains forward-biased. Since the drop in voltage across it is 0 volts, the output remains at 0 volts, and all the current flows through the conducting (forward-biased) diode. If both inputs are made +10 volts, however, the output rises to +10 volts. Both diodes are now reverse-biased and no current flows through them. The combinations of voltages can be concisely stated using a voltage truth table. The table for the diode gate considered is shown in Figure 6–6. All voltages are ideal where the

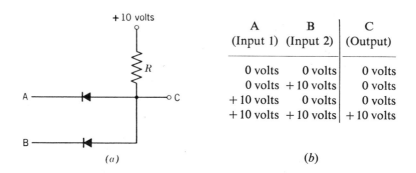

A (Input 1)	B (Input 2)	C (Output)
0 volts	0 volts	0 volts
0 volts	+10 volts	0 volts
+10 volts	0 volts	0 volts
+10 volts	+10 volts	+10 volts

(a)   (b)

Figure 6–6.   (a) Diode gate and (b) voltage truth table.

drop across the forward-biased diode is considered zero and the reverse current flow is considered zero.

Using the previous definition of logical 1 and 0, 0 volts = 0 and +10 volts = 1, we can construct the corresponding logic truth table shown in Figure 6–7.

A (Input 1)	B (Input 2)	C (Output)	
0	0	0	0 volts ≡ 0
0	1	0	+10 volts ≡ 1
1	0	0	
1	1	1	

Figure 6–7. Diode gate logic truth table for AND gate (positive logic).

The function has a 1 output only when A and B are 1. As a logical expression this reads C = AB. This is an AND function and the gate is therefore an AND gate. An output is present (1) only when both inputs are present (1).

Although this interpretation is the most popular one, the choice of +10 volts as logical 1 and of 0 volts as logical 0 was arbitrary. Had this choice been reversed, a different logical truth table would have resulted from the voltage truth table derived (see Figure 6–8).

A (Input 1)	B (Input 2)	C (Output)	
1	1	1	0 volts ≡ 1
1	0	1	+10 volts ≡ 0
0	1	1	
0	0	0	

Figure 6–8. Diode OR gate logic truth table (negative logic).

The output function is a 1 when both inputs are 1, or when A is 1 and B is 0, or when A is 0 and B is 1. Stated as an equation,

$$C = AB + AB' + A'B$$
$$= A(B + B') + A'B$$
$$= A(1) + A'B$$
$$= A + A'B$$
$$= A + B \quad \text{(remember the identity proved in Chapter 5)}$$

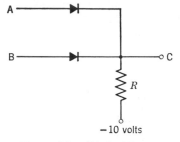

Figure 6–9. Diode OR gate.

For this second definition of logic levels the function turns out to be an OR function, so that now the gate can be considered an OR gate. To distinguish between the two definitions the first is called *positive* logic because the logical 1 was chosen to be the more *positive* voltage ($+10$ volts as compared to 0 volts). The second logic choice is called *negative* logic because here the logical 1 was chosen to be the more *negative* voltage (0 volts compared to $+10$ volts). The gate discussed so far is an AND gate for positive logic.

Another popular gate using diodes as gating (logic) elements, and 0 volts and $+10$ volts as the logic levels, is shown in Figure 6–9.

This gate is different in that the inputs are applied to the anode side of the diode, and the resistor is returned to -10 volts. If both inputs are at 0 volts the output is near 0 volts (a few tenths of a volt below zero because of the voltage drop across the forward-biased diode). With either input at 0 volts and the other at $+10$ volts, the output is at $+10$ volts (see Figure 6–10). The forward-biased diode

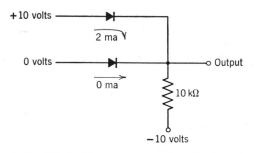

Figure 6–10. Diode OR gate with 0-volt and $+10$-volt inputs.

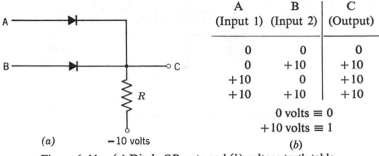

A (Input 1)	B (Input 2)	C (Output)
0	0	0
0	+10	+10
+10	0	+10
+10	+10	+10

0 volts ≡ 0
+10 volts ≡ 1

(a)   −10 volts   (b)

Figure 6–11.   (a) Diode OR gate and (b) voltage truth table.

raises the output voltage to +10 volts.   The diode with 0 volts at its input is now reverse-biased and conducts no current.

When both diodes have +10-volt input, the output is also +10 volts.   The voltage truth table for this circuit containing the 0-volt and +10-volt input signals and the ideal 0-volt and +10-volt output signals is shown in Figure 6–11.

Defining 0 volts as logical 0 and +10 volts as logical 1 gives the corresponding positive logic truth table (Figure 6–12).   The function

A (Input 1)	B (Input 2)	C (Output)	
0	0	0	0 volts = 0
0	1	1	+10 volts ≡ 1
1	0	1	
1	1	1	

Figure 6 12.   Diode OR gate logic truth table (positive logic).

is 1 when A + B is 1 so that the gate is an OR gate.   Since logical 1 is the more positive voltage the gate is an OR gate for positive logic. As expected, the logic truth table for negative logic will represent the AND function (see Figure 6–13).   As a summary the two gates are shown for positive logic operation in Figure 6–14.

Problem 6–1.   Prepare a voltage truth table and logic truth table for a negative logic OR gate.

Problem 6–2.   For the circuit shown in Figure 6–15 indicate appropriate logic voltages and prepare a voltage truth table.

A (Input 1)	B (Input 2)	C (Output)	
1	1	1	0 volts ≡ 1
1	0	0	+10 volts ≡ 0
0	1	0	
0	0	0	

Figure 6–13.   Diode AND gate logic truth table (negative logic).

Loading in Multistage Logic.   When logic is performed using AND and OR gates, the number of cascaded stages is limited.   This limitation comes from desired operating speeds and voltage levels. The positive logic gates of Figure 6–14 will be used to show how the limitations come about.   Consider the operation where an AND gate is connected to an OR gate (Figure 6–16).

When inputs A or B are 0 (0 volts), the voltage at point C is $+V_D$,

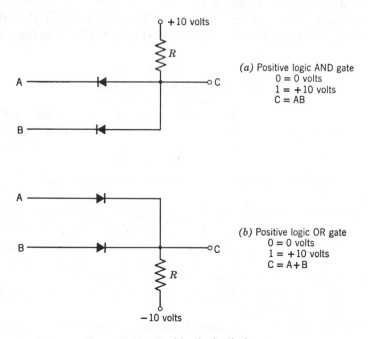

Figure 6–14.   Positive logic diode gates.

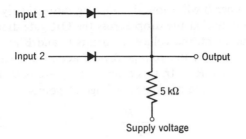

Figure 6–15.   Diode circuit for Problem 6–2.

the voltage drops across the forward-biased diode. If D is a 1
(+10 volts), the output at E is at $+10 - V_D$, or very near +10 volts.
For these inputs the gates operate properly. Now consider the
operation when both A and B are 1.   The two AND gate diodes are
back-biased and the voltage at point C should go to +10 volts, as
did the AND gate operating alone.   Does it go to +10 volts as
desired?   No, because it is not connected into an open circuit.
The OR gate has a finite input impedance and loads down point C.
A partial diagram with input A and B diodes removed (they are

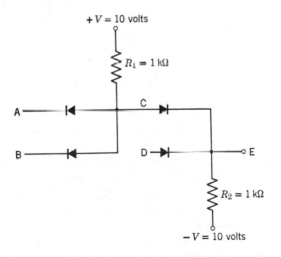

Figure 6–16.   Diode AND–OR gates.

cut off, remember?) will show this loading more clearly (see Figure 6–17.   Assuming that the drop across the OR gate diode shown is zero for the moment, the voltage at points C and E are determined by the voltage divider action of resistors R_1 and R_2.   In this example they are both 1 kohm and the computed voltage of points C and E is

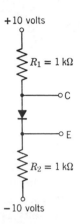

+10 volts

$R_1 = 1$ kΩ

C

E

$R_2 = 1$ kΩ

−10 volts

Figure 6–17.
Partial circuit of
AND–OR gates.

$$\frac{R_2}{R_1 + R_2}(20) - 10 = 0 \text{ volts}$$

But 0 volts is the logical 0 voltage, and for two 1 inputs to the AND gate we should have a 1 output (+10 volts).   Obviously the gate will not operate properly as shown.   An improvement can be obtained by making R_2 larger than R_1. If R_2 is ten times larger than R_1 the voltage at C and E will be

$$\frac{10R_1}{R_1 + (10R_1)}(20) - 10 = \tfrac{10}{11}(20) - 10$$

$$= 18.2 - 10 = 8.2 \text{ volts}$$

This is probably a high enough voltage for the gate to operate properly.   But what would happen if the AND gate were fed into two OR gates.   The load of two OR gates would be that of two R_2 resistors in parallel.   In that case the output would be

$$\frac{5R_1}{R_1 + 5R_1}(20) - 10 = \tfrac{5}{6}(20) - 10 = 16.6 - 10 = 6.6 \text{ volts}$$

where $R_2 = \frac{1}{2}(10R_1)$.   This voltage may not be high enough for proper operation.   Why not make R_2 larger?   It could certainly be chosen to make the output voltage sufficiently high.   The reason R_2 cannot be made indiscriminately large is the speed of operation restriction.   There is a small amount of stray capacitance (C) at the output of the gate due to wiring, diodes, etc.   If we represent the gate simply as in Figure 6–18, we can see the effect of R_2.

When the two inputs go low (to 0 volts) the output should also go to 0 volts.   However, the OR gate diodes get reverse-biased and the output will drop to 0 volts as the capacitor discharges through R_2. Thus the R_2C time constant will determine how fast the output goes

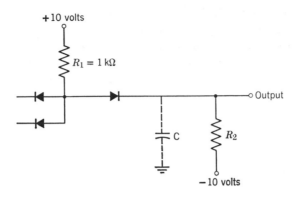

Figure 6–18.   Diode AND–OR gate with stray capacitance included.

down to 0 volts.   For a C of 100 μμf and R_2 of 100 kohms the time constant is

$$R_2 C_2 = (100 \times 10^{-12})(100 \times 10^9)$$
$$= 10 \times 10^{-6}$$
$$= 10 \ \mu sec$$

If it took four time constants to reach a sufficiently low voltage, the gate could not be operated faster than every 40 μsec, or at 25 kcps. The values chosen were particularly high, but a limit on the size of R_2 should be apparent.

Looking back at the circuit, we find there is another way to keep the AND gate from being loaded down.   If R_1 is made small compared to R_2, the output voltage level could still be kept high.   But this solution also has its drawbacks.   Consider the current through the input diodes for $R_1 = 1$ kohm.   The maximum value is slightly less than 10 volts/1 kohm or 1 ma.   If R_1 is decreased to 100 ohms to improve the output voltage level, the diode must carry almost 10 ma.   Obviously we cannot decrease R_1 too much without putting undue restrictions on the choice of the logic diodes.   Preferably the diodes and circuits should operate with as little power as possible since so many will be needed in the computer.   So we are left with the conclusion that in using AND and OR gates the number of logic gates in cascade is limited.   One solution to this problem is to use inverters to prevent too much loading.   The inverter is basically an amplifier and therefore builds up the signal again so that the loading

is corrected.   Try the diode circuit problem before considering how
the inverter operates.

Problem 6–3.   What are the actual output voltages for the circuit of
Figure 6–19 for the following cases:

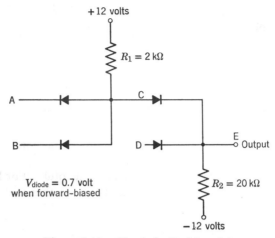

Figure 6–19.   Circuit for Problem 6–3.

1. A = 1   2. A = 1
   B = 0   B = 0
   D = 1   D = 0

3. A = 1   4. A = 1
   B = 1   B = 1
   D = 0   D = 1

6–2.   Transistor Inverter Gate

The inversion operation requires the use of an "active" device
such as a vacuum tube or transistor.   A signal applied to the grid
of a vacuum tube results in an amplified, inverted signal.   The
transistor counterpart has the signal applied to the base-emitter
circuit and results in an amplified, inverted signal at the collector-
emitter output (common-emitter configuration).   In a computer

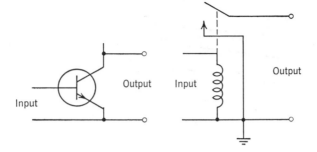

Figure 6-20.   Ideal transistor switch.

circuit the logical inversion is the principal function of the transistor, the amplification being used to correct for "loading" between gates.

A review of transistor characteristics with emphasis on the features of importance to switching circuits would be helpful.   For logic use the transistor must represent the states 0 or 1, so that they are well distinguished.   The best conditions possible are the states when the transistor is fully OFF and fully ON.   Comparing the operation under these conditions to the operation of a switch as the ideal, we can see how well a transistor operates in a switching circuit.

Figure 6-20 provides a comparison of the features of the transistor- and relay-operated switch.   When the input turns the switch ON, the relay causes the contact to close so that the output becomes ground potential.   The transistor switch, however, is not at true ground potential, for there is a voltage drop across the collector-emitter junction when the transistor is turned fully ON.   When the relay leaves the contacts open, there is a perfect open circuit.   In the transistor counterpart, a minority current flows during cutoff, again causing a deviation from ideal conditions.   The outstanding features of the transistor, however, which allow acceptance of these slight offsets are its very fast switching time—less than a microsecond, compared to milliseconds for the relay—and its long life—billions of operations, compared to hundreds of thousands for the relay.

A common-emitter characteristic will more clearly define the transistor deviations from "ideal" and the basic operation as a switching element.   A typical characteristic is that of Figure 6-21.

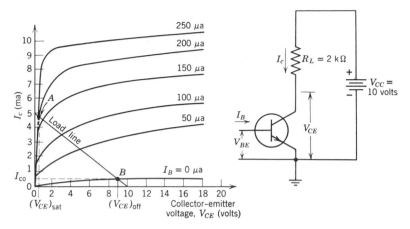

Figure 6–21.   Common-emitter characteristic.

Adding a load resistor for operation defines the regions in which the transistor operates.   When fully ON the transistor current is increased to a limited value or saturated value.   The voltage drop across the transistor under this condition is called a saturated voltage, or $(V_{CE})_{sat}$.

Point A, the intersection of the load line with the transistor characteristic, is the operating point when the transistor is fully ON (or saturated).   From the curve the saturation voltage of the output is only a few tenths of a volt.   These few tenths of a volt are the deviation from the ideal value of zero for the switch contacts.   It is still a well-distinguished value from the OFF value (point B of Figure 6–21).   Point B, the intersection of the load line and the transistor curve for the OFF condition ($I_B = 0$), shows a lower OFF voltage than the supply value of 10 volts.   This drop in voltage is due to the flow of minority carriers under reverse-bias conditions.   The cutoff current I_{co} causes a drop across the load resistor, $I_{co}R_L$, reducing the OFF voltage from the value under ideal switch conditions.   The difference between cutoff and saturation voltage can be well distinguished so that we could generally refer to the ON voltage as 0 volts and OFF voltage as the full supply value.   Where necessary, as for accuracy, the actual value $(V_{CE})_{sat}$ or $(V_{CE})_{off}$ will be used.   When the ideal values are used it is only because the logic function is being described and the small voltage deviation would have no

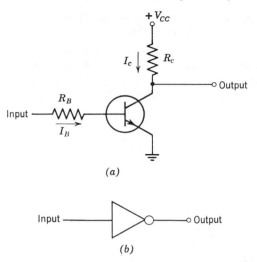

(a)

(b)

Figure 6–22.   Inverter (a) circuit and (b) logic diagram.

significantly clearer meaning in the discussion.   However, it should be clear that these ideal values are only used in discussion but that actual circuit operation results in deviation from ideal.

In switching states the transistor passes through the linear region of the characteristic.   The time in this region is so short that a switching transistor is said to operate in either the saturation or cutoff regions only.   Transistor switching time is quite complex to analyze and will not be considered here.   Only the important fact that it can range from around a microsecond down to a few nanoseconds for most good switching transistors should be kept in mind. There are a growing number of books dealing with the details of designing inverters with consideration of switching times.   Outside texts should be consulted for this topic as well as for many others not covered in great detail in the basic treatment of ideas given in this book.

A simple inverter circuit is shown in Figure 6–22.   The input resistor is chosen to set the base current so that with the minimum input voltage the value of base current is sufficient to "drive" the transistor into saturation (for the value of collector current drawn). The collector resistor must not be chosen too high to cause an appreciable drop in output voltage when I_{co} flows (OFF condition).

Voltage and logic truth tables are simple to define and are provided for completeness (see Figure 6–23).

When the input is 0 volts there is no turn-on voltage and only the minority current I_{co} flows. The output voltage is $V_{CC} - I_{co}R_c$. Since I_{co} ranges from nanoamperes (10^{-9} amp) to microamperes (10^{-6} amp) and R_c is a few kilohms, the voltage drop $I_{co}R_c$ is usually negligible. For $+10$-volt input the transistor is driven ON. When fully ON the voltage across the forward-biased base-emitter junction is around 0.5 volt. It varies slightly with large changes in input current. The input drive current is approximately $(V_{in} - 0.5)/R_B$. Typical values for R_B of 10 kohm and V_{in} of 10 volts give a base current of $(10 - 0.5)/10(10^3) = 0.95$ ma. In general, the base-emitter voltage is designated $(V_{BE})_{on}$ for the ON condition. The output voltage for the ON condition is $(V_{CE})_{sat}$, as previously mentioned, and the collector current is $I_c = (V_{CC} - (V_{CE})_{sat})/R_c$. Typical values of $R_c = 2$ kohm, $V_{CC} = 10$ volts, and $(V_{CE})_{sat} = 0.3$ volt result in $I_c = (10 - 0.3)/2 = 4.85$ ma.

A (Input)	A′ (Output)
0 volts	$+10$ volts
$+10$ volts	0 volts

(a) Voltage truth table

A (Input)	A′ (Output)	
0	1	0 volts $\equiv$ 0
1	0	$+10$ volts $\equiv$ 1

(b) Positive logic truth table

A (Input)	A′ (Output)	
1	0	0 volts $\equiv$ 1
0	1	$+10$ volts $\equiv$ 0

(c) Negative logic truth table

Figure 6–23. Inverter, voltage and logic truth tables.

Try the following two problems analyzing inverter circuits.

Problem 6–4.   Calculate I_c and I_B for the circuit in Figure 6–24.

Problem 6–5.   Calculate I_c and I_B for the circuit of Figure 6–24 if the supply voltage is changed to $+12$ volts, R_B to 20 kohm and V_{in} to $+12$ volts.

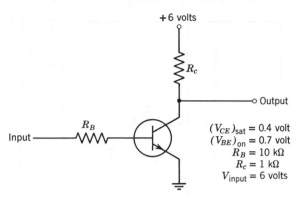

+6 volts

R_c

Output

Input

R_B

$(V_{CE})_{sat} = 0.4$ volt
$(V_{BE})_{on} = 0.7$ volt
$R_B = 10$ kΩ
$R_c = 1$ kΩ
$V_{input} = 6$ volts

Figure 6–24. Inverter circuit for Problems 6–4 and 6–5.

6–3. Transistor NAND, NOR Gates

Having separately considered the diode OR, AND gates and the transistor inverter, the two can be combined as one gate for convenience. In practice, AND gates and OR gates alone "load down" in cascaded sections. The amount of other gates driven from a single gate is also quite limited in practice. Amplification or load matching requires the use of transistor inverters for every few diode gates. The NAND gate (or NOR gate) was developed to provide a single building block which can provide all the logic functions.

The basic gate can be formed by adding an inverter after the logic gate (see Figure 6–25). Recalling that the logic gate shown is an AND gate for positive logic, the complete function would be an AND-INVERSION or NAND function. For negative logic the same gate would perform the NOR function. A second form of this gate is made using the positive logic OR gate followed by a *PNP* transistor inverter. This circuit is shown in Figure 6–26. A practical version of the *NPN* logic-inverter gate and its voltage and logic truth tables are shown in Figures 6–27 and 6–28.

The positive logic definitions give a logic truth table whose output is 1 when $A'B' + A'B + AB'$ occur:

$$C = A'B' + A'B + AB'$$
$$= A'(B' + B) + AB'$$
$$= A' + AB'$$
$$= A' + B'$$

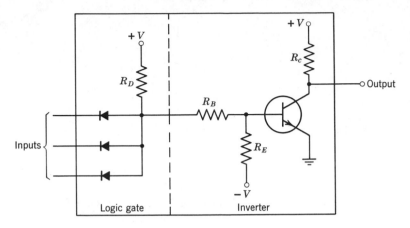

Figure 6–25. Logic-inverter gate (*NPN*).

By De Morgan's theorem,

$$A' + B' = (AB)'$$
$$C = (AB)' \qquad \text{NAND function}$$

For negative logic the output equation is simply

$$C = A'B'$$

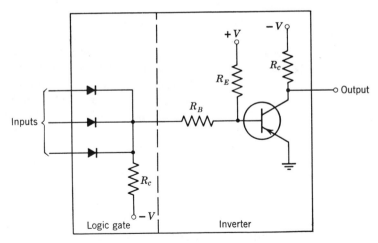

Figure 6–26. Logic-inverter gate (*PNP*).

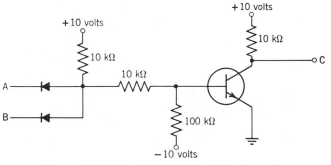

Figure 6–27. Practical *NPN* logic-inverter gate.

which De Morgan's theorem shows to be equivalent to

$$C = (A + B)' \qquad \text{NOR function}$$

A (Input 1)	B (Input 2)	C (Output)
0 volts	0 volts	+ 10 volts
0 volts	+ 10 volts	+ 10 volts
+ 10 volts	0 volts	+ 10 volts
+ 10 volts	+ 10 volts	0 volts

(*a*) Voltage truth table

A (Input 1)	B (Input 2)	C (Output)
0	0	1
0	1	1
1	0	1
1	1	0

0 volts ≡ 0
+ 10 volts ≡ 1

(*b*) Positive logic truth table (NAND gate)

A (Input 1)	B (Input 2)	C (Output)
1	1	0
1	0	0
0	1	0
0	0	1

0 volts ≡ 1
+ 10 volts ≡ 0

(*c*) Negative logic truth table (NOR gate)

Figure 6–28. *NPN* logic-inverter gate, voltage and logic truth tables.

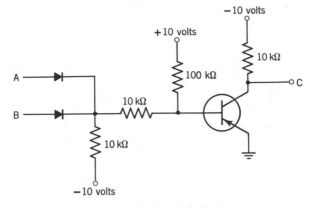

Figure 6–29.   Practical *PNP* logic-inverter gate.

Considering the practical *PNP* logic-inverter gate we find the opposite functions exist (see Figures 6–29 and 6–30).

From the positive logic truth table we find that C = 1 when A'B' = 1, or C = A'B'. By De Morgan's theorem this is also C = (A + B)', a NOR function. For negative logic the output is 1 when A'B' + A'B + AB' is 1. Again using the reduction to A' + B' and De Morgan's theorem, we have C = (AB)', a NAND function.

A (Input 1)	B (Input 2)	C (Output)
0 volts	0 volts	− 10 volts
0 volts	− 10 volts	− 10 volts
− 10 volts	0 volts	− 10 volts
− 10 volts	− 10 volts	0 volts

(*a*) Voltage truth table

A (Input 1)	B (Input 2)	C (Output)
1	1	0
1	0	0
0	1	0
0	0	1

0 volts ≡ 1
− 10 volts ≡ 0

(*b*) Positive logic truth table (NOR gate)

A (Input 1)	B (Input 2)	C (Output)	
0	0	1	0 volts $\equiv$ 0
0	1	1	-10 volts $\equiv$ 1
1	0	1	
1	1	0	

(c) Negative logic truth table (NAND gate)

Figure 6–30. *PNP* logic-inverter gate, voltage and logic truth tables.

Now that we have a good idea of how a NAND gate functions overall, and how it should work, we can take a more detailed look at some design considerations.   This will also help us later on in the chapter when more complicated circuits are considered based on the inverter operating principles.   Analysis of the circuit operation can be broken down into two cases, one case for turning the transistor ON and the second for keeping it OFF.   Here we are concerned primarily with the details of transistor currents and voltages to insure that the transistor is fully saturated when ON under the worst possible conditions and fully OFF with I_{co} having no detrimental effect.

Considering the *NPN* circuit only (the *PNP* circuit is exactly the same except for opposite voltage polarity and opposite current direction) for the ON condition, all inputs to the gate are at $+V$ volts. Figure 6–31 shows the details of current and voltage for this logic case.   Of primary consideration is that I_B be sufficient for the

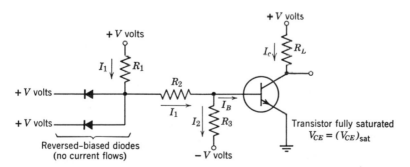

Figure 6–31. Detailed *NPN* NAND gate circuit for ON condition.

required I_c to saturate the transistor. The general expressions for I_B and I_c are

$$I_B = I_1 - I_2, \quad I_1 = \frac{V - (V_{BE})_{\text{on}}}{R_1 + R_2}, \quad I_2 = \frac{V + (V_{BE})_{\text{on}}}{R_3}$$

$$I_B = \frac{V - (V_{BE})_{\text{on}}}{R_1 + R_2} - \frac{V + (V_{BE})_{\text{on}}}{R_3}$$

$$I_c = \frac{V - (V_{CE})_{\text{sat}}}{R_L}$$

For saturation the ratio of I_c to I_B (circuit β) must be less than the actual transistor current gain (h_{FE}):

$$h_{FE} > \frac{I_c}{I_B} \quad \text{(using } I_c \text{ and } I_B \text{ as just given)}$$

A set of typical values for this gate are listed next with the resulting check to see whether the circuit will saturate as desired:

$$R_1 = 10 \text{ kohm} \qquad\qquad V = +10 \text{ volts}$$
$$R_2 = 10 \text{ kohm} \qquad\qquad (V_{CE})_{\text{sat}} = +0.2 \text{ volt}$$
$$R_3 = 100 \text{ kohm} \qquad\qquad (V_{BE})_{\text{on}} = +0.5 \text{ volt}$$
$$R_L = 10 \text{ kohm} \qquad\qquad h_{FE} = 20$$

$$I_B = \frac{10 - 0.5}{(10 + 10)10^3} - \frac{10 + 0.5}{(100)10^3} = \frac{9.5}{20} - \frac{10.5}{100} \text{ ma}$$

$$I_B = 0.475 - 0.105 = 0.370 \text{ ma} = 370 \text{ μa}$$

$$I_c = \frac{10 - 0.2}{(10)10^3} = \frac{9.8}{10} \text{ ma} = 0.98 \text{ ma} = 980 \text{ μa}$$

Check:

$$h_{FE} > \frac{I_c}{I_B} \quad \text{(required saturation condition)}$$
$$\text{Is } 20 > 980/370?$$

Yes—therefore circuit will saturate properly when turned ON. If the transistor were chosen with lower h_{FE} or if load requirements were increased (more I_c drawn), the ON condition would have to be rechecked to be certain that the circuit will operate properly. The worst conditions occur when the transistor h_{FE} is smallest. Since h_{FE} is temperature-dependent and decreases with decreasing tem-

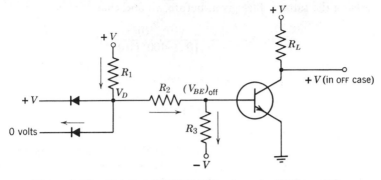

Figure 6–32. Detailed *NPN* NAND gate under OFF condition.

perature, it will have to satisfy the ON condition under the lowest possible temperatures the circuit may encounter. For the OFF condition the circuit must hold the transistor nonconducting even for a noise pulse of specified amplitude. Voltage and current nomenclature is shown in Figure 6–32. Notice that only one diode need be forward-biased (conducting) for the transistor to be held OFF.

As the voltage across the forward-biased diode is the small value $+V_D$, the voltage at the transistor base is the result of a voltage divider between R_3 and R_2. Considering $V_D \approx 0$ volts, the simplified divider is shown in Figure 6–33. Solving for $(V_{BE})_{off}$ we obtain

$$(V_{BE})_{off} = - \frac{R_2}{R_2 + R_3} V$$

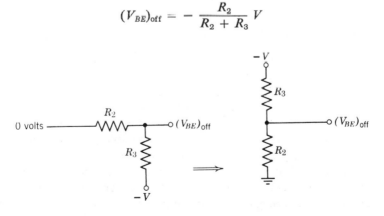

Figure 6–33. Simplified divider for OFF condition.

Using the same values given before we find that

$$(V_{BE})_{\text{off}} = -\frac{(10)\,(10)^3}{(10 + 100)\,(10)^3}\,10$$

$$= -\frac{100}{110}\text{ volts}$$

$$= -0.91\text{ volt}$$

This means that the base-emitter is reverse-biased by almost 1 volt, insuring that the transistor is turned OFF. Since it requires about $V_{BE} = +0.5$ volt to turn ON a transistor, the total noise voltage that would not affect the circuit is 0.91 + 0.5 or 1.41 volts. Any voltage less than this value which occurs because of pick up of noise by the circuit would not affect the desired OFF condition. Although the transistor is OFF, minority current I_{co} flows through R_L and must be small enough not to cause an appreciable voltage drop across R_L [$(V_{CE})_{\text{off}}$ is $+V$ volts, ideally]. The worst case occurs at highest operating temperatures as I_{co} increases with increasing temperature. For a typical I_{co} of 1 μa and R of 10 kohm, the voltage drop from 10 volts is $1 \times 10^{-6} \times 10 \times 10^3 = 0.01$ volt or 10 mv. This is small enough compared to 10 volts to be disregarded.

Problem 6–6. Using the following values of resistance and voltage, show whether h_{FE} of 20 is sufficient to fully saturate the transistor shown in Figure 6–31: $R_1 = 2$ kohm, $R_2 = 1$ kohm, $R_3 = 10$ kohm, $R_L = 1$ kohm, $V = 12$ volts.
Problem 6–7. For the OFF condition, as shown in Figures 6–32 and 6–33, calculate $(V_{BE})_{\text{off}}$ using the values given in Problem 6–6.

Transistor Logic Gating (DCTL). Transistor logic circuits use the transistor as the logic input element rather than the diode. It can operate faster than the diode-transistor gate discussed. Some benefits of transistor logic gates (called DCTL for direct-coupled transistor logic) are lower possible operating voltages resulting in lower power dissipation per gate, and compatability to less expensive cost using micrologic manufacturing techniques. Since it is possible to manufacture many transistors in one operation (in the same size case that previously held only one transistor), a complete gate with many inputs can be made in a single package.

One form of transistor gate is shown in Figure 6–34. It could be

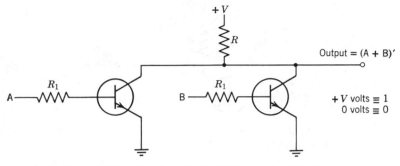

Figure 6–34. Transistor logic NOR gate (positive logic).

described as analogous to two switches in parallel.   If any switch is closed (transistor ON) the output is at 0 volts $[+ (V_{CE})_{sat}]$.   Thus, if either A or B is a 1 ($+V$ volts) the conducting transistor causes the output to go low.   Only when both inputs are 0 (0 volts) and all transistors are OFF does the output rise to $+V$.   A voltage and logic truth table shows that this is a NOR gate for positive logic (see Figure 6–35).   It should be apparent by this time that it would also be a NAND gate for negative logic.

A	B	Output
0 volts	0 volts	$+V$ volts
0 volts	$+V$ volts	0 volts
$+V$ volts	0 volts	0 volts
$+V$ volts	$+V$ volts	0 volts

(a)

A	B	Output
0	0	1
0	1	0
1	0	0
1	1	0

$+V$ volts $\equiv 1$
0 volts $\equiv 0$

(b)

Figure 6–35.   (a) Voltage and (b) logic truth tables of transistor NOR gate (positive logic).

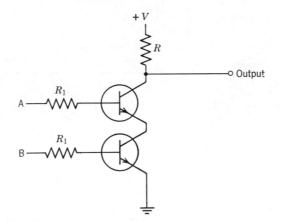

Figure 6–36.   Transistor logic NAND gate (positive logic).

The other compatible transistor-gated circuit is that of Figure 6–36.   It is a NAND gate for positive logic (and NOR gate for negative logic).   This circuit can be described as analogous to two switches in series.   If either switch is open the circuit will not conduct.   Only if both input A and B are present (both switches closed) is the output affected.   The voltage and logic truth tables of Figure 6–37 describe the circuit logical operation.   If either input is 0 volts

A	B	Output
0 volts	0 volts	$+V$ volts
0 volts	$+V$ volts	$+V$ volts
$+V$ volts	0 volts	$+V$ volts
$+V$ volts	$+V$ volts	0 volts

(a)

A	B	Output	
0	0	1	$+V$ volts $\equiv 1$
0	1	1	0 volts $\equiv 0$
1	0	1	
1	1	0	

(b)

Figure 6–37.   (*a*) Voltage and (*b*) logic truth tables of transistor NAND gate (positive logic).

that transistor does not receive a base turn-on current and remains cut off.   If both inputs are $+V$ the output is that of two saturated collector-emitter voltage drops.   With silicon epitaxial transistors this could easily be as low as 0.1 volt per transistor.   Thus for a five-input gate the voltage for the 0 condition would be $+0.5$ volt. As distinguished from this, $+3$ volts could be used as the 1-voltage level.

An interesting difference between the transistor-gated circuits and the diode-transistor logic circuits is that in the former both circuits may be used compatibly in the same system because they both use the same type of transistor and thus the same voltage levels as inputs. The NAND and NOR gates using diodes were of opposite transistor type (for one type of logic, positive or negative) and used different logic voltage levels.

An example of how the transistor gate can be used is shown implementing the half-adder function in Figure 6–38.   Recall that the sum and carry-out expressions were

$$SUM = AB' + A'B = (AB + A'B')'$$
$$CARRY\ OUT = AB$$

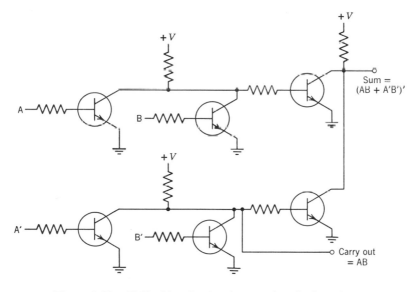

Figure 6–38.   Half-adder circuit using transistor logic gating.

Problem 6–8. Draw a DCTL circuit to implement the Boolean function AB' + A'BC.

Problem 6–9. Draw a DCTL circuit to implement the Boolean function (A + B)AB'C'.

Summary

The chapter presented AND, OR, INVERTER, NAND, and NOR gates. Although AND and OR gates are used to implement logic functions, the problem of loading limits how much they can be applied. More often a designer will use NAND or NOR gates to develop the logic function because he has clearly defined loading factors on both signal amplitude and speed. The advent of microelectronics has increased standardization of circuits.

PROBLEMS

1. Draw the circuit diagram of a positive logic OR gate using +10 volts and 0 volts as voltage levels. Prepare a voltage truth table and logic truth table of the circuit.

2. Prepare a voltage and logic truth table for a positive logic OR gate using 0 volts and −10 volts as voltage levels.

3. Repeat Problem 6–3 for R_1 = 1 kohm and R_2 = 5 kohm.

4. Draw the circuit diagram of a negative logic diode-transistor NOR gate.

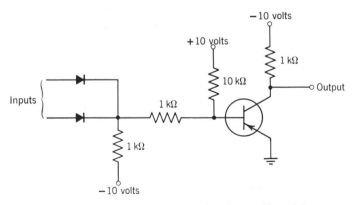

Figure 6–39.   NAND gate circuit for Problem 6–9.

5. Prepare the voltage and logic truth tables for a negative logic NAND gate.

6. Repeat Problem 6–6 using $R_1 = 5$ kohm, $R_2 = 2$ kohm, $R_3 = 12$ kohm, and $R_L = 500$ ohms.   All other values are the same.

7. Repeat Problem 6–7 using the values of Problem 6.

8. Draw a voltage truth table and logic truth table for a NOR gate using $+10$ volts and 0 volts as logic levels.   Is positive logic or negative logic used?

9. For the NAND gate in Figure 6–39 draw the voltage truth table and indicate whether positive or negative logic is used.

10. Draw a DCTL circuit to implement the logic equation

$$W = X'YZ + XZ' + YZ.$$

0111

Computer circuits

After the computer logic circuits covered in Chapter 6, the next type of computer circuit to study is the class of multivibrator circuits. The most popular of these is the bistable multivibrator, or flip-flop, which can be used as memory element, in counters, and in shift registers. Logic circuits are used to perform logical operations as expressed in Boolean equations. A bistable circuit allows data to be stored or shifted from one location to another, either in parallel (all bits at once) or serially (bit by bit). A bistable circuit is also used in counters to provide arithmetic counting (accumulating).

The monostable multivibrator, or one-shot, is used in timing and pulse-shaping operations. It provides a fixed-duration pulse when triggered, which is useful when one operation is to follow another after a fixed-delay interval or when pulse intervals have to be re-shaped into either narrower or wider pulses.

An astable multivibrator, or clock, is used to provide a fixed-frequency square wave which is used to control the rate at which operations are carried out by the computer. The similarity and differences between the three multivibrator circuits are covered in detail in the present chapter. Basic applications of these circuits to computer operations are covered in Chapter 8.

Finally, the Schmitt trigger circuit is described in detail and some applications are considered. A Schmitt trigger is a shaping circuit which converts a slowly varying waveform into one with sharply rising and falling slope for use in digital circuitry.

7–1. Bistable Multivibrator Circuit

The basic multivibrator circuit is shown in Figure 7–1. This circuit is stable in either of two possible conduction states. If Q_1 is

150

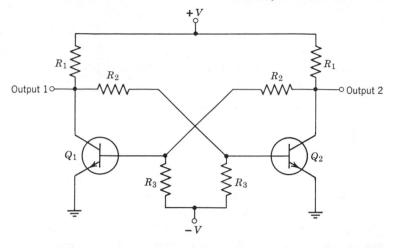

Figure 7–1.   Multivibrator circuit.

made conducting and Q_2 cutoff (nonconducting) the circuit will remain that way indefinitely after the triggering signal is removed (assuming power is not turned off).   If the circuit had been set to Q_2 conducting and Q_1 nonconducting it will remain in this state indefinitely.   These two possible stable states or bistable states are dependent on the cross-coupling connections made by resistors R_2, in this case.   If one of the cross-coupling elements was a capacitor the circuit would only be able to maintain one stable state, and if both coupling elements were capacitors the circuit would have no stable state and would oscillate back and forth, this being the astable operation.

In order to understand the operation of a bistable device consider the circuit of Figure 7–2.   Two inverters are connected in a loop.

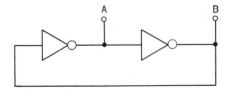

Figure 7–2.   Bistable circuit using two inverters.

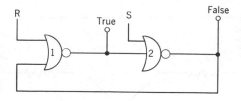

Figure 7–3.   Bistable circuit with SET (S) and RESET (R) inputs.

If the input to the first (B) is a 1, the output (A) is a 0.   A 0 into the second would result in a 1 output, which is precisely what we assumed it to be.   Now assume that the input to the first inverter (B) is a 0. The output of that inverter, A, is a 1 and the output B is then a 0, as assumed.   Either of these cases leads to stable operation and each condition is called a stable state.   In fact, it should be clear that A and B are always opposite and that the outputs could be labelled A and A′, TRUE and FALSE, 1 and 0, etc.

The bistable circuit is always in one of the two stable states.   How is it changed to operate in the other stable state?   To understand this let us consider using two NOR gates rather than inverters (Figure 7–3).

If R and S inputs are FALSE or 0, the operation is the same as that just described.   Assume that the TRUE output is at the 1 condition (and FALSE therefore at the 0).   By definition, the TRUE output being a 1 is called the SET condition of the circuit; the FALSE output being a 1 is the RESET condition.   R and S are the RESET and SET inputs as will now be shown.   When S becomes a 1, it causes the TRUE side to be a 1, thereby SET'ing the circuit. Since R and S cannot (or should not) be 1 at the same time, the R is presently a 0.   With TRUE output at 1 the FALSE output is made 0 (by the TRUE signal applied to NOR gate 2).   When the SET signal is removed (goes back to 0), the FALSE output connected as the input to NOR 1 holds the TRUE output at 1, thereby providing stable operation in the SET state.   To RESET the bistable circuit the R input goes to 1, causing the FALSE output to be a 1, which makes the TRUE output 0.   When R goes back to 0, the circuit now remains in the stable RESET state with TRUE output at 0 and FALSE output at 1.

As a summary, we can define the two outputs of a bistable circuit as TRUE and FALSE (they are *always* opposite) and the two stable states as SET and RESET, where SET is defined as TRUE = 1 and FALSE = 0, and RESET is defined as TRUE = 0 and FALSE = 1.

With this general description in mind let us now go back to the details of the bistable circuit. Although the circuit using two NOR's worked properly, it can only operate with dc voltage levels. To provide more flexible operation it is also operated with alternating current or pulse inputs for which a more detailed circuit is considered.

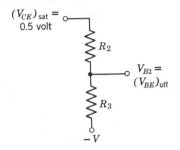

Figure 7–4.   Partial circuit for holding transistor cutoff.

The bistable circuit is symmetrical so that the circuit of R_1, R_2, and R_3 for holding Q_1 conducting is the same as that for holding Q_2 conducting.   Similarly, the circuit parts that hold Q_1 cutoff would be duplicated in those that hold Q_2 cutoff in the other stable condition.   In analyzing the operation with Q_1 conducting and Q_2 cutoff, we satisfy describing the requirements for having Q_2 conducting and Q_1 cutoff, the alternate stable condition.

When Q_1 is conducting the voltage at the collector is the saturation voltage, about 0.5 volt.   The voltage at the base of Q_2 under these conditions is determined by the voltage divider R_2 and R_3.   A partial circuit under this condition is shown in Figure 7–4.

Assuming $(V_{CE})_{sat} = 0$ volts, for a good approximation of V_{B2} we find that

$$V_{B2} = -\frac{R_2}{R_2 + R_3} V$$

Generally $R_2 \ll R_3$ and $V \gg V_{sat}$ so that the voltage at the base of Q_2 (with Q_1 conducting) is negative, thereby holding Q_2 cutoff or nonconducting.   Continuing, with Q_2 cutoff the voltage at the base of Q_1 can be determined.   Looking at Figure 7–5, we find that in order to have Q_1 conducting the base voltage must be $(V_{BE})_{on}$ or approximately 0.7 volt.   The important factor for the conducting transistor is that it be driven into saturation. The base drive current is $I_B = I_1 - I_2$, where

$$I_1 = \frac{V - 0.7}{R_1 + R_2} \quad \text{and} \quad I_2 = \frac{V + 0.7}{R_3}$$

These equations show that R_1 and R_2 have to be low enough to provide sufficient base drive current, whereas R_3 has to be large so that little drive current developed is bled away from the base. For saturation the base drive must be greater than I_c/β, $(\beta I_B = I_c)$. Meeting these conditions alone provides satisfactory operation of the bistable circuit. As long as one transistor is made conducting it holds the other nonconducting through R_2, and R_3 to $-V$. The nonconducting transistor, in turn, provides that through $+V$, R_1, and R_2 the conducting transistor gets adequate base drive current. One other criteria may also be applied in selecting R_1, R_2, and R_3. To have a reasonably high voltage at the collector of the nonconducting transistor, R_2 must be larger than R_1 so that the voltage divider from $+V$ to $(V_{BE})_{on}$ provides a proper voltage level. From the partial circuit of Figure 7–6 and the assumption that $(V_{BE})_{on} \approx 0$, a good approximation of V_{C2} is

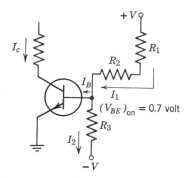

Figure 7–5. Partial circuit for holding transistor conducting.

$$V_{C2} = \frac{R_2}{R_1 + R_2} V$$

To complement or invert the state of the flip-flop a ground (0 volts) might be applied to the collector of the nonconducting transistor or the base of the conducting transistor. Once the ground is removed the circuit will remain in this other stable state. As shown so far, the bistable circuit is useful mainly as a memory element, "remembering" the state it was last put into. To provide for more general use of the circuit in counting and shifting operations, an input triggering network is used.

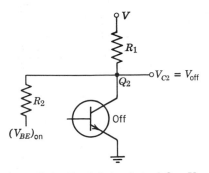

Figure 7–6. Partial circuit to define V_{off}.

To drive the conducting transistor into cutoff a negative signal may be applied to the base. Capacitive coupling is used to allow pulsing the base when the voltage changes without holding the circuit clamped. The basic input circuit is a differentiating circuit with a diode to clip the pulse of one polarity (see Figure 7–7). If this were used as the input network it would allow only the negative-going voltage change to drive a conducting transistor OFF. As opposed to grounding the collector or base through a direct signal path and holding the circuit in a fixed state during the pulse time, the input circuit provides a cutoff signal through an ac path (responds to signal changes) and does not hold the circuit in a fixed state. The duration of the negative pulse need be only long enough for the conducting transistor to turn OFF. If ac SET and RESET inputs of this type are used, the flip-flop may be controlled by application of a pulse to the proper control terminal (SET or RESET). If pulses are applied to both simultaneously, however, the circuit will provide cutoff pulses to both transistors and will not work properly.

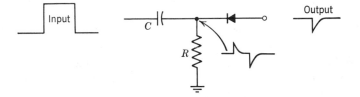

Figure 7–7. Input network for multivibrator circuit.

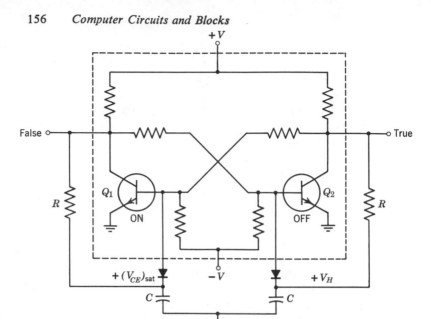

Figure 7–8.   Flip-flop with steering circuit.

For counting operation where a single pulse complements the flip-flop, a steering arrangement must be used so that only the conducting transistor is turned OFF.   The non-conducting transistor is turned ON through the cross-coupling network of the flip-flop. To "sense" the state of the flip-flop and feed the negative pulse to the conducting transistor only, each resistor of the steering network is returned to a transistor collector.   This is shown in Figure 7–8, where the flip-flop is blocked in, with the steering circuit outside.

Considering the junctions of the resistor, capacitor, and diode for each transistor input, the capacitor feeding the conducting transistor charges up to $(V_{CE})_{sat}$ and the other to V_H.   If the signal amplitude is selected to operate the circuit properly ($V_{trigger} = V_H$) only the conducting transistor receives a negative pulse.   When the trigger pulse goes positive, the positive differentiated signal is blocked from appearing at either base.   The negative step of the triggering signal causes the voltage across the capacitor feeding the nonconducting transistor to change by V_H volts.   But since the capacitor junction voltage was initially at $+V_H$ it goes down to 0 volts. Since the base of the nonconducting transistor is normally a few volts negative, the diode remains reverse-biased and no pulse appears at the base. For the conducting side, the negative voltage step V_H caused the diode to conduct since it was originally at $(V_{BE})_{on}$ at the base and the negative pulse at the base causes the conducting transistor to turn OFF. Only the conducting transistor receives a negative turn-off signal. When it turns OFF it causes the nonconducting transistor to turn ON through the bistable cross-coupling network completing the inversion or complementing of the circuit. On the next trigger pulse the circuit will complement again as the steering is charged oppositely ($+V_H$ again with the nonconductive side) and the bistable returns to the previous state. Thus, every trigger pulse causes the flip-flop to complement on the negative-going slope input providing a complementing flip-flop which may be used for counting.

The steering network may be connected to provide another important operation in a digital system. Shifting data (bits of fixed word length) around in a computer is often very useful. A bistable stage may be used as a shift stage and a number of shift stages connected to form a shift register. The steering network directs the input trigger pulse to the base of the conducting transistor when connected as shown in Figure 7–8. If the R resistors were connected to collectors of another stage, the network would be steered by the collector voltages of this other stage. If the other stage had a 1 output from the TRUE side and 0 from the FALSE, these signals connected to the steering resistors could force the present stage to go to the state of the other stage when a shift pulse is applied to the trigger input. Had the outputs of other stage been FALSE = 1 and TRUE = 0, this would have been forced on the present stage when the shift pulse was applied. In other words, the information stored in one stage is shifted into a second by application of a shift pulse. Examples of this are given in Chapter 8.

Problem 7–1. Draw the circuit diagram of a flip-flop circuit using *PNP* transistors.

Problem 7–2. For a flip-flop circuit like that of Figure 7–1, calculate the base and collector voltages of the OFF transistor using

$$R_1 = 1 \text{ kohm} \qquad R_2 = 2 \text{ kohm}$$
$$R_3 = 10 \text{ kohm} \qquad V = +10 \text{ volts}$$

Problem 7–3.   Draw the circuit diagram of a *PNP* flip-flop including complementary steering network.

7–2.   Monostable Multivibrator Circuits

The monostable circuit of the multivibrator class has as indicated one stable state, which means that the conditions of one transistor ON and the other OFF is stable only for a particular pair.   For example, Q_1 = OFF and Q_2 = ON may be the defined stable state. As long as no signal is applied to the circuit it remains in that state. When an input pulse is applied the state is changed to Q_1 = ON and Q_2 = OFF.   This state is not stable and the circuit will remain in this condition for only a set period of time, which may be a fraction of a microsecond to a few seconds.   After this period of time, the circuit returns to its stable state, remaining there indefinitely or until another triggering pulse is applied.   The monostable circuit of Figure 7–9 reflects the basic multivibrator arrangement with one cross-coupling resistor replaced by a capacitor.   This change and the connection of resistor R to $+V$ convert the bistable circuit to a monostable circuit.

The input trigger network shown is a differentiating circuit for the input pulse applied.   The diode prevents the positive-going part of the signal from getting to the base of Q_2.   Only the negative-going part of the input pulse reaches the base, and because Q_2 is the conducting transistor in the stable state the input pulse results in Q_2 being turned OFF.

In the stable operating state transistor Q_1 is OFF and Q_2 ON. When the trigger pulse causes the voltage at the base of Q_2 to go negative, turning Q_2 OFF, the cross-coupling from the collector of Q_2 results in Q_1 being turned ON.   Thus, the OFF pulse need be present only long enough for Q_1 to turn ON.   When Q_1 turns ON it discharges capacitor C, the resulting negative step causing the voltage at the base of Q_2 to go negative by the same amount.   This result is due to the fact that the voltage across a capacitor cannot change instantaneously, therefore a negative step on the Q_1 side of the capacitor is accompanied by a negative step of the same magnitude on the Q_2 side of the capacitor.   The capacitor will now start recharging towards $+V$ volts with a time constant RC.   When it

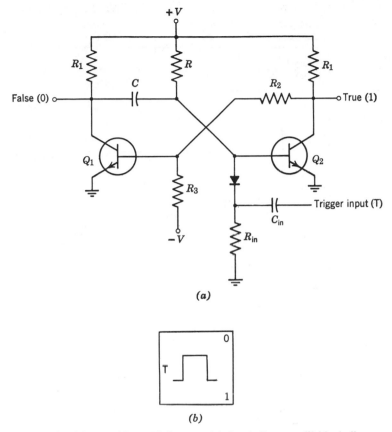

(a)

(b)

Figure 7–9.   Monostable multivibrator: (*a*) circuit diagram, (*b*) block diagram.

reaches $(V_{BE})_{on}$ volts it will cause Q_2 to turn ON again.   Transistor Q_1 will be turned OFF since the voltage divider of R_3 and R_2 results in a negative voltage at the base of Q_1 when the collector side of R_2 is near ground (Q_2 saturated).   A good picture of the operation of the monostable is obtained from looking at the waveforms shown in Figure 7–10.   The time period in the unstable state depends on RC as shown and is approximately equal to $0.7RC$ seconds of time.   (This value is a good approximation as long as $+V$ and $-V$ are of equal voltage magnitude.)

The main use of the monostable multivibrator in computer circuits

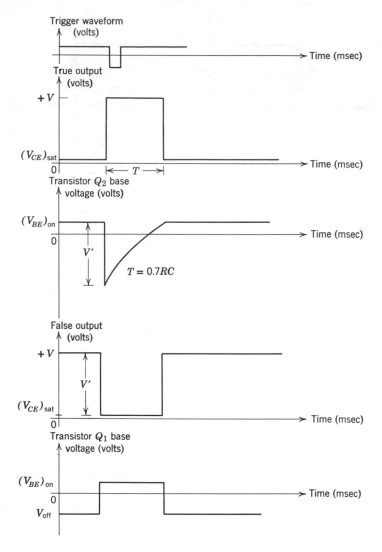

Figure 7–10.   Monostable waveforms.

is waveshaping or signal retiming and providing fixed delays.   The output of the TRUE side is a positive pulse of fixed width.   When a signal of variable pulse width is applied, the monostable output is a fixed-width pulse.   For example, if a few signal pulses applied to a logic gate do not fully coincide, the output pulse width will vary. Although this logic pulse may vary in width, the output of a mono-stable circuit, which it is applied to, provides pulses of fixed width or pulse time.   Another example may be an output from a memory device where a narrow, poorly shaped pulse is obtained from the readout circuitry.   Reshaping into a pulse of longer duration with a monostable provides a more useful signal for operation with other circuits in the computer.   Where pulses at a fixed frequency are applied, the output of the monostable is at this same frequency, but the output signal duty cycle (time OFF/time ON ratio) is under the control of the monostable time period $T = 0.7RC$.   This time period is used in pulse generators to provide an output pulse at variable duty cycle without affecting the signal frequency.   Using a variable R or C in the circuit allows the pulse width to be adjusted for calibrated control of the duty cycle.

With the indicated NPN circuit the monostable is triggered on the negative-going voltage change.   The output taken from the TRUE collector goes from near 0 volts when the transistor is saturated (stable condition) to near $+V$ volts during the monostable pulse time.   Here are two examples of how the monostable operates for both NPN and PNP circuits.

Example 7–1.   For the following NPN monostable multivibrator (Figure 7–11) draw the output waveform for the given input wave-form.

Solution: First the monostable time constant $T = 0.7RC$ must be calculated.   The R is 10 kohm and C is 0.7 μf, giving

$$T = 0.7 \, (10 \times 10^3) \, (0.7 \times 10^{-6}) \text{ sec}$$
$$= 0.49 \times 10^{-2} = 4.9 \times 10^{-3}$$
$$\approx 5 \text{ msec}$$

Since the monostable is triggered every time the input goes negative, the resulting output waveform is that of Figure 7–11c.

Example 7–2.   For the given PNP circuit draw the output waveshape for the input trigger signal shown (see Figure 7–12).

Solution: The time constant of $T = 0.7RC$ is found to be $T = 0.7$ $(1.2 \times 10^3)(1.2 \times 10^{-6}) = 1$ msec.   The circuit is triggered when-ever the input pulse goes positive (PNP circuit), so that the resulting output waveform is that of Figure 7–12c.

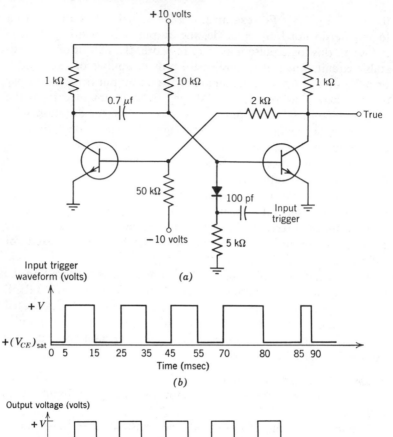

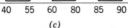

Figure 7–11.   Monostable circuit and waveforms for Example 7–1.

Problem 7–4.   Draw the TRUE output waveform for the following circuit (Figure 7–13) and input waveform.

Problem 7–5.   Draw the output waveshape for the FALSE output of the following circuit (Figure 7–14) when triggered by a 1-kc square wave.

Problem 7–6.   Calculate the monostable time constant for the circuit given in Figure 7–15.

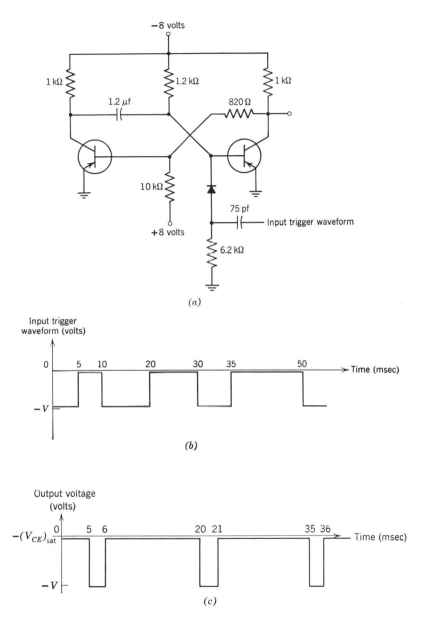

Figure 7–12.   Monostable circuit and waveforms for Example 7–2.

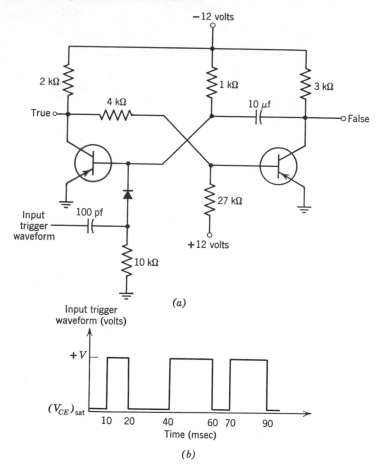

Figure 7–13.   Circuit and input waveform for Problem 7–4.

7–3.   Astable Multivibrator Circuits

An important part of computer or digital circuit operation is the timing signals.   A basic oscillator provides timing signals for controlling all the operations of the system.   One simple means of obtaining a clock signal is to use a multivibrator circuit which is designed to have no stable operating state.   This forces the circuit

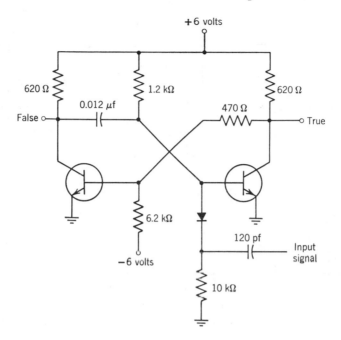

Figure 7–14.   Circuit for Problem 7–5.

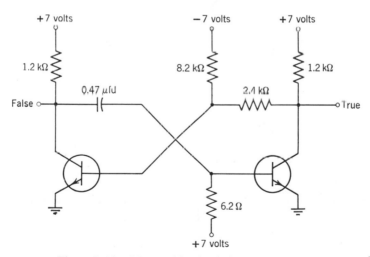

Figure 7–15.   Monostable circuit for Problem 7–6.

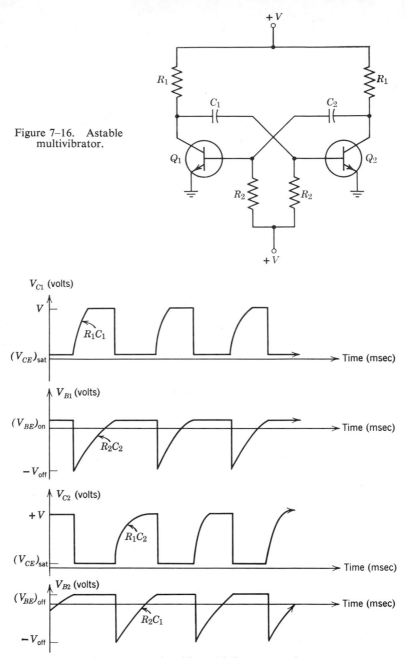

Figure 7–16. Astable multivibrator.

Figure 7–17. Astable multivibrator waveforms.

to continually alternate back and forth between two semistable (quasistable) states, the alternating rate resulting in the clock frequency of the multivibrator circuit. Such a circuit, called an "astable multivibrator," is shown in Figure 7–16. The figure is drawn to represent the basic multivibrator arrangement where the cross-coupling elements are capacitors C_1 and C_2. When a capacitor is used as the cross-coupling element, it provides an output that remains in a fixed state (ON or OFF) for only a set period of time. In the monostable circuit one coupling capacitor provides only one stable state. In the astable configuration the two coupling capacitors permit no stable state, the outputs remaining in either state for only a set period of time. This time can range from fractions of a microsecond to a few seconds. Compare this to the output of the bistable circuit that remains in a fixed state indefinitely (as long as no outside signal is applied to change it), or the monostable multivibrator which stays in one state until triggered and in the other state for only a fixed interval of time.

To analyze the operation of the astable circuit consider Q_1 to be conducting (ON) and Q_2 nonconducting (OFF). Under this condition the voltages at the collectors are $V_{C1} = (V_{CE})_{sat}$ and $V_{C2} = +V$. With the capacitor C_1 connected to ground through conducting transistor Q_1, resistor R_2 will charge C_1, the charging time constant being R_2C_1. When V_{B2} reaches a voltage of $(V_{BE})_{on}$ (≈ 0.7-volt), transistor Q_2 will turn ON. Capacitor C_2 will discharge through the transistor, the negative step appearing at the base of Q_1 since the voltage across a capacitor cannot change instantaneously.

This negative step from $(V_{BE})_{on}$, the base voltage when Q_1 was ON, turns Q_1 OFF. Thus, Q_1 and Q_2 have alternated states temporarily. Capacitor C_2 will be charged by the other resistor R_2 from the initial negative voltage until it reaches $(V_{BE})_{on}$, the charging time constant being R_2C_2. For the interval of time that the capacitor is charging the two outputs remain in their present states. After the charging time they again alternate states, for the negative step resulting when C_1 discharges through Q_1 causes transistor Q_2 to turn OFF. The base and collector waveforms for the two transistors are shown in Figure 7–17 and provide a good picture of the charging operation in controlling the length of time in each state. In the case where $C_1 = C_2$ the waveform is symmetrical and the output is a square wave. A good approximation of the time in each state is $T = 0.7R_2C$.

Since one cycle is two of these times and the repetition frequency is $f = 1/T$, the clock rate can be calculated from

$$f = \frac{1}{2(0.7R_2C)} = \frac{1}{1.4R_2C}$$

The frequency can be adjusted by reducing the value of capacitor C to raise the frequency or by raising the value of the capacitor to lower the frequency.

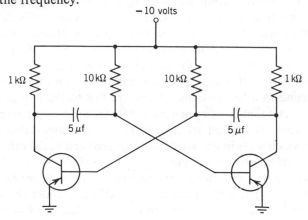

Figure 7–18.   Astable multivibrator for Example 7–3.

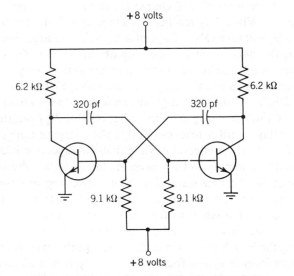

Figure 7–19.   Astable circuit for Problem 7–7.

A close look at the waveforms of Figure 7–17 shows that the outputs of the multivibrator are always opposite (as would be expected). The time constants of the collector waveforms show that R_1 is smaller in value than R_2 so that the collectors quickly rise up to the steady level $+V$. If the resistor value did not allow the collector to rise to $+V$ before the transistor is again turned ON, the given frequency equation would be in error and in particular would give too low a frequency result. Under usual operating conditions the collector rises up to a steady voltage level so that the circuit operates as described and the clock rate or frequency of oscillation is that given by the equation above. The oscillator may be synchronized, if desired, by an external signal applied to the collector if negative-going, or to the base if positive-going.

Example 7–3. Calculate the operating frequency of the following *PNP* astable oscillator (Figure 7–18).

Solution: The timing elements are $R = 10$ kohm and $C = 5$ μf. Using the frequency equation $f = 1/1.4RC$, we find the clock rate to be

$$f = \frac{1}{1.4(10 \times 10^3)(5 \times 10^{-6})}$$

$$f = \frac{1}{7 \times 10^{-2}} = \frac{100}{7} = 14.28 \text{ cps}$$

Problem 7–7. Calculate the clock rate for the circuit shown in Figure 7–19.

Problem 7–8. Calculate the clock rate for the circuit in Figure 7–20.

7–4. Schmitt Trigger

The Schmitt trigger (Figure 7–21) operates as a regenerative amplifier, to provide a pulsed-shape output for a slowly varying sloped input. When the input voltage exceeds a threshold level (this level may be selected when the circuit elements are chosen), the input transistor turns ON and begins to turn the output transistor OFF. This action is regenerative; the output in going OFF further turns the input ON which turns the output OFF more quickly, resulting in a pulsed waveshape (fast rise and fall times). Alternately, when the input signal goes below a second threshold level

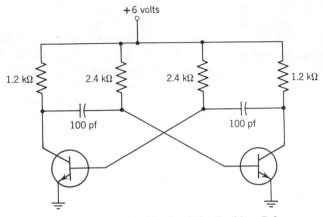

Figure 7–20.   Astable circuit for Problem 7–8.

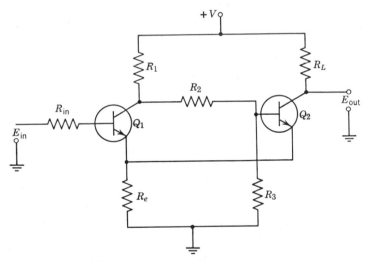

Figure 7–21.   Schmitt trigger circuit.

(also a design value) the first transistor switches, regeneratively turning the second ON which further turns the first OFF, etc.   The waveform of input and output for a typical case of sinusoidal input is shown in Figure 7–22.

Where the input is a 60-cps sinusoidal signal, with very slowly rising and falling slopes (order of milliseconds), the output rise and fall times may be in the order of a fraction of a microsecond.   The output signal occurring at the same frequency rate as the input has a sharp slope suitable for use with digital circuits.   In the particular case where the ON and OFF threshold levels are chosen as 0 volts, the output waveform to a sinusoidal input is a square wave at the same frequency as the input.

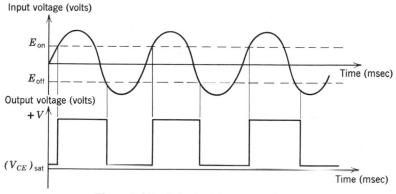

Figure 7–22.   Schmitt trigger waveshapes.

The following operating description refers to the circuit of Figure 7–21.   With no input applied to the Schmitt circuit Q_1 is OFF and Q_2 is ON.   A partial circuit is useful to analyze the voltage levels around transistor Q_2.   This is shown in Figure 7–23.   The voltage

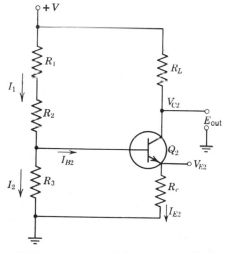

Figure 7–23.   Partial output circuit of Schmitt trigger.

at base 2 in general will depend on the value obtained from the voltage divider of resistor R_3 in parallel with the input resistance of the transistor emitter follower (Q_2 feeding R_e) and R_1 and R_2 in series.   If the current gain of the transistor times the value of R_e is large enough compared to R_3, the base voltage is simply

$$V_{B2} = \frac{R_3}{R_1 + R_2 + R_3} V$$

Since $V_{BE2} = V_{B2} - V_{E2}$ we can solve for V_{E2} as $V_{B2} - V_{BE2}$. V_{BE2} for the conducting transistor is approximately 0.7 volts so that the ratio of $R_3/(R_1 + R_2 + R_3)$ will set the voltage at the conducting transistor emitter.   Looking back to Figure 7–21, we see that this voltage is also that of the nonconducting emitter.   For input transistor Q_1 to turn ON, the input must exceed V_{E2} by V_{BE} volts.   Thus, the voltage level or threshold level at which the Schmitt trigger will "fire" regeneratively turning Q_1 ON and Q_2 OFF is for the simple analysis

$$\frac{R_3 V}{R_1 + R_2 + R_3} \text{ volts}$$

This approximation neglects many small effects of differences in $(V_{BE})_{on}$ between transistors, loading effects of the transistor feeding R_e on resistor R_3, etc.   Although these other factors are of importance to a good engineering design, they do not aid in the understanding of the basic circuit.

The regenerative nature of the turn ON should now be considered. When the input signal goes above V threshold by $(V_{BE})_{on}$, transistor Q_1 begins to conduct causing the voltage V_{C1} to go down.   Transistor Q_2 going OFF let the voltage V_{E2} go further negative, turning Q_1 ON. V_{C1} going negative cuts down the input drive current to transistor Q_2, further cutting Q_2 OFF.   This regenerative action will continue until Q_1 is conducting in the saturation region and transistor Q_2 is in cutoff.

The analysis of the operation when the signal causes Q_1 to turn OFF and Q_2 ON is aided by the partial diagram of Figure 7–24. The voltage at the base of Q_2 must be low enough to hold Q_2 OFF. Since V_{E2} is the same voltage as V_{E1}, the additional voltage, V_{CE1} of saturated transistor Q_1, must be attenuated by R_3 and R_2 to less than $(V_{BE})_{on}$.   In general, $(V_{CE})_{sat}$ is less than $(V_{BE})_{on}$ so that an attenuation by 5 or 10 will surely hold Q_2 OFF.   It should be realized though that the larger the attenuation factor, the lower R_3, resulting in more current being bled from the base drive current when Q_2 is ON.   The threshold voltage to turn Q_1 OFF can be found by calculating V_{E1} (V_{E1} is simply $I_{E1}R_e$).   Since I_{E1} is approximately I_{C1} when the transistor is saturated ($I_{B1} \ll I_{C1}$ for high current gain), by neglecting the current drawn through R_2 and R_3 and the voltage drop of the saturated transistor, the current $I_{E1} \cong V/(R_1 + R_e)$, gives a threshold voltage of

$$V_{E1} = \frac{R_e}{R_1 + R_e} V$$

This equation results from the previous simplifications that the voltage is due to the voltage divider of R_e and R_1.

When the input voltage goes below V_{E1}, transistor Q_1 begins to turn OFF.   As V_{C1} rises because there is less current flowing through R_1, the voltage at the base of Q_2 (V_{B2}) begins to rise turning Q_2 ON.   Current flow through Q_2 makes the voltage V_{E2} rise, causing Q_1 to be further cut off.   The regenerative action continues until now Q_2 is saturated and Q_1 is OFF.

A typical use of a Schmitt trigger is the squaring of a slowly varying waveform.   One example would be squaring of a sinusoidal signal as shown in Figure 7-22.   As mentioned, if the threshold points are both at 0 volts, the resulting wave is a square wave.   In a practical circuit the two levels cannot be made exactly the same, the voltage difference between turn ON and turn OFF of Q_1 being considered a hysteresis voltage.   The resulting waveform, then, is not a square wave but is still at the frequency of the input signal and has sharp rise and fall times for use with computer circuitry.   The fact that this pulse-type signal is locked to the frequency of the sinusoidal signal is quite often the important feature of the output signal of the Schmitt trigger.

Another common use of the Schmitt circuit is to square up a noisy signal coming from the output of a memory read device. Signals for this operation are shown in Figure 7-25.   Although the output waveform is not at all symmetrical, it has as many pulses as the input signal has, which exceed the threshold level.   Thus, any noise signals below the threshold levels are rejected and those that are accepted are sharpened up by the circuit.   Finally, it should be realized that if the emitter resistor R_e is returned to a negative voltage

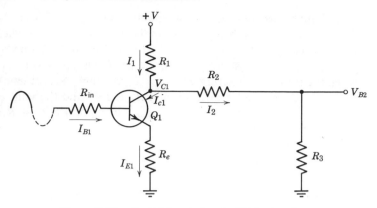

Figure 7–24.   Partial input circuit of Schmitt trigger.

rather than ground potential, the threshold levels may be chosen to lie below zero so that the circuit operation is more flexible.

Problem 7–9.   Draw the output waveform resulting when a 400-cps sinusoidal signal is applied to a Schmitt trigger.   Use $E_{on} - E_{off} = 0$ volts.   Indicate the time base clearly.

Problem 7–10.   Draw the output waveform resulting if the input to a

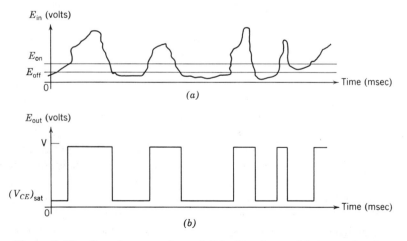

Figure 7–25.   Squaring operation of Schmitt trigger: (*a*) input signal to Schmitt trigger, (*b*) output signal of Schmitt trigger.

Schmitt trigger circuit is that shown in Figure 7–26.   Use $E_{on} = +2$ volts; $E_{off} = -1$ volt.

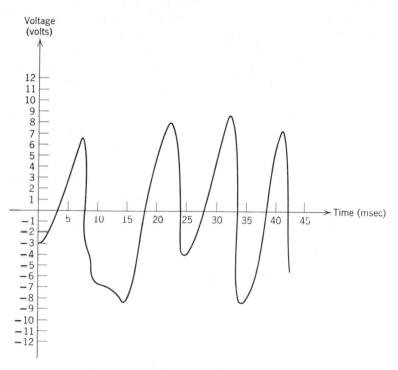

Figure 7–26.   Waveform for Problem 7–10.

Summary

Multivibrator circuits are important in computer operation.   Of these the bistable circuit is by far the most popular.   In operation the circuit state may be changed in a number of ways.   When SET or RESET the circuit is forced to assume a specific state.   When SET the TRUE output is 1 and when RESET the FALSE output is 1. A flip-flop may be connected as a complementing stage, changing state whenever an input pulse is applied to the trigger input.   A flip-flop may also be used as a shift stage.   For this operation the steering resistors are not connected to the transistor collectors of that stage but to those of another stage.   When a shift pulse is applied to the trigger input, the data stored in the other stage is shifted into the stage considered. Applications of the flip-flop as counter and shift register stages are given in the next chapter.

The monostable multivibrator (one-shot) has only one stable operating state and is used to provide a fixed-duration pulse. The pulse time or delay time of the monostable is fixed by an RC time constant. Simple designs allow for delays from microseconds to seconds. As a general rule the delay time is calculated from $T = 0.7RC$.

The astable multivibrator (clock) is an oscillator whose operating frequency is fixed by an RC time constant. The frequency may be calculated from $f = 1/1.4RC$ cps. Both equations just given are restricted as indicated in the chapter.

A Schmitt trigger circuit is used to "square up" a slowly varying waveform. The circuit is regenerative, switching in a very short time. Circuit design allows setting the threshold voltages at which the circuit switches.

PROBLEMS

1. Draw a circuit diagram of a *PNP* bistable multivibrator. Label all components, input lines, and output lines.

2. Draw the collector waveform of a complementary flip-flop triggered by a 200-kc square wave. Show input waveform on the same time scale and indicate time and voltage scales clearly. Assume *PNP* transistors are used.

3. Draw the circuit diagram of a *PNP* monostable multivibrator and indicate values for the timing R and C components for a circuit time constant of 20 msec.

4. Draw the TRUE output waveform of the circuit shown in Figure 7–27 for a 10-kcps square-wave input signal. Include input waveform on the same time axes.

5. Draw the FALSE output waveform for the circuit of Figure 7–13 when the monostable is triggered by a 100-cps square wave.

6. Calculate the output clock frequency for the astable multivibrator shown in Figure 7–28.

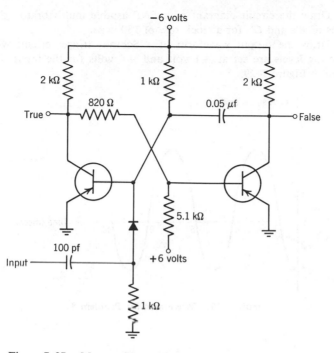

Figure 7–27. Monostable multivibrator circuit for Problem 4.

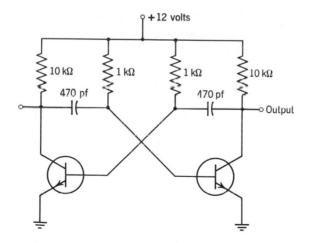

Figure 7–28. Astable multivibrator circuit for Problem 6.

7. Draw the circuit diagram of a *PNP* astable multivibrator giving values of *R*'s and *C*'s for a clock rate of 150 kcps.

8. Draw the output waveform of a Schmitt trigger circuit whose triggering levels are set at $+1$ volt and $+6$ volts for the input signal shown in Figure 7–29.

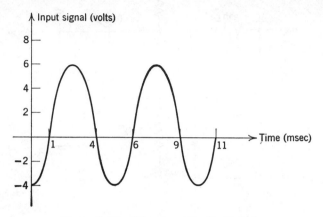

Figure 7–29.   Waveform for Problem 8.

1000

Counters and shift registers

Monostable circuits have many applications in computers. Bistable multivibrators are used in binary counters to provide timing for various computer operations and in shift registers to move binary data throughout the computer units. When other than binary counts are needed, the basic binary counter can be modified to a feedback counter. The astable multivibrator is used to provide the clock signal to operate the counters and shift registers. Monostable multivibrators are used to shape various signals to have longer duration times if too short and shorter duration times if too long or to shape a signal occurring at a fixed-delay interval after the monostable circuit is triggered.

8–1. Binary Counters

A flip-flop block diagram is shown in Figure 8–1. The 1 and 0 output lines refer to the collector output of each transistor with the 1 or TRUE side chosen arbitrarily. Once chosen, the SET input is one that causes the TRUE side to go to the logical 1 condition and the RESET input one that results in the FALSE side being in the logical 1 condition. The trigger or complementing input is that described in Chapter 7.

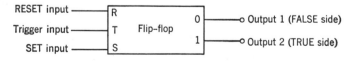

Figure 8–1. Flip-flop block diagram.

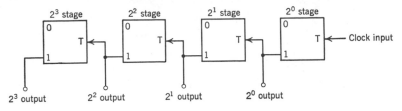

Figure 8-2. Binary counter block diagram.

Used in a counter, the flip-flops are interconnected with each successive one taking its trigger input from the output of the preceding stage.   A four-stage binary counter is shown in Figure 8-2. An input signal is applied to the 2^0 stage.   The output of each stage, numbered by the stage order (2^0, 2^1, etc.), is taken from the TRUE side of the flip-flop.   Notice that for this case the trigger for each succeeding stage is also from a TRUE side.   Each time the clock input goes negative, the 2^0 stage is complemented.   Consider all stages RESET (TRUE outputs all 0).   The first input pulse causes the 2^0 output to go from 0 to 1.   For the *NPN* circuit considered so far, the stage will complement only when the input voltage has a negative slope.   Using positive logic ($+V = 1$, 0 volts = 0), we find the flip-flop will complement when the input goes from 1 to 0 ($+V$ to 0 volts).   Since the first input trigger pulse causes the output of the 2^0 stage to go from 0 to 1, the 2^1 stage does not complement. Only the 2^0 stage changes state.   On the second input pulse the 2^0 stage again complements but this time going from 1 to 0.   This causes the 2^1 stage to complement, the 2^1 output going from 0 to 1. No further stage is triggered.   Putting these steps in tabular form will show the pattern clearly (see Table 8-1).

Notice that the binary count is equivalent to the input pulse number and progresses in an increasing direction.   The first pulse results in the count 0001 (reading the 2^0 or LSD, least significant digit, on the right), the second in 0010, the third in 0011, the fourth in 0100, etc., up to binary 15—1111.   On the next pulse the count goes back to binary 0 and the sequence starts all over again.   With four stages the count repeats every sixteen pulses.   Generally, there are 2^n counts with an *n*-stage counter.   For the four stages used here the count goes 2^4, or 16 steps.

As an aside, the arrows in Table 8-1 indicate when the 1 to 0

Table 8–1.   Count-Up Operation (four stages)

Input Pulses	2^3 OUTPUT	2^2 OUTPUT	2^1 OUTPUT	2^0 OUTPUT
0	0	0	0	0
1	0	0	0	1
2	0	0	1	0
3	0	0	1	1
4	0	1	0	0
5	0	1	0	1
6	0	1	1	0
7	0	1	1	1
8	1	0	0	0
9	1	0	0	1
10	1	0	1	0
11	1	0	1	1
12	1	1	0	0
13	1	1	0	1
14	1	1	1	0
15	1	1	1	1
16 or 0	0	0	0	0

change triggers a succeeding stage.   Notice that the 2^0 stage goes through 8 cycles, the 2^1 only 4, the 2^2 only 2, and the 2^3 one.   This fact can be interpreted as a decreasing cycle rate for higher-order stages.   For sixteen pulses the first stage cycles eight times for $16/2^1$, the next four times or $16/2^2$, the third stage by two or $16/2^3$, and the fourth by one or $16/2^4$.   This decreasing cycle rate can also be shown in a timing diagram such as Figure 8–3.   Here the input clock is shown with the TRUE output of each stage below it.   It can be seen that the frequency of each stage is less by a factor of 2.   Thus, the connection shown in Figure 8–2 is also that of a frequency divider. If the input frequency, for example, had been 256,000 cps, the frequency of the 2^3 stage OUTPUT would be only 16,000 cps, or 256 kc/16.   The arrows in Figure 8–3 indicate the negative slopes which trigger the next stage.

Getting back to counting, the count-up stages shown in Figure 8–2 form a count-up register.   This register can be used as a binary

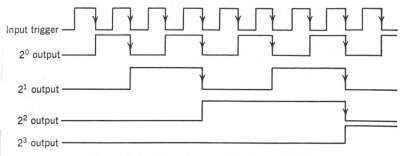

Figure 8–3. Waveforms of frequency divider.

accumulator or adder.   If five pulses are fed to the input, the count goes to 0101—or binary five.   If four more pulses are now fed in, a total count of 1001 results.   Thus, addition of two numbers may be performed using the counter as an accumulator to sum the number of pulses.   In order to do subtraction, the register would have to count in the reverse direction or count down.   To provide this facility, the interconnection shown in Figure 8–4 is used.   As seen, the trigger pulses are taken from the FALSE side of the proceeding stage for count-down operation.   However, because we still use the TRUE side as the output, we find that although the triggering still occurs when the trigger pulse goes from 1 to 0, since this is taken from the FALSE side, a table showing the TRUE output will indicate that triggering occurs on the 0 to 1 change.   Table 8–2 shows the count-down operation.

Looking at Table 8–2, we find the arrows again indicate that each successive stage operates at a slower rate.   (Either connection, as a count-up or count-down register, will provide operation as a frequency divider.)   For arithmetic operation one connection (using

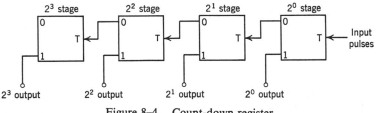

Figure 8–4. Count-down register.

Table 8–2.   Count-Down Operation (four stages)

Input Pulses	2^3 TRUE	2^2 TRUE	2^1 TRUE	2^0 TRUE	Decimal Output Count
0	0	0	0	0	16 (or 0)
1	1	1	1	1	15
2	1	1	1	0	14
3	1	1	0	1	13
4	1	1	0	0	12
5	1	0	1	1	11
6	1	0	1	0	10
7	1	0	0	1	9
8	1	0	0	0	8
9	0	1	1	1	7
10	0	1	1	0	6
11	0	1	0	1	5
12	0	1	0	0	4
13	0	0	1	1	3
14	0	0	1	0	2
15	0	0	0	1	1
16 (or 0)	0	0	0	0	0 (or 16)

TRUE side as trigger) provides addition and the other subtraction. Although most large general-purpose computers use standard binary adders, some special-purpose computers use the counter as an accumulator as described here.   The following problems help point out some important features to be considered in using bistable multivibrator circuits.

Problem 8–1.   Draw the circuit diagram of a *PNP* bistable multivibrator.

Problem 8–2.   Since the *PNP* flip-flop triggers on a positive-going voltage change, draw the output of the FALSE (0) side of the flip-flop for the following trigger signal (see Figure 8–5).

Problem 8–3.   Draw the interconnection block diagram for a five-stage count-down register.

Problem 8–4.   Draw the count-down table for a five-stage register using *PNP* stages.

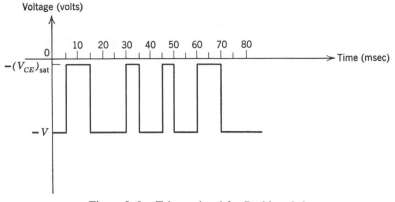

Figure 8–5.   Trigger signal for Problem 8–2.

8–2.   Shift Registers

We previously considered the steering network of the flip-flop and found that it directed the turn-off pulse to the conducting transistor only.   This occurs when the steering resistors are connected to the collectors of the flip-flop transistors.   Another possible arrangement is to connect the steering resistors to the collectors of another flip-flop stage (see Figure 8–6, circuit diagram).   Then the other stage will determine how the first stage will change when a trigger pulse is applied.   The resulting operation allows shifting of the stored information (binary 1 or 0) from one stage into another.   Depending on the connection, the information may shift to the stage on its right or on its left.   Thus, the circuit may be a shift-right register or a shift-left register, depending on the connection.   Examples of each are shown in Figures 8–7 and 8–8, respectively.   The steering resistor points are indicated on the block diagram by the letters X and Y.   In Figure 8–6 a circuit schematic indicating the lettering and corresponding circuit point is given.

Notice that X input is always connected to the FALSE side and Y input always to a TRUE.   Information or data fed into one side of the register is sent down the register one bit at each shift pulse. Since the data moves one bit at a time, the operation is termed "serial."   At each shift pulse *all* data moves *one* bit over; the direction depends on whether the register is wired up for shift-left

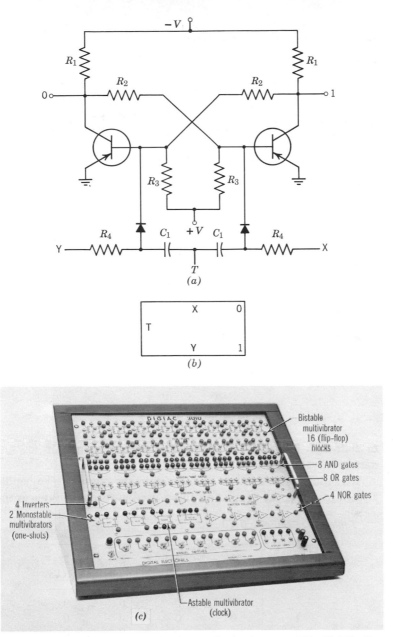

Figure 8–6. (a) Flip-flop circuit (with shift steering network). (b) Flip-flop block. (c) Computer blocks for study of logical operations. (Courtesy of Digital Electronics, Westbury, New York.)

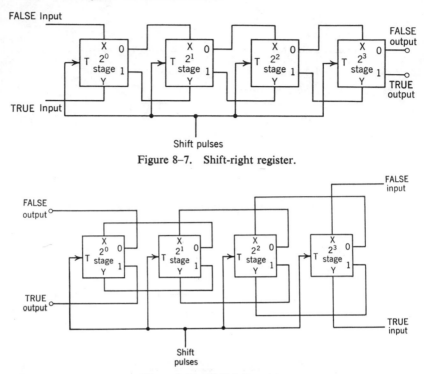

Figure 8–7.   Shift-right register.

Figure 8–8.   Shift-left register.

or shift-right operation.   Table 8–3 shows an example of how the data moves through the shift register for an input of 0110.

After four pulses the data is shifted into the register.   To handle a word properly, the number of pulses used must be the same as the

Table 8–3.   *Shifting 0110 into a Four-Stage Shift-Right Register*

Input Pulses	2^0 TRUE	2^1 TRUE	2^2 TRUE	2^3 TRUE
	0	0	0	0
1	0	0	0	0
2	1	0	0	0
3	1	1	0	0
4	0	1	1	0

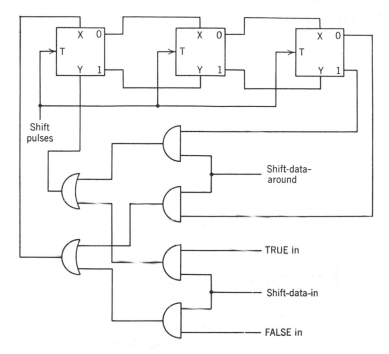

Figure 8–9.   Shift-in and shift-around operation.

number of register stages.   In addition to shifting information into a register, it is often desirable to maintain information in the register. This can be done by shifting the data around and back into the input. The connection for three stages with this shift-around facility is shown in Figure 8–9.   The logic circuits used provide the means of doing one or the other operation—shift in or shift around.   At each shift operation time three shift pulses are applied to the shift pulse line.   If the shift-data-around input is present (and shift-data is not present), the data being fed into the first register stage (2^0) is that from the 2^2 stage.   After three shift pulses the same word is present as before the shift operation.   Thus, data is shifted around and saved.   When new data is to be entered into the register, the shift-around must be blocked.   In this case the shift-data-in signal is present (and shift-around is not) so that the new input data is applied to the input stage.   After three shift pulses a new data word is stored in the register.   The shift-data-around and shift-data-in commands must always be opposite for proper operation.

8–3.   Feedback Counters

Using the counters considered so far only allows for counting in binary multiples.   Often some other count factor is needed.   The most common would be ten, so that the count is some decade multiple for use with decimal operations.   There are a number of techniques for altering the binary count.   The use of feedback to advance the count is one popular method.   If a certain count is desired, the number of stages is chosen to provide the next higher binary count and count feedback is used to advance the count by the extra steps.   For example, to count 6 a three-stage counter (count of 8) may be used with feedback advancing the counter by two steps.   Eight minus two leaves the desired six counts.   Just as a three-stage binary counter resets to zero after eight pulses and starts over, the count-of-6 counter will also go back to zero after six steps and repeat the count.   Figure 8–10 shows a possible circuit arrangement.   A count-of-6 counter is often called a "Modulus 6" (normally abbreviated to MOD 6) counter, with the modulus of the counter indicating that it resets on that particular pulse.   Since the trigger input is operated by a specific voltage change (negative or positive), it should be considered in the design.   When positive logic is used the 1 is the more positive voltage and 0 the less positive. Therefore, going from 1 to 0 results in a negative step.   With negative logic, the 1 being less positive than the 0, a change from 1 to 0 results in a positive-going step.

Example 8–1.   Design a count-of-25 (MOD 25) counter using feed-

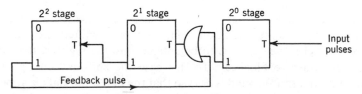

Fig. 8–10.   Count-of-6 (MOD 6) counter using feedback (concept representation only).

back.   The flip-flops are triggered by a negative-going pulse and use positive logic.

Solution: With positive logic a change from 1 to 0 gives a negative step and a change from 0 to 1 a positive step.   Assume all stages reset at the start.   The next binary count above 25 is 32, so five stages are needed.   To reduce 32 to 25 the number of steps advanced must be $32 - 25$, or 7.   To advance 7 requires triggering the 2^0 (1), 2^1 (2), and 2^2 (4) stages, since $1 + 2 + 4 = 7$.   The circuit used is shown in Figure 8–11.   Notice that the feedback is taken from the 0 output in this example.   The 0 or FALSE side when RESET is 1 and at the count of sixteen goes from 1 to 0, providing the negative pulse to trigger the monostable multivibrator.   When triggered the monostable 1 output provides a pulse to SET the 2^0, 2^1, and 2^2 stages, advancing the count by 7.   It is essential that when the state of any stage is changed it does not trigger another stage (unless that was the intent).   In this example the first three stages go from 0 to 1, a positive step which does not trigger a stage.   Table 8–4 lists the count for each input pulse.

The feedback was taken from the last stage because only that stage changes once per cycle.   Had the feedback in Example 8–1 been taken from the 2^3 stage output, it would have advanced the count by 2×7, or 14, since that stage changes twice during every cycle.   This advance points out another consideration in the design but also another way of advancing the count.   Where the count is to be advanced by a multiple of 2 the feedback could be taken from a lower-order stage than the last.   Example 8–2 provides a description of this method.

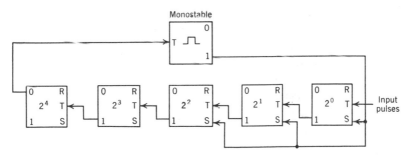

Figure 8–11.   Count-of-25 (MOD 25) counter for Example 8–1.

Table 8-4.   Count-of-25 (MOD 25) Counter Steps

Input Pulses	2^4 TRUE	2^3 TRUE	2^2 TRUE	2^1 TRUE	2^0 TRUE	
0	0	0	0	0	0	
1	0	0	0	0	1	
2	0	0	0	1	0	
–	–	–	–	–	–	
–	–	–	–	–	–	
7	0	0	1	1	1	
8	0	1	0	0	0	
–	–	–	–	–	–	
–	–	–	–	–	–	
–	–	–	–	–	–	
15	0	1	1	1	1	
16	1	0	0	0	0	⎰ FALSE 2^4 going
	1	0	1	1	1	⎱ from 1 to 0 SETS 2^0, 2^1, 2^2 stages
17	1	1	0	0	0	
18	1	1	0	0	1	
–	–	–	–	–	–	
–	–	–	–	–	–	
24	1↘0	1↘0	1↘0	1↘0	1↘0	
25 or 0						

Example 8-2. Develop the circuit diagram and count table of a MOD 26 counter. Use positive logic and negative triggering pulses.

Solution: To obtain 26 counts requires a five-stage counter (32 maximum counts) with feedback to advance by six pulse steps. The advance of 6 could be obtained by using the FALSE output of the 2^4 stage feeding back to the 2^1 and 2^2 stages. It could also be obtained by feedback from the 2^3 stage to the 2^0 and 2^1 since this would advance the count twice by 3. The table and block diagrams for this second method are shown in Table 8-5 and Figure 8-12, respectively.

Problem 8-5. Draw the block diagram and table of a MOD 12 counter. The flip-flops used are *PNP* (trigger on positive-going pulse) and use negative logic.

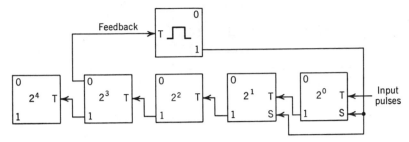

Figure 8–12.   Count-of-26 (MOD 26) counter for Example 8–2.

Table 8–5.   Count Table for Example 8–2

Input Pulses	2^4 TRUE	2^3 TRUE	2^2 TRUE	2^1 TRUE	2^0 TRUE	
0	0	0	0	0	0	
1	0	0	0	0	1	
2	0	0	0	1	0	
–	–	–	–	–	–	
–	–	–	–	–	–	
7	0	0⌐	1	1	1	
8	0	1←	0	0	0	⎫ Count ad-
	0	1	0	1	1	⎭ vanced by 3
9	0	1	1	0	0	
–	–	–	–	–	–	
–	–	–	–	–	–	
–	–	–	–	–	–	
–	–	–	–	–	–	
20	1	0⌐	1	1	1	
21	1	1←	0	0	0	⎫ Count ad-
	1	1	0	1	1	⎭ vanced by 3
22	1	1	1	0	0	
23	1	1	1	0	1	
24	1	1	1	1	0	
25	1	1	1	1	1	
26 or 0	0	0	0	0	0	

↑
Arrow indicates when
2^3 stage triggers monostable

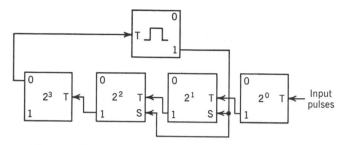

Figure 8–13.   Decade counter using single advance pulse.

Problem 8–6.   Draw the block diagram of a MOD 19 counter for *NPN* flip-flops using negative logic.

Problem 8–7.   Repeat Problem 8–6 for a MOD 39 counter.

Problem 8–8.   Make a count table for Problem 8–7.

Problem 8–9.   Draw the block diagram of two different MOD 24 counters using feedback.   Indicate trigger polarity and type of logic used.

A decade or count-of-10 counter can also be made using feedback. Because it is so popular, the decade counter is being treated separately here.   As with the feedback counters described so far, a count of 10 can be obtained using four stages with a count advance of 6. The count advance of 6 can be obtained by once triggering the 2^1 and 2^2 stages, or triggering the 2^0 and 2^1 stages twice.   Each of these methods and their count table are shown in Figures 8–13 and 8–14 and Tables 8–6 and 8–7.

Quite often the decade counter must also provide the binary equivalent count for each decimal pulse.   Then a decoding gate can

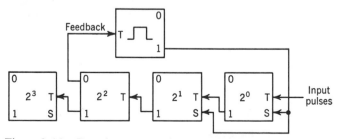

Figure 8–14.   Decade counter using two advance pulses per cycle.

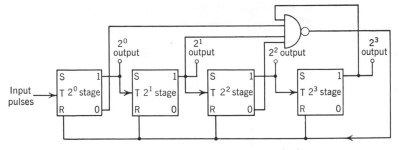

Figure 8–15.   Decade counter for binary equivalent count.

be used to sense the end count (10 in this case) to reset the counter
to zero.   One circuit of this kind is that of Figure 8–15 and its count
table is given in Table 8–8.

Table 8–6.   Count Table of Decade Counter of Figure 8–13

Input Pulses	2^3 TRUE	2^2 TRUE	2^1 TRUE	2^0 TRUE	
0	0	0	0	0	
1	0	0	0	1	
2	0	0	1	0	
3	0	0	1	1	
4	0	1	0	0	
5	0	1	0	1	
6	0	1	1	0	
7	0	1	1	1	
8	1	0	0	0	} Count advanced
	1	1	1	0	} by 6
9	1	1	1	1	
10 (or 0)	0	0	0	0	

↑
Arrow indicates
when 2^3 stage
triggers monostable

The NAND gate goes low when the count of 1010 (decimal 10) is
reached and resets all four stages.   The table shows that only the 2^1
and 2^3 flip-flops need be reset to return the count to zero.   All the

Table 8–7.   Count Table of Decade Counter of Figure 8–14

Input Pulses	2^3 TRUE	2^2 TRUE	2^1 TRUE	2^0 TRUE	
0	0	0	0	0	
1	0	0	0	1	
2	0	0	1	0	
3	0	0 ⌐	1	1	
4	0	1 ⌐	0	0	⎫ Count advanced
	0	1	1	1	⎰ by 3
5	1	0	0	0	
6	1	0	0	1	
7	1	0	1	0	
8	1	0 ⌐	1	1	
9	1	1 ⌐	0	0	⎫ Count advanced
	1	1	1	1	⎰ by 3
10 (or 0)	0	0	0	0	

↑
Arrow indicates
when 2^2 stage
triggers monostable

Table 8–8.   Decade Count Table of Figure 8–15

Input Pulse	2^3 TRUE	2^2 TRUE	2^1 TRUE	2^0 TRUE
0	0	0	0	0
1	0	0	0	1
2	0	0	1	0
3	0	0	1	1
4	0	1	0	0
5	0	1	0	1
6	0	1	1	0
7	0	1	1	1
8	1	0	0	0
9	1	0	0	1
10	1	0	1	0
↓	↓	↓	↓	↓
0	0	0	0	0

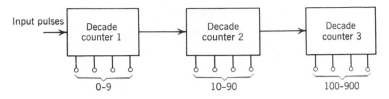

Figure 8–16.   Decade counters for scale-of-10 counting.

stages were reset to insure that the count starts at zero at all times. This need not have been done.   The table also shows that the binary count for each decimal step is exactly the binary equivalent of that decimal count.   This was not true for the feedback counters for every step.   Look back and check to see that this is true.   Using binary-to-decimal converters, the decimal count is available for each step.   This type of circuit might be used to drive the output display lights which indicate the count as a decimal number.   A few decade counters may be used to provide scale-of-10 counting (see Figure 8–16).

Summary

A basic part of every digital computer is a counter.   Complementary flip-flop stages may be connected to provide either count-up or count-down operation.   The number of unique counts is 2^n for n stages; e.g., 8 counts with 3 stages (2^3), 32 counts with five stages (2^5).

When other than a binary count is desired, count feedback may be used to advance the count.   For a MOD 28 counter, for example, a five-stage counter ($2^5 = 32$) would have to be advanced by $32 - 28$, or 4 counts to provide recycling every 28 counts.

Another application of the bistable stage is as a shift register. Data stored in one register may be shifted into another for serial operation.   Some applications using a shift register will be shown in Chapter 10, which covers the arithmetic unit.

PROBLEMS

1. Draw the block diagram for a five-stage count-down register.
2. Draw the block diagram for a four-stage shift-left register.

3. Draw a logic diagram of a MOD 20 counter.

4. Draw a logic diagram of a MOD 12 counter.

5. Prepare a count table for the MOD 12 counter of problem 4.

6. Draw logic diagrams of two different MOD 3 counters.

7. Draw the logic diagram of a decade counter (other than those in this chapter).

8. Draw the logic diagram of a MOD 24 counter.

Section Three

COMPUTER UNITS

1001

Computer timing and control

Although a computer seems to "think" and act automatically, in actuality it only performs very simple steps in a set order. The control unit is the part of the computer that provides the basic timing signals to operate all units of the computer. Although the stored program directs the main flow of operations to be performed, the control unit still provides for all the little steps that must be taken for each command executed.

The difference between a "wired" operation and the operation with a stored program should be appreciated. By "wired" we mean those that are carried out automatically by special circuits of the computer. For example, the multiply and divide operations may be "wired" so that a single multiply or divide command starts the operation and all the little steps needed to carry out the command are provided by the control unit. If the computer had only add or subtract commands, the multiply and divide could still be performed as a number of steps of a stored program. The difference is mainly speed of execution, the wired operation being faster.

The control unit may vary considerably from one computer to another, depending on what commands are wired and the type of internal memory, whether serial or parallel operations are performed, etc. Although details of a control unit can become involved, there are basic parts that may be studied. These include counters, diode matrices, decoding gates, and registers. When all operation is controlled by a master clock (astable oscillator, for example), the computer operates synchronously. If synchronous operation is too slow (it requires waiting a set time interval to begin the next step), asynchronous operation is used where the next step occurs immediately after the present one is completed.

Before considering the overall operation of a control unit, some of the basic parts will be studied.

9–1. Timing Signals

Just as a specific count time was decoded by the NAND gate of Figure 8–15, specific time intervals may be obtained by decoding the outputs of counter stages.   A two-stage counter can have 2^2, or four, different count combinations.   Each of these occurs at a different time interval.   By decoding each combination in order, a set of pulses in time sequence can be obtained for use in the computer. Figure 9–1 shows the counter and decoding gates for two stages. Figure 9–2 provides timing waveforms of the output gates.   The important feature to note in Figure 9–2 is that the outputs 0, 1, 2, 3 are high sequentially in the numbered order.   As timing signals they can be used to provide each step in proper sequence, since only one is ON at any time.   For example, in adding two numbers together the 0 step might mean clear the adder register, the 1 step add the first number to register A, the 2 step add a second number to the first with the result in the adder register, and the 3 step read the result into the computer memory for storage.   In other words, the small steps of the computer are controlled by such timing and decoding gates.   The computer program only indicates whether addition, subtraction, etc., is to be performed, in what order, and on which information.   For each smaller operation the computer follows this set pattern of steps.   When the steps are not a binary multiple number, a feedback counter may be used to provide the desired number of steps per cycle.   Although this method is good for small numbers of steps, it requires a considerable number of decoding gates for larger numbers.   In this example four gates were needed with a two-stage counter for four steps.   For 64 steps, a six-stage counter with 64 gates, each having six inputs, would be needed.   With diode inputs the number of diodes required in the decoding gates would be 64×6, or 384 diodes.   A method of reducing this number using a diode matrix is given later in this chapter.

Another method of obtaining sequential pulses for timing is from

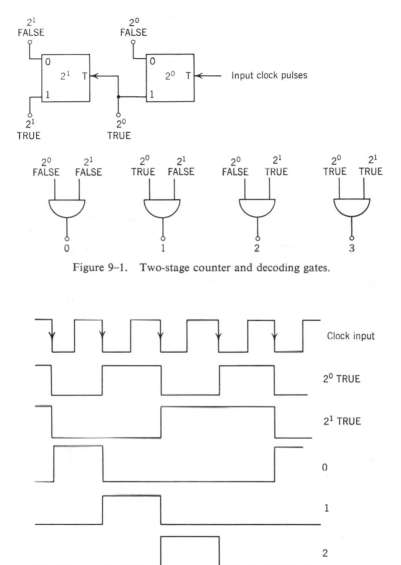

Figure 9–1.   Two-stage counter and decoding gates.

Figure 9–2.   Waveforms for Figure 9–1.

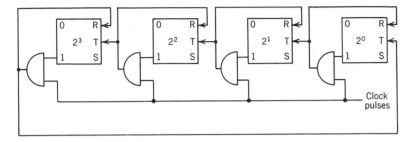

Figure 9–3. Ring counter.

the outputs of a ring counter. The ring counter is different from other counter types in that the TRUE output of only one stage is high at any time. Actually, the arrangement of flip-flops is more like a shift register, but the circuit is conventionally called a ring counter. A four-stage ring counter circuit is shown in Figure 9–3.

Assuming that only one stage has a 1 at the start, each pulse of the clock causes the next higher stage to become 1 while the preceding stage is reset to 0. The output waveforms for the ring counter (Figure 9–4) show that it also provides sequential timing signals. Although the circuit required four flip-flops, as compared to two with decoding, the ring counter did not require any decoding gates to develop the sequential timing signals.

Another form of ring counter is that of a shift register, with a single 1 being shifted around. The block diagram is shown in

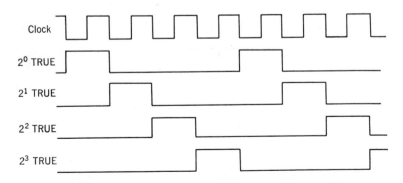

Figure 9–4. Ring counter output waveforms.

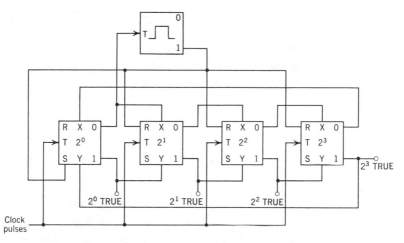

Figure 9–5.   Ring counter using shift register.

Figure 9–5.   With a single 1 in the register, the result of applying clock pulses to the trigger inputs is to advance the 1 by one stage for each clock pulse.   A basic cycle with each TRUE output going ON once in sequence (2^0 to 2^3) repeats every four clock pulses.   The output waveforms are exactly the same as those shown in Figure 9–4.

As a means of insuring that only a single 1 is present, the monostable multivibrator is triggered whenever the 2^0 stage goes to 1. The output pulse of the monostable SETs the 2^0 stage and RESETs all others.   After starting, the proper counter operation will be assured within one cycle if, for example, a noise pulse has caused a second 1 to appear.   Since proper operation requires all other stages to be 0 when the 2^0 stage is a 1, the monostable circuit should normally not change anything.   Notice that the monostable as used here only corrects for more than one 1 in all stages.   If no stage had a 1, the circuit would not provide any outputs, a fact that should be readily apparent.

Problem 9–1.   Draw the block diagram of a five-stage ring counter and show the output waveform for each stage below a 1-kcps clock signal.

Problem 9–2.   Draw the block diagram of a three-stage counter and the eight decoding gates. Label the input signals for each gate.

Problem 9–3. Draw a sketch of the output waveshapes for each gate of Problem 9–2 below the clock input waveform. Assume that *NPN* flip-flops and positive logic are used.

9–2. Encoding and Decoding Matrices

Another means of decoding a binary number into a unique signal for use in a computer is a diode matrix. Some examples for input-output operation will be given.

A diode matrix for a three-variable decoder is shown in Figure 9–6. Since both the TRUE and FALSE of each input is provided, half the inputs will be 1 and half will be 0 at all times. For each input combination (there are 2^3, or 8) a different output line is high. Only one output, however, is high at any time. All other input combinations have at least one diode input at 0 volts which clamps that output line to 0 volts. The darkened diodes are those that have high-voltage inputs $(+V)$ and are back-biased (for the 1 0 1 condition). The low (0-volt) input at $(2^2)'$ keeps the top four output lines clamped low, the low input at (2^1) keeps the bottom two output lines clamped low, and the $(2^0)'$ input keeps the 1 0 0 line clamped low. Only the 1 0 1 line, for the example considered, has a high output voltage. Notice that $2^3 \times 3$, or 24, diodes were needed. For 2^n output combinations $2^n \cdot n$ diodes would be needed. With a six-stage counter (64 counts) this would still require $2^6 \cdot 6$, or 384, diodes, as with single decoding gates.

An arrangement of "treeing" the inputs will reduce the number for 8 output combinations to 14. The tree connection is named for its physical appearance (see Figure 9–7), as is the diode matrix for its similarity to the ordered arrangement of rows and columns of a mathematical matrix.

To develop the tree connection concept an arrangement of relay switches is used as in Figure 9–8. (Refer back to the relay logic operation described in section 5–2.) There are 3 relays used—relay A has two contacts, one normally closed (NC) and one normally open (NO); relay B has two contact pairs (four contacts); relay C has four contact pairs (eight contacts). If relays A and C are selected (relays energized), corresponding to an input of A, not B, and C

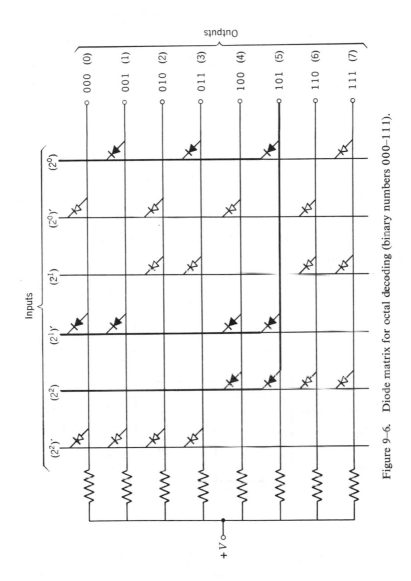

Figure 9–6.   Diode matrix for octal decoding (binary numbers 000–111).

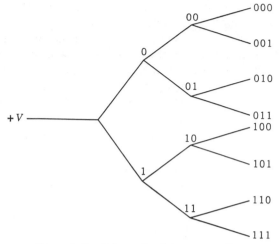

Figure 9–7.   Schematic of tree connection.

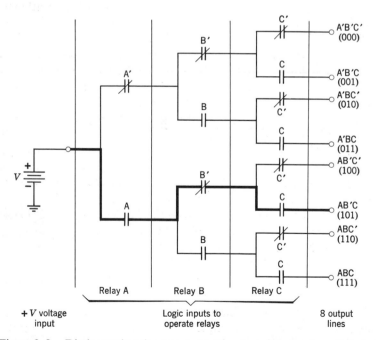

Figure 9–8.   Diode matrix using tree connection to reduce number of diodes.

(logically AB′C), the +V voltage will pass through the now closed NO contact of A, the normally closed contact of B, and the now closed NO contact of C, as shown by the darkened lines in Figure 9–8.

With the given circuit we obtain outputs of open lines (0 volt) on all but one line, the selected line, which is at +V volts.   It is thus possible to select one of the eight output lines using only 14 contacts with the tree arrangement.   Extending this idea, for six inputs the tree decoder would require $2^1 + 2^2 + 2^3 + 2^4 + 2^5 + 2^6$ or 126 contacts as compared to 384 contacts for the straight connection matrix.   Although the tree arrangement offers advantages it is not directly applicable to diode connections.   However, partial decoding, decoding part of the total output signal, may be applied to reduce the number of diodes.   Since diodes are now the more popular selection device we return to the discussion of diode matrices.

The diode matrix may be used either to decode a binary code into a single output line or to take a number of single lines and encode that into a unique binary count.   As a decode example, consider a digital system which uses excess-three code in doing arithmetic operations.   If the final results are to be displayed on an output light as a decimal number, each excess-three combination (there are 10 for the decimal digits) must light up a different decimal digit. The matrix in Figure 9–9 is fed by a four-stage buffer register.   This is a register which holds the binary number while it is being decoded for display and allows the rest of the computer to continue operating. While the computer is doing other operations or even computing a new number to display the present value remains in the buffer register.   When a new value is to be displayed the excess-three number either is shifted into the buffer register one bit at a time or is dumped (all bits at once), depending on whether the computer operated serially or in parallel on readout.

Since the input to the matrix is from a flip-flop stage, both TRUE and FALSE inputs are available.   In the diagram the decode of decimal eight is shown.   Since a straight decode is used, forty diodes are needed.   The decimal number chosen to be displayed by the matrix may be operated by a light driver (transistor amplifier) to prevent loading the matrix.

Figure 9–10 gives an encoder matrix for octal numbers.   In the circuit arrangement shown an input of 0 volts from one of lines 0–7 causes the equivalent binary number to be inserted into the input

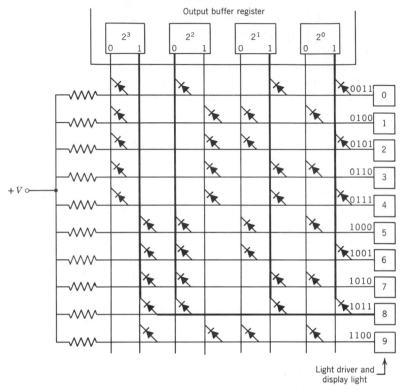

Figure 9–9.   Decoder matrix for excess-three numbers.

buffer register.   The darkened lines indicate the operation for encoding the octal number 5.   Notice that the supply voltage shown
back-biases all the diodes so that they have no effect on the register
stages.   Only an input going low (to 0 volts) will change the number
stored in the buffer register.

9–3.   Control Operation

Operation of the control unit depends greatly on the details of the
computer—whether it operates in serial or parallel, what type of
memory it has, what types of input/output are used, how arithmetic
operations are performed, etc.   It also depends on how the computer
is programmed.   The machine language used in Chapter 2 is for a

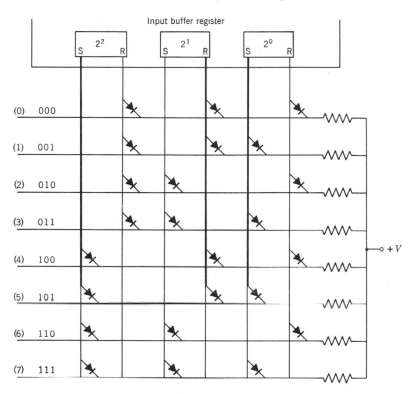

Figure 9-10.   Encoder matrix for octal numbers.

one-address machine.   Two-, three-, and four-address machines have also been built and will be described after some fundamental ideas have been considered.   We shall use the one-address machine as our example to make these ideas clear.   Recall first that the solution to a problem to be run on a computer requires a listing of computer operations called the program.   In its elementary form the program contains machine language statements similar to those described in Chapter 2.   Although originally placed on punched card or tape, the program is stored in the computer memory before it is executed.   One program step is handled at a time, starting from the first, with the possibility of branch instructions resulting in the elimination of some steps or the repetition of others.

With the program instructions stored in memory, the computer must now perform a basic set of steps to operate on these instructions. It must first read the instruction from memory into the control unit (FETCH). In the control unit the parts of the instruction are separated and appropriate control (command and timing) signals are generated to perform the instruction (EXECUTE). The basic FETCH-EXECUTE is then continually repeated until a HALT or STOP instruction is received. As shown in Figure 9–11, some basic parts of the control section are (*a*) a storage register which holds the address or location of the NEXT instruction to be performed and (*b*) a storage register which holds the PRESENT instruction being performed including the operation or command and the address of the operand.

During the FETCH operation the word stored at the address of the NEXT address register is read from memory into the INSTRUCTION register. The NEXT address register is also advanced by one count. If the instruction located at address 152 has just been read, the next address from which to obtain the next instruction is 153. With the FETCH operation finished, the EXECUTE phase is performed. The operation part of the word in the instruction register is used to "tell" the control and timing circuits what specific signals are to be generated. If the op code is 10, for example, the

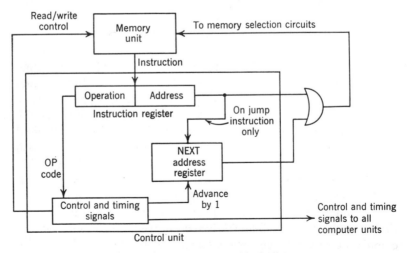

Figure 9–11.   Control unit, block diagram.

decoder circuits will activate the clear-add line and will qualify a number of timing signals to carry out this operation in the various computer units.   Then the word stored at the address indicated by the address part of the instruction is read and added to the accumulator of the arithmetic unit after the accumulator has been reset to zero.   At the end of the EXECUTE cycle the FETCH cycle begins and, following the example given, the instruction at address 153 is read and is placed in the INSTRUCTION register; the NEXT address register is advanced by 1 to 154.

This procedure is only altered when a branch instruction is performed.   If the instruction is an unconditional branch (44), the FETCH operation is still the same and the NEXT address register is advanced by 1.   If this instruction is read from location 362, for example, the NEXT instruction register will be advanced to 363. During EXECUTE, however, the operation decoded to mean perform an unconditional branch will cause the address part of the instruction to be dumped or shifted into the NEXT address register. If this address is 325, the stored 362 is replaced by the new 325 address.   Since this completes the EXECUTE step, the machine now goes to FETCH, brings the word stored at 325 into the instruction register, and then advances the NEXT address register to 326. As far as the FETCH operation is concerned, no change has taken place and the machine continues using instructions from consecutive address locations after 325.   Had the branch instruction been conditional (45, 46, 47), the operation would have been: Look at the number in the accumulator—if it is that specified by the branch ($-$ for 45, $+$ for 46) or if the value is zero (47), take the address part of the instruction and place it in the NEXT address register; if not, just go on to the next FETCH operation.

The control unit contains decode gates or matrices to select the control lines for the operation code presently in the instruction register.   The timing signals are taken from counters and decoding gates which generate a few operating patterns, each of which is wired to perform the specific operation—add, subtract, multiply, divide, etc.

A computer having a two-address instruction code operates somewhat differently.   The instruction code is made up of three parts— op code, operand address, and next instruction address.   It uses the operand address in conjunction with the op code to perform the

EXECUTE operation. During the FETCH operation the next instruction address is fed to the memory unit to obtain the next program instruction. No update of instruction address is necessary since each program instruction contains the address of the next instruction. The branch instruction is different in that one of the two address parts of the instruction is used to specify where to obtain the next instruction from. If the branch condition is met or if no condition exists, the next instruction address may be used. If the branch condition is not met, the operand address specifies where to obtain the next instruction.

With a three-address instruction, two are used to specify where to obtain both operands for an arithmetic operation. For example, an addition instruction will contain the address of word A and the address of word B (where A and B are to be added). The third address might indicate the address for the next instruction or it might be used to indicate where the result of the arithmetic operation is to be placed. A four-address instruction will allow specifying where words A and B are located, where to store the result of that operation, and the address of the next instruction to be performed. Obviously, the more addresses used, the larger the instruction word and the fewer the program steps needed. For a drum memory in which each read operation is cyclical (must wait half a drum revolution on the average), fewer read operations will result in faster overall performance.

Upon decode of a HALT command, the computer will go out of the automatic type of operation just described and into a manual operation during which the machine operator can make changes. With larger computers stoppage after every program would be wasteful, and generally the end of a program only requires a new program to be specified (as with a branch command) to keep the computer operating.

Since the memory may not hold enough different programs to keep the machine operating continuously, the next few program steps might be to read in new cards or tape containing another program and data and then a branch to this new program. When errors occur which the machine is able to determine, it can branch out of calculations on the program in operation and read in another one. In this way larger computer facilities are continuously operating, doing a wide assortment of problems in succession.

Summary

Some of the basic parts of the control unit were discussed. These included counters with decoder gates, ring counters, and diode matrices. Sequential pulses are generated for timing operations controlling the order in which operations occur.

Diode matrices may be used to encode signals—take a number of input lines and convert a signal on any one into a binary count—or to decode signals—take a binary count and convert each count into an output on a different line.

A basic machine cycle is the FETCH-EXECUTE. During FETCH the computer calls for a new instruction to perform. In EXECUTE the operation is carried out. Because there are single- and multiple-address machines, the following summary of their meaning is given.

1 address instruction	Op Code + Operand Address
2 address instruction	Op Code + Operand Address + Next Instruction Address
3 address instruction	Op Code + Operand Address + Operand Address + Next Instruction Address
	or
	Op Code + Operand Address + Operand Address + Result Address
4 address instruction	Op Code + Operand Address + Operand Address + Result Address + Next Instruction Address.

The main difference between all these is whether a next instruction address register is needed or not.

PROBLEMS

1. Using OR or AND gates only prepare the interconnection diagram to decode all combinations of a three-stage counter.

2. Using only NAND gates prepare the decoder gating interconnection diagram for a two-stage counter.

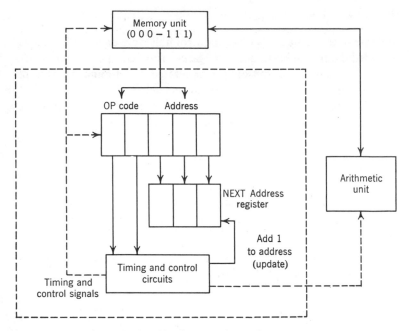

Figure 9–12.   Simple control unit for problem 5.

3. Draw the circuit diagram of a diode matrix to decode the three counts of a MOD 3 counter.

4. Draw the circuit diagram of a diode matrix to encode four input lines of BCD information into the binary count of a four-stage register.

5. A very simple model of the control part of a computer is shown in the Figure 9–12. The instruction register is two bits and address register three bits. For two bits only four commands are possible. Use the following for this example:

$$0\ 0 = \text{Add}$$
$$0\ 1 = \text{Subtract}$$
$$1\ 0 = \text{Branch if minus}$$
$$1\ 1 = \text{Store in memory}$$

With only three bits there are eight different memory cells which can be specified.   For this simple system prepare a detailed description of what occurs during the FETCH and during the EXECUTE part of the cycle for each step of the following program.   Only binary numbers are used in this simple setup.   Rather than add more bits to allow more operation codes, halt will be indicated by the word HALT in place of any real instruction.   The program should be started at location 0 0 0, and the accumulator is assumed here to be clear.

	Instruction	
Location	Operation	Address
0 0 0	0 0	1 0 1
0 0 1	0 1	1 1 0
0 1 0	1 0	1 1 1
0 1 1	1 1	1 1 0
1 0 0	HALT	
1 0 1	0 1	1 1 1
1 1 0	1 1	1 1 1
1 1 1	HALT	

6. Repeat problem 5 for the following program.   Again assume the accumulator is clear when the program starts at 0 0 0.

Location	Operation	Address
0 0 0	0 0	0 0 0
0 0 1	0 0	1 0 0
0 1 0	1 1	0 0 0
0 1 1	HALT	
1 0 0	0 0	0 0 1

1010

Computer arithmetic operations

10-1. General Arithmetic Section Operation

The arithmetic unit of a digital computer contains the logic circuitry for performing additions, subtractions, multiplications, and divisions. Information to be processed by the computer is generally placed in memory first and taken into the arithmetic unit at some later time. Answers from the arithmetic section are returned to the memory unit. Because of the high speed of arithmetic operations (a clock rate of around 1 mcps is typical) and the lower speed of taking data into the computer (anywhere from a few cycles per second to around 10,000 cps), the function of the memory as a speed buffer is essential. In fact, the high speed of the arithmetic section often necessitates a special high-speed memory—called a "scratch-pad memory"—for use solely with the arithmetic unit. A separate, larger-capacity, slower-speed memory is also used for overall computing functions and program storage.

Since multiplication and division in a general-purpose digital machine is done by repeated additions and repeated subtractions, respectively, the arithmetic operations performed need only be those of addition and subtraction. However, a large amount of additional logic and data-handling circuitry is required for these operations. Other more complex functions such as square root and trigonometric are either obtained from stored tables (requiring large data storage) or calculated from iterative formula under the control of a stored program. These iterative operations only require using the four basic arithmetic functions so that with the use of logic gating, timing

216

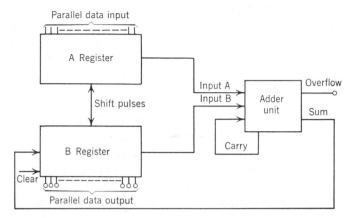

Figure 10-1.   Arithmetic adder operation, simplified block diagram.

control, and stored program the add and subtract operation provides
the computer with all essential mathematical operations.

In Chapter 3 the addition operation was considered for the straight
binary code as well as for a few other codes.   Subtraction was also
considered using ONE's complement.   Neither topic considered the
addition and subtraction of numbers with sign included.   Only the
absolute value of a number was operated on.   This additional, but
very real, factor will be examined in the present chapter, as will the
details of multiplication and division as handled by a computer.

First, though, we should consider the makeup of the arithmetic
section in terms of registers, adders, and logic for doing all these
operations.   Figure 10-1 shows a simplified block diagram of part
of a typical arithmetic section.   Register A in particular receives
information from the memory, and register B feeds the result of the
arithmetic operation back to the memory.   A serial addition is
accomplished by shifting the two numbers to be added, least significant digit first, through the adder.   The sum, appearing serially at
the output of the adder, is shifted back into the B register so that
register B now contains the result of the addition.   If subtraction
were being done the adder unit would be replaced by a subtractor,
but data flow would be the same.   Actually, since the sum and
difference expressions are identical, only the borrow or carry terms
will be different.   The block diagram indicates that the input data is

handled in parallel form, whereas the addition takes place serially. The parallel processing feature is indicated since it is generally desirable to move in and out of the memory as fast as possible in order to operate more quickly. Data could have been read in bit serial if speed were not important. In fact, if the data in memory were transferred serially, register A would not be needed because the data in the accumulator (register B) could be shifted into the adder unit as the input data from memory is also shifted directly into the adder unit. Since speed is often important, most larger machines include parallel operations in the adder section as well. The biggest detriment is the higher cost. Whereas the unit shown contains only one adder, parallel operation requires the greater amount of logic and adders to perform parallel addition and is considerably more costly.

An overflow signal is used in sign determination, which will be discussed. The carry signal indicated is the delayed carry signal from the previous bits added. Data is loaded into the adder unit in three steps. Register B is reset to zero by a clear pulse. The first number to be added is dumped into register A and then serially shifted into the adder unit, added to B, and stored in B. At a later time the second number is dumped into A, completing the loading of the unit. A basic pattern is thereby established, namely, parallel transfer into A and then shift pulses to both A and B. Three cycles of this pattern are necessary to do an addition. On the first the parallel shift or dump temporarily places a number in register A and the shift pulses then move that number to register B (through the adder). On the second dump time another number is placed in A and on the second shift time the two numbers are added, the result going into the accumulator. Finally, on the third dump time the result of the addition is read back into memory. The last shift time has no effect on the operation and can be ignored here. Although this process may seem very slow, it is reflective of all operations in computers. For the present case, assuming a 1-Mcps clock rate, the dump time will be 1 μsec and the shift time for a ten-bit word will be 10 μsec, so that the three cycles for addition will be 33 μsec. At this rate the number of additions per second will be $1/(33 \times 10^{-6})$, or 30,000. It is this fast speed allowing many thousands of operations per second that is one of the outstanding features of digital computers. Multiplications and divisions, requiring repeated steps

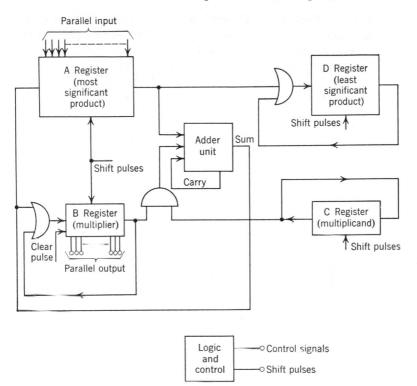

Figure 10-2.   Arithmetic unit with multiplication operation.

for each operation, are necessarily slower.   Where speed is critical, fully parallel operating machines are used.   Where speed is of little importance, cost can be saved by using serial operation throughout.

To perform the multiplication or division operation, two more registers may be used.   Calling these the C and D registers, Figure 10-2 shows that there are some other logic modifications.   These will be discussed in detail later in the chapter.   For now, the B register holds the multiplier number and the C the multiplicand. Since the product of two ten-bit numbers may be twenty bits long, the product is formed and stored in registers A and D, with A holding the more significant half.   The same basic pattern of dump and shift may be used to perform the multiplication operation.   Under control of the multiplier digit in the output of register B, the multiplicand

is added to zero initially.   On the next shift this partial sum is added
to the partial sum depending on the next multiplier digit.   When
the multiplier is 0 the number in A is added to zero and put back
into A.   When the multiplier is 1 the multiplicand is added to the
partial sum in A.   It will be explained later that a shift by one digit
is necessary each time around.   The multiplicand in the C register
is used over and over and must be maintained throughout the multiplication steps.   This is done using shift around to replace the
number in C as it is shifted out.   Shift around is used when information is to be saved.   Logic is required to determine when new
information is to be shifted in or the old shifted around.

10–2.   Arithmetic Section Addition/Subtraction

Addition.   When adding two numbers with sign, certain decisions
are made—seemingly automatic—to obtain the correct answer.   If
both numbers are of the same sign, the two numbers are added and
the sign carried along.   When the signs are not alike, the two
numbers are subtracted and the sign of the larger is used with the
answer.   All this is simple to state and to carry out for a human
operator.   However, the digital operation must be carried out
according to defined rules of operation.   How does the arithmetic
section "know" which number is larger and when to bother looking
for a larger number.   One approach to implementing the addition
is straightforward.   Compare the signs first to see whether they are
like or unlike.   If like, add the numbers and use that same sign; if
unlike, form both $A - B$ and $B - A$ in two separate subtractors.
An overflow shows that the term subtracted was the larger, indicating
that the sign of the subtracted term and the difference value of the
other subtraction must be used, for this is the positive difference
value.   Since this method is not the simplest or the one used most
often, it will not be further detailed, to avoid confusing the issue.
A slight modification of this method would be to use ONE's complement for negative numbers to avoid the need of subtractor units.
The procedure is essentially the same.

A simple procedure for mechanizing addition and subtraction with
sign is described next.   The rules required for the particular method
are the following.   Utilizing the 1 and 0 terms to specify the plus
and minus sign, this procedure *specifically requires* using 1 for

negative sign and 0 for positive sign.   Positive numbers are written with the 0 sign in the most significant position with the positive absolute value, and negative numbers are written with the 1 sign in the most significant position and the ONE's complement form of the number.   Both numbers should be written with equal digits and of sufficient number to include the sum number without mixing up the sign with the number part.   All this can be more easily seen in the following examples.   It should be pointed out, though, that these are rules for procedure and do not complicate the mechanization. As we shall see, the whole procedure only requires using the specified format and adding the two numbers and their signs—all as if they were number digits.   This being true, the mechanization is no more complicated than that of adding two binary numbers together— without considering sign.   In doing problems on paper the correct format must be assured.   Once set up, however, the operation is carried out mechanically as if no sign were present.   The answer read is in the prescribed format.

Example 10–1.   Write the following numbers in the prescribed format.

(a) $+7$ (b) $+12$ (c) -3 (d) -9 (e) -21

Solution:

(a) $+7$ is 0   1 1 1   or   0111
      $\uparrow$ $\underbrace{\qquad}$
      $+$ sign binary 7

(b) $+12$ is 0   1 1 0 0

(c) -3 is 1   0 0
      $\uparrow$ $\underbrace{\qquad}$
      $-$ sign   1's complement of 3 $\rightarrow$ 3 is $(11)_2$

                                   1's complement of 3 is $(00)_2$

(d) -9 is 1   0 1 1 0 $\rightarrow$ 9 is $(1001)_2$

                    1's complement is $(0110)_2$

(e) -21 is 1   0 1 0 1 0   [where $21 = (10101)_2$]
      $\uparrow$ $\underbrace{\qquad\qquad}$
      $-$ sign   1's
                      com-
                      plement
                      of 21

Example 10–2. Add the following two positive numbers.

  (a) +6, +1   (b) +9, +4   (c) +2, +8   (d) +8, +9

Solution:

(a) +6   0 1 1 0

      +1 $\longrightarrow$ 0 0 0 1

      +7   0 1 1 1   *Answer:* +7

(b) +9   0 1 0 0 1

      +4 $\longrightarrow$ 0 0 1 0 0

     +13   0 1 1 0 1   *Answer:* +13

(c) +2   0 0 0 1 0   +2 should be 0010

      +8 $\longrightarrow$ 0 1 0 0 0   to keep the same number

    +10   0 1 0 1 0   of places for both

                                  Answer: +10

(d) +8 = 0 1 0 0 0

     +9 = 0 1 0 0 1

However, because the answer will require five bits, the numbers should be written using five bits (the fifth and most significant bit for each is zero, which is trivial for this case but more important when the complement is taken with negative numbers).

      +8   0 0 1 0 0 0

      +9 $\longrightarrow$ 0 0 1 0 0 1

    +17   0 1 0 0 0 1   *Answer:* +17

Note that although you have to be careful in setting up the problem, when an adder is used it has fixed number of places and automatically handles the data properly. For example, with a ten-bit adder register, one bit is for sign, one is to allow for largest answers, and eight bits are for the numbers to be summed. When using this machine the operator knows that the largest number he can add is eight digits in length and that the higher-order digits are zero when the number added has fewer digits.

Example 10–3. Add the following two numbers where the larger is positive.

  (a) +6, −3   (b) +8, −4   (c) +9, −6   (d) +8, −5

Solution:

(a) +6   0 1 1 0
    −3   1 1 0 0   (where 3 is 011)
    ―――   ――――――――
    +3   1 0 0 1 0
                └――――→ 1   (end-around carry)
               ――――――――
                0 0 1 1
                ↑   ⏝
                | 3   *Answer:* +3
                +   sign

(b) +8   0 1 0 0 0
    −4   1 1 0 1 1   (where 4 is 0100)
    ―――   ――――――――――
    +4   1 0 0 0 1 1
                └――――→ 1   end-around carry
               ――――――――――
                0 0 1 0 0
                ↑   ⏝
                | 4
                + sign   *Answer:* +4

(c) +9   0 1 0 0 1
    −6   1 1 0 0 1   (where 6 is 0110)
    ―――   ――――――――――
    +3   1 0 0 0 1 0
                └――――→ 1   end-around carry
               ――――――――――
                0 0 0 1 1
                ↑   ⏝
                | 3
                + sign   *Answer:* +3

(d) +8   0 1 0 0 0
    −5 →   1 1 0 1 0
    ―――   ――――――――――
    +3   1 0 0 0 1 0
                └――――→ 1   end-around carry
               ――――――――――
                0 0 0 1 1
                ↑   ⏝
                | 3
                + sign   *Answer:* +3

Example 10–4. Add the following two numbers where the larger-magnitude number is negative.

(a) $+9, -12$ (b) $+6, -7$ (c) $+15, -18$ (d) $+2, -4$

Solution:

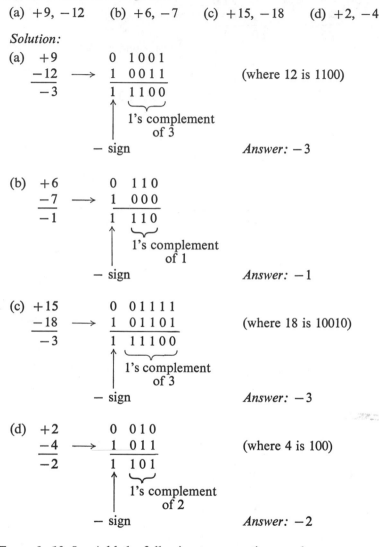

(a) $+9$ 0 1 0 0 1
     -12 ⟶ 1 0 0 1 1   (where 12 is 1100)
     -3 1 1 1 0 0
                    1's complement
                      of 3
             — sign   *Answer:* -3

(b) $+6$ 0 1 1 0
     -7 ⟶ 1 0 0 0
     -1 1 1 1 0
                    1's complement
                      of 1
             — sign   *Answer:* -1

(c) $+15$ 0 0 1 1 1 1
     -18 ⟶ 1 0 1 1 0 1   (where 18 is 10010)
     -3 1 1 1 1 0 0
                    1's complement
                      of 3
             — sign   *Answer:* -3

(d) $+2$ 0 0 1 0
     -4 ⟶ 1 0 1 1   (where 4 is 100)
     -2 1 1 0 1
                    1's complement
                      of 2
             — sign   *Answer:* -2

Example 10–5. Add the following two negative numbers.

(a) $-3, -4$ (b) $-9, -6$ (c) $-12, -10$
(d) $-8, -14$ (e) $-13, -16$

Solution:

(a)   −3   1   1 0 0
      −4 ⟶   1   0 1 1
      ─────   ───────
      −7   1 0 1 1 1
                    └──→ 1   end-around carry

                   1   0 0 0
                   ↑   ⌣⌣⌣
                   | 1's complement
                   | of 7
                 − sign   *Answer:* −7

(b)   −9   1   0 1 1 0
      −6   ⟶   1   1 0 0 1
      ─────   ─────────
     −15   1 0 1 1 1 1
                     └──────→ 1   end-around carry

                   1   0 0 0 0
                   ↑   ⌣⌣⌣⌣
                   | 1's complement
                   | of 15
                 − sign   *Answer:* −15

(c) −12   1   1 0 0 1 1   (where 12 is 01100)
     −10   ⟶   1   1 0 1 0 1   (where 10 is 01010)
     ─────   ───────────
     −22   1 1 0 1 0 0 0
                      └────────→ 1   end-around carry

                   1   0 1 0 0 1
                   ↑   ⌣⌣⌣⌣
                   | 1's complement
                   | of 22
                 − sign   *Answer:* −22

Note that 12 and 10 were written using five digits, since the answer required five. Where the problem was done using the same number of significant digits for number and answer, the sum did not require an extra place. The extra place could have been required in the number and the correct answer obtained.

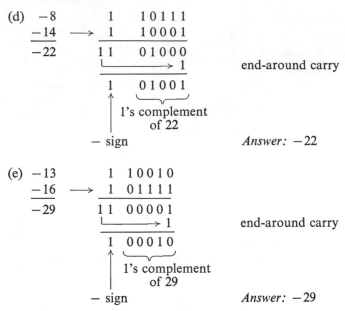

(d) −8   1   1 0 1 1 1
    −14 ⟶   1   1 0 0 0 1
    ─────   ─────────────
    −22   1 1   0 1 0 0 0
                 └─────────⟶ 1   end-around carry
                ─────────────
                 1   0 1 0 0 1
                 ↑   ⌣‿‿‿⌣
                 │   1's complement
                 │   of 22
              − sign   *Answer:* −22

(e) −13   1   1 0 0 1 0
    −16 ⟶   1   0 1 1 1 1
    ─────   ─────────────
    −29   1 1   0 0 0 0 1
                 └─────────⟶ 1   end-around carry
                ─────────────
                 1   0 0 0 1 0
                 ↑   ⌣‿‿‿⌣
                 │   1's complement
                 │   of 29
              − sign   *Answer:* −29

These examples should have shown that adding the sign digit as if it were a number digit leads to the correct answer for all possible combinations of sign and magnitude when the prescribed rules of operation are used.

Problem 10–1. Write the binary form of the following numbers as in Example 10–1.

1. +3	2. −11	3. −17
4. +26	5. −19	6. +17

Problem 10–2. Add the following two numbers using the method of Examples 10–2 through 10–5.

1. +6, +12	2. +8, −6	3. +6, −8
4. +13, −13	5. +9, −12	6. −8, −12
7. −2, +4	8. −16, +13	9. −10, −12
10. −21, +25		

Subtraction. Doing subtraction by the method just indicated is valid but slightly more confusing. Rather than go into any detail, an example of each of the four types is given. No new understanding of the technique is considered but rather a completion of the use of the method.   Subtraction is performed by adding the 1's complement.

Example 10–6.   Subtract the following two positive numbers:
  (a) +6 minus +4   (b) +4 minus +6

Solution:

(a)   +6   0 1 1 0   0 1 1 0
  (−) +4 → (−) 0 1 0 0 → (+) 1 0 1 1
      +2   1 0 0 0 1
                             ⌞——→ 1
                            0 0 1 0   *Answer:* +2

(b)   +4   0 1 0 0   0 1 0 0
  (−) +6 → (−) 0 1 1 0 → (+) 1 0 0 1
      −2   1 1 0 1   *Answer:* −2

Example 10–7.   Subtract the following two numbers:
  (a) +6 minus −2   (b) +2 minus −6

Solution:

(a)   +6   0 0 1 1 0   0 0 1 1 0
  (−) −2 → (−) 1 1 1 0 1 → (+) 0 0 0 1 0
      +8   0 1 0 0 0 *Answer:* +8

(b)   +2   0 0 0 1 0   0 0 0 1 0
  (−) −6 → (−) 1 1 0 0 1 → (+) 0 0 1 1 0
      +8   0 1 0 0 0 *Answer:* +8

Example 10–8.   Subtract the following two numbers:
  (a) −4 minus −6   (b) −3 minus −2

Solution:

(a)   −4   1 1 0 1 1   1 1 0 1 1
  (−) −6 → (−) 1 1 0 0 1 → (+) 0 0 1 1 0
      +2   1 0 0 0 0 1
                             ⌞———→ 1
                          0 0 0 1 0 *Answer:* +2

(b)   −3   1 1 0 0   1 1 0 0
  (−) −2 → (−) 1 1 0 1   → (+) 0 0 1 0
      −1   1 1 1 0 *Answer:* −1

Example 10-9. Subtract the following two numbers:

(a) −6 minus +2   (b) −2 minus +6

Solution:

(a)   −6   1   1 0 0 1   1 1 0 0 1

  (−) +2   (−) 0   0 0 1 0   →   (+) 1 1 1 0 1

        −8   1 1 0 1 1 0

                                                                  └──────→ 1

                                                          1 0 1 1 1   *Answer:* −8

(b)   −2   1   1 1 0 1   1 1 1 0 1

  (−) +6   →   (−) 0   0 1 1 0   →   (+) 1 1 0 0 1

        8   1 1 0 1 1 0

                                                                  └──────→ 1

                                                          1 0 1 1 1   *Answer:* −8

As extra practice try the following problem for subtraction.

Problem 10-3. Using the method shown in Examples 10–6 through 10–9, subtract the following numbers.

1. +7 minus +3   2. −8 minus +4
3. −5 minus −6   4. +9 minus +12
5. −4 minus −2   6. −6 minus +9
7. +12 minus −8   8. +15 minus −17

10-3. Computer Multiplication

Operating as fast as it does, the computer is capable of doing multiplication by repeated additions. Although with decimal numbers this may be quite lengthy, it is not so with binary. For example, 74 × 86 would require adding 74 six times and then 74 eight times, one digit position higher. In binary, since the digit can only be zero or one, the maximum number of additions for each place is one and a ten-bit number would require only ten addition steps. At 1 μsec per step this would be 10 μsec total, or a rate of 100,000 multiplications per second. Since other considerations must be made— timing, data shifting, etc.—fewer multiplications are performed, but the rate is still so high and the implementation so easy that the method is readily used by general-purpose computers. To distinguish between the method people use and the method the machine uses, the first will be called "pencil multiplication" and the latter "machine multiplication." An example of each, using the same numbers, is given to show the difference and to point out how the machine implements this operation.

Example 10–10.   Do a pencil multiplication of the binary numbers 1 0 1 1 and 1 0 0 1.
   Solution:

$$
\begin{array}{ll}
1\,0\,1\,1 & \text{multiplicand} \\
\underline{1\,0\,0\,1} & \text{multiplier} \\
1\,0\,1\,1 & \\
0\,0\,0\,0 & \text{partial} \\
0\,0\,0\,0 & \text{products} \\
\underline{1\,0\,1\,1\quad\;} & \\
1\,1\,0\,0\,0\,1\,1 & \text{product}
\end{array}
$$

Example 10–11.   Show a machine multiplication of the same two numbers as in Example 10–10.
   Solution:

1.	1 0 1 1		
2.	1 0 0 [1]	◄───────	multiplier digit place
3.	1 0 1 1		add (since multiplier digit is 1)
4.	1 0 1	1	shift data and multiplier right
5.	0 0 0 0	↓	add 4 and 5
6.	0 1 0 1	1	sum in registers A and D
7.	0 1 0	1 1	shift right
8.	0 0 0 0	↓ ↓	add 7 and 8
9.	0 0 1 0	1 1	
10.	0 0 0 1	0 1 1	shift right
11.	1 0 1 1	↓ ↓ ↓	add 10 and 11
12.	1 1 0 0	0 1 1	PRODUCT in A and D

most significant   least significant
part in A   part in D

   Answer: 1100011

As the last example shows, the machine method is a repeated addition and shift right.   In terms of the registers shown in Figure 10–2, the B register holds the multiplier number and the C holds the multiplicand.   On the first addition (with register A cleared) the multiplicand is added to the value in A (zero at first) and the sum obtained is placed back into A.   All registers are now shifted right so that the A, B, and D registers are shifted one extra place to the right and the C is shifted around so that the multiplicand is saved. With the extra shift in A and D the data is moved one place over so that the next sum is added in at a higher-order position.   Moreover, by shifting register B one extra place the next multiplier bit (0 in this case) is used to qualify adding the multiplicand or not on the next add time.   This procedure is repeated as many times as the number of bits per register or word.   Here it is repeated four times.   Follow the next two examples and then try a few problems yourself.

Example 10–12.   Show the machine multiplication of 1 0 1 0 1 × 1 0 1 1 0.   Do the pencil multiplication as a check.

Solution:

```
1 0 1 0 1|              multiplicand
1 0 1 1 0|              multiplier

0 0 0 0 0|              add zero to A
  0 0 0 0| 0            shift right
1 0 1 0 1| ↓            add multiplicand to A

1 0 1 0 1| 0
  1 0 1 0| 1 0          shift right
1 0 1 0 1| ↓ ↓          add multiplicand to A

1 1 1 1 1| 1 0
  1 1 1 1| 1 1 0        shift right
0 0 0 0 0| ↓ ↓ ↓        add zero to A

0 1 1 1 1| 1 1 0
  0 1 1 1| 1 1 1 0      shift right
1 0 1 0 1| ↓ ↓ ↓ ↓      add multiplicand to A

1 1 1 0 0| 1 1 1 0      PRODUCT
```

Answer: 111001110

Check:

```
1 0 1 0 1
1 0 1 1 0
```

```
0 0 0 0 0
1 0 1 0 1
1 0 1 0 1
0 0 0 0 0
1 0 1 0 1
```

```
1 1 1 0 0 1 1 1 0     Answer
```

Example 10–13. Show a machine multiplication of $1 0 1 \times 1 1$. Check using pencil multiplication.

Solution:

```
1 0 1|
0 1 1|
```

```
1 0 1|          add
  1 0| 1        shift right
1 0 1| ↓        add
```

```
1 1 1| 1
0 1 1| 1 1      shift right
0 0 0| ↓ ↓      add
```

```
0 1 1| 1 1
```

Answer: 1111

Check:

```
1 0 1
0 1 1
```

```
1 0 1
1 0 1
```

```
1 1 1 1
```

Problem 10–4. Show a machine multiplication of the following numbers (check each using pencil multiplication).

1. 1 1 0
    × 1 0

2. 1 0 1 1
    × 1 0 1 1

3. 1 1 0 1 0
    × 1 0 0 1 0

4. 1 0 0 0 1
    × 1 0 0 1

5. 1 1 0 1 1
    × 1 0 1 0 0

10–4.   Computer Division

Division can be accomplished in a manner similar to multiplication in that a repeated subtraction and shift left is used.   For this operation only three registers are needed, for the answer (quotient) requires as many (or few) places as the numbers processed.   Recall that with multiplication two ten-bit numbers can give a twenty-bit answer, requiring the additional register.   Using the same registers as for multiplication but redefining their usage for the division operation, Figure 10–3 shows the simplified logic and registers to perform the function.   Needless to say, a large computer with other requirements works the logic gating and registers differently, but the operation might still be the same—repeated subtraction and shift left.   The diagram of Figure 10–3 provides a basis for seeing how the data is handled in division.   Register A is the input register of the arithmetic section.   The divisor is read into A and then shifted to B (register B having been cleared first).   The division operation is now ready to start, since the registers are loaded.   (Loading a register, either parallel or serial, means filling it with information.)   The subtractor of A − B (dividend minus divisor) provides a

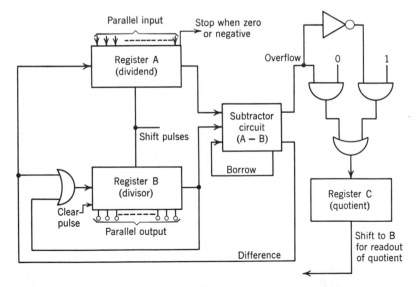

Figure 10–3.   Computer division, simplified block diagram.

difference output and an overflow output.   If the overflow is a 0 the divisor is smaller than the part of the dividend it is being divided into, and the only number of times it could go into the dividend part is 1. If the overflow is 1 the subtraction went negative or the divisor was smaller and goes into that part of the dividend 0 times.   Register C receives this digit for each subtraction, and after the dividend remaining goes to zero or negative the division is complete.   Example 10–14 shows the operation numerically.

Example 10–14.   Divide 328 by 8 using the computer or machine method.   Check using a pencil solution.

Solution:

1.	1 0 1 0|0 1 0 0 0	dividend (A)
2.	1 0 0 0	divisor (B)
3.	0 0 1 0|0 1 0 0 0	subtract (1) − (2)
4.	0 0 1 0 0|1 0 0 0	shift left (no overflow— 1 into C)
5.	1 0 0 0	subtract (4) − (5)
6. overflow ⟶	1 1 1 0 0	overflow means 0 to C
7.	0 0 1 0 0|1 0 0 0	restore (4)
8.	0 0 1 0 0 1|0 0 0	shift left
9.	1 0 0 0	subtract (8) − (9)
10.	0 0 0 0 0 1|0 0 0	no overflow (1 into C)
11.	0 0 0 0 0 1 0|0 0	shift left
12.	1 0 0 0	subtract (11) − (12)
13. overflow ⟶	1 1 0 1 0	overflow (0 to C)
14.	0 0 0 0 0 1 0 0|0	restore (11) and shift left
15.	1 0 0 0	subtract (14) − (15)
16. overflow ⟶	1 1 1 0 0	overflow means (0 to C)
17.	0 0 0 0 0 1 0 0|0 0	restore (14) and shift left
18.	1 0 0|0	subtract (17) − (18)
19.	0 0 0 0 0 0 0|0	no overflow (1 to C)

dividend difference is now all zero
∴ STOP

Answer is read from beginning 101001

Check:

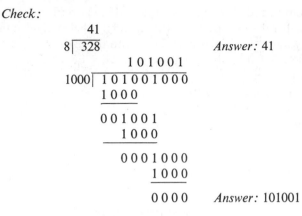

$$\begin{array}{r} 41 \\ 8\overline{)\ 328} \end{array} \qquad\qquad \textit{Answer: } 41$$

Although the theory is simple, the detailing on paper is lengthy. Try the following problem to help clear up the procedure.

Problem 10–5. Show a machine division of the following numbers. Check using pencil method.

1. $101\overline{)11001}$ 2. $17\overline{)68}$ 3. $111\overline{)101010}$

4. $9\overline{)81}$

Summary

The arithmetic unit contains circuitry to carry out addition, subtraction, multiplication, and division, to name the basic operations. Some circuits were shown to carry out these operations, although many others exist in practice.

In addition (or subtraction) the two numbers to be added are shifted through an adder (subtractor) circuit and the resulting sum output is shifted back into the output register. The output may be read out in parallel for storage in the memory unit.

In multiplication (division) the two numbers are processed by addition (subtraction) and shift-right (shift-left) operations.

The addition or subtraction of two numbers including sign can be easily implemented using a 0 or 1 to represent the sign in the most significant digit and performing the operation as if the sign bit were a number.

PROBLEMS

1. Write the binary form (as in Example 10–1) of (a) +27, (b) −36.
2. Write the binary form (as in Example 10–1) of (a) +72, (b) −56.
3. Add the following two numbers, using the method of Examples 10–2 through 10–5: (a) +22, +16, (b) +25, −15.
4. Repeat problem 3 for (a) −19, −33, (b) −18, +15.
5. Subtract the following numbers using the method of Examples 10–6 through 10–9: (a) +18 minus +8, (b) +25 minus −16.
6. Repeat problem 5 for (a) −36 minus +14, (b) −24 minus −12.
7. Show a machine multiplication of 1 0 0 1
$$\times 1\ 1$$

8. Show a machine multiplication of 1 1 0 1 0
$$\times 1\ 0\ 1$$

9. Show a machine division of $1010\overline{)1100100}$ and check using pencil method.
10. Repeat problem 9 for $10\overline{)1010}$.

1011

Computer memory

11–1. General Memory Description

A computer memory plays a very important part in how effective a
computer is.   A fast memory allows for quicker operation providing
more solutions.   Large memory capacity allows handling more data
and doing more complex operations.   Low memory cost allows the
computer to be a practical reality.   These three factors—speed, size
or capacity, and cost—vary considerably for the different types of
memories used and are important criteria in the selection of a suitable
memory.

A digital memory can be simply defined as any element that can
maintain either of two stable states indefinitely (as long as power is
not shut off).   A flip-flop falls under this definition.   Because of the
large capacity required of even a small computer memory system
and because of the size and cost of a flip-flop circuit, flip-flop circuits
are not used for large-scale memory storage.   Flip-flop registers are
used as intermediate or buffer memories between sections of a computer handling one word of information at a time.   A memory
system may handle hundred to hundred thousands of words (a fixed
number of bits define a word).   A word may be a few bits long or as
many as 36, 48, or 64 bits for some computers.   For discussion in
this book consider a word to be ten bits unless otherwise stated.
Two very popular memory devices are magnetic cores and magnetic
drums.   Although such devices as magnetic tape, paper tape, and
punched card are also memory devices, their use is primarily that of
providing data into the computer and saving data from the computer.
They are best classed as input/output equipment.   This distinction

comes about from considering whether the memory unit is used *directly* by the arithmetic unit or not. Those used directly will be called computer memories. Those storing data which is fed into the internal computer memory or taking data from the internal computer memory are considered input or output equipment. These latter units are discussed in Chapter 12. Other less popular internal computer memories exist, such as optical, tunnel diode, multi-aperture core or transfluxor, twistor, cryogenic, thin-film, ferrite, etc. Some of these will be discussed briefly. They are basically faster or smaller, are generally more costly, and are presently (September 1965) under research or in limited practical use. Awareness of these types is important, for they may someday gain prime importance. The present popularity of the magnetic core and, to a lesser extent, of the magnetic drum requires more detailed consideration of their usage. In addition, these latter two are organized differently and will provide for a discussion of the types of memory organization, an important factor in their usage.

A number of different expressions are used in connection with memory operation. "Bit serial" means that each bit is taken sequentially, or one at a time. "Word serial" indicates that each word is read out sequentially, or one word at a time. "Bit parallel" would mean that a group of bits are read out at one time and "word parallel" that a group of words are read simultaneously. "Access" is the operation of getting a word or bit out of memory. Time of access or access time is a very important factor in the speed of a memory unit and indicates the amount of time involved in getting data from the memory. For example, finding page 459 in a book takes a certain amount of looking time. With the book closed after each look the amount of time to find a certain page will vary. If you have to advance one page at a time, getting to page 625 will take much longer than getting to page 27. Advancing in this prescribed manner is considered a sequential operation. In a similar manner a computer memory that must be looked at or read in a prescribed order is sequential access. As opposed to this, the pages could be indexed and you might be able to turn directly to the page asked for. In such a case, the time to find one page is the same as to find another. Such a memory operation is called "random access." Obviously the random access is much faster than the sequential access memory. Since there is a trade-off between speed and economy in operating these memory types, different combinations of bit or word and sequential or random access operation are chosen to best fit the particular problem.

11–2. Magnetic Core Memory

Because the magnetic core memory is at present the most popular computer memory element, it will be the first one considered. Before discussing the organization of such a memory and its properties, the memory characteristic of a magnetic core must be considered. The magnetic core is generally a round toroid very much like a doughnut in shape. It is so small in size that many thousands can be held in a

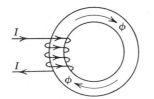

Figure 11–1.   Flux flow in magnetic core.

sewing thimble. The core is made of ferromagnetic material of specified characteristic. A few turns of wire wound around a magnetic core carrying a current will produce a magnetic flux. If the current is passed in one direction through the wire, the flux direction (north-south poles) can be determined by the right-hand rule. A typical configuration showing flux, current, and direction is that of Figure 11–1. As the current is increased the flux first increases linearly (equal flux change for a fixed current change), then changes less and less for each current interval, and finally there is no flux change for an increase in current. At this point the core is *saturated* and will allow no further increase in flux as current is increased. Actually, there is always a very slight increase in flux, but for our purposes the core is fully saturated. Thus, the core will "store" or "remember" the signal applied long after it has been removed. There, of course, must be two distinct states if it is to be used as a binary memory element.

Continuing the discussion of magnetization of a core, we can reverse the current direction in the winding of the core, causing the magnetic flux to be reduced even further until it goes to zero and then becomes negative. "Negative" means that the north-south poles of the core are reversed and that the flux flows in the opposite direction. Flux is usually considered as flowing from a north pole

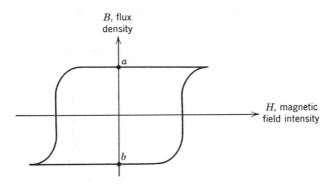

Figure 11–2.   *B–H* curve of magnetic core for storage use.

to a south pole.   The flux fully saturates in the opposite or negative direction.   If the current is now decreased the amount of flux decreases, until the current is completely removed and residual flux is flowing in the opposite direction.

An important consideration in using the magnetic core is how to "read out" the state of the core.   We know that it is magnetized and flux is flowing in one of two directions—one being arbitrarily designated binary ZERO, the other binary ONE.   Which way is it magnetized?   Since there is a constant flux flowing, it is difficult to know which way.   The flux must be made to change to "sense" the direction.   Only a change in flux can induce a voltage in a stationary element.   However, in causing it to change it is no longer magnetized as before.   In order to read the stored information it is necessary to "destroy" it.   This is referred to as destructive readout.   To make it possible to use the same information a number of times, additional operations must be added to "rewrite" the data to "save" it.   With these general ideas in mind let us now go back and look more closely at how the magnetic core operates and is organized in a memory system.

A ferrite core used in a computer memory has a "square" loop characteristic as shown in Figure 11–2.   Points *a* and *b* show the amount of flux remaining after the drive signal is removed.   Consider point *a* as the 1 state and *b* as the 0 for memory use.   To "switch" the core from one binary state to the other requires a driving signal of correct polarity and intensity.   A core and drive

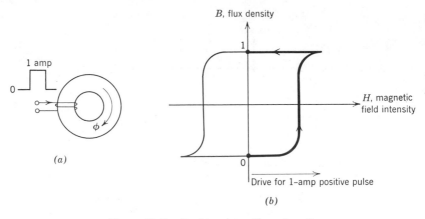

Figure 11–3.   Positive drive (from 0 to 1).

winding are shown in Figure 11–3*a*.   The wire is wrapped around
the core, and by the right-hand rule the magnetization direction may
be obtained.   For a fixed number of turns of wire the current is
directly proportional to H.   Figure 11–3*b* shows how the core is
magnetized for the given signal input.   After the drive signal goes
back to zero the core remains at binary ONE.   Applying a pulse to

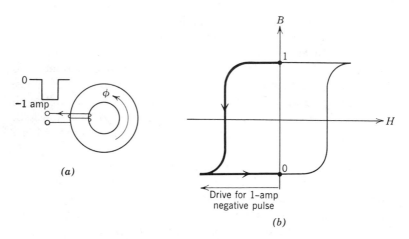

Figure 11–4.   Negative drive (from 1 to 0).

the same core in the negative direction will bring the core back to binary ZERO.   See Figure 11–4.

When the core is pulsed it takes a certain amount of time to switch states, depending on the intensity of the driving pulse and its rate of change.   Fast cores are operated in less than one-millionth of a second, or 1 μsec.   Slow operation is around 10 μsec.   Thus, access time for magnetic cores is from 1 to 10 μsec.   Let us use 1 μsec as the switching time for this discussion.   When a magnetic core is used in a memory, it can be set to the ONE state or reset to the ZERO state by pulsing it with a correct polarity current signal.   Since the core element is made as small as possible, it is wound with only one turn, with the wire generally being as fine as human hair.   It is desirable to operate the core with as few wires as possible to obtain the smallest unit.

When reading a core, the core may not maintain state after the read operation.   If the core changes state, as sensed by a pickup wire, consider the core having been in the ONE state.   If it does not change state, consider it having been in the ZERO state.   The change of flux when going from ONE to ZERO induces a voltage in a pickup wire or sense wire indicating the storage of a ONE in the sensed memory element.   No voltage out indicates that a ZERO was stored.   In either case the core is at ZERO after a read time. This type of readout is destructive since it destroys the stored information.   A ONE stored in the core can only be read once. If the core is read again it will read ZERO.   In comparison, a flip-flop output can be gated with an AND gate which allows a read pulse through if the TRUE side is at ONE.   In reading, the flip-flop state is unchanged.   Unfortunately, magnetic core readout must be destructive.   To provide a more permanent storage operation the data must be written back into the core after each read operation. This means that the basic operation of the core memory requires a read-write cycle.   Every time a core is read, the data is written back in.   When a ONE is read, a ONE is written back in.   When a ZERO is read, the core is left alone.   Resetting the core requires only a read pulse to insure that it is in the ZERO state.

A major consideration in organizing the core memory is to keep track of where data is stored.   One method requires labeling each individual core, so that any specific core may be read.   This is a bit-organized core memory.   To reduce the amount of selection needed the cores may be arranged into words (ten bits per word, for example) and each word may then be separately selected. In this case ten times less specification is needed and the data is read out or written in a word at a time. This is a word-organized core memory. The problems and solutions using both bit-organized and word-organized are considered next.

Two main problems in organizing the data of a core memory are the large number of wires needed for exclusive read, write, and sense of data, and the large amount of selection circuitry needed to provide the control and operation of the memory. A single core may require separate read, write, and sense lines. For a 1024-word memory (memories are usually numbered in binary powers, 2^{10} being 1024) this would mean over 3000 wires. Even with small-sized cores, 3000 wires take up considerable space. A very clever technique using an x–y-coordinate selection scheme has been adopted. To select any specific core requires choosing the proper x coordinate and y coordinate of the desired core. Figure 11–5 shows the general setup of such a scheme for a 100-core array. To pick out core 12, for example, requires selecting both x_1 and y_2. Either alone is not sufficient. Only core 12 is selected, since no other receives two selection signals. If these 100 cores were individually selected 100 wires would be needed. Using the x–y-coordinate scheme takes

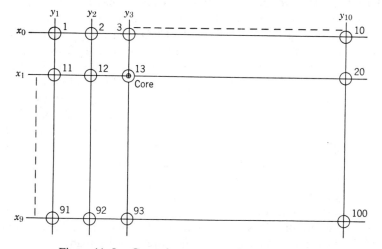

Figure 11–5.   General core array using x–y selection.

only twenty wires, a saving of $\frac{4}{5}$, or 80%. A 1024-core memory would need only sixty-four wires as compared to 1024 wires, a saving of $\frac{15}{16}$, or 94%. Obviously the x–y-coordinate selection method proves better suited to the larger-sized memory system. For this reason it has become the accepted method for all large computer systems. Additional savings in "hardware" or circuitry is also made possible with the x–y selection scheme. Whereas 100 driver gates are needed for the 100-core system, only twenty gates are needed for the x–y core selection system.

Looking at the practical problem of core selection, we find the x–y scheme requires two coincident signals to select a core. Since the core is not switched until a certain magnitude pulse is applied, each half-select pulse alone must be of insufficient magnitude to switch the core and both pulses of sufficient magnitude. Figure 11 6 shows the core B–H curve and the half-select signals. Since the pulses are current pulses the scheme is popularly known as coincident-current selection. Each select line therefore receives only a half-select current, the coincidence of two half-select current pulses at one core causing the core to switch. The sensing of a core is also made very simple by using one wire for all cores. The

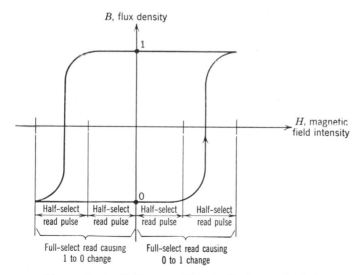

Figure 11–6. B–H curve with coincident-current select.

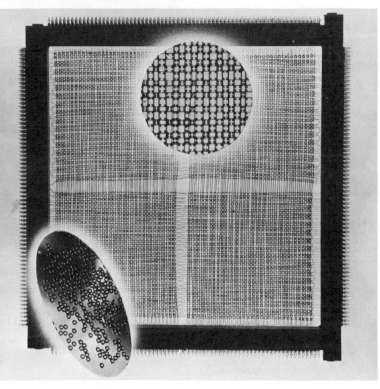

Figure 11-7. Magnetic core plane.

selection circuit specifies which core is being read. A flux change indicates the storage of ONE and results in the pickup of a voltage pulse at read time. No flux change indicates the storage of a ZERO and results in no voltage pulse. The same two read wires may now be used to write the ONE back in, if that was the data stored, by feeding two coincident pulses of opposite polarity. Current in the opposite direction produces flux flow in the opposite direction (opposite that for the ZERO condition) switching the core to the ONE state. Figure 11-7 shows a single magnetic core plane and some details of the core windings.

A practical core array for a 1024-core memory is shown in Figure 11-8. There are thirty-two rows and thirty-two columns, each having a driver gate to operate the core line. To provide easy

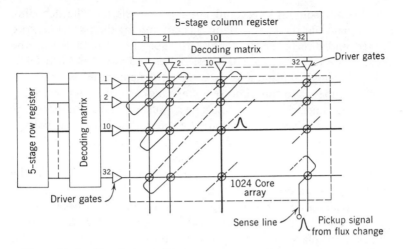

Figure 11-8.   Practical coincident-current magnetic core storage circuit.

selection a buffer register is used to store the five-bit number representing one of the thirty-two rows and a decoding matrix to pick out the one driver selected.   To specify a particular core requires ten

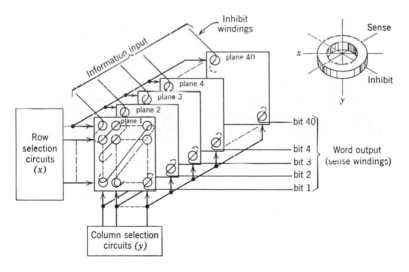

Figure 11-9.   Word-organized core memory.

bits, five for column select and five for row select.   The decoding matrix picks out the one row and one column for the particular core desired and directs the read pulse to those lines so that only the chosen core receives two half-select pulses and switches (if in ONE state).   A single sense line is used for all the cores and is wound in such a manner as to cancel noise voltage pickup produced by driving sixty-three other cores with half-select pulses.   Core number 10 is selected on the diagram as shown by the darker lines, and voltage pulse is shown on the sense line.   Knowing which core was selected, the voltage indicates that a ONE was stored.   A write operation must follow in order to put the ONE back into the core to make the overall operation nondestructive.

Where larger amounts of data are desired and word organization would reduce the amount of circuitry, the cores are arranged in core planes, each plane containing a single bit of the word.   A ten-bit word requires ten planes.   If each plane has 1024 cores, then 1024 words may be stored.   Ten planes of 1024 bits means that 10,240 cores are used.   Because the magnetic core, wiring, and drive circuitry are expensive, this memory represents a sizable investment. Core memory is probably the most expensive popular memory used. To complete the picture, a 1024-bit plane is smaller than a quarter of an $8\frac{1}{2} \times 11$-inch page, and recent developments have put 4096 bits in less space.   The thickness of the memory is about ten of these pages when such things as wiring are included.   Most of this size is due to wiring of the memory.

Although the write operation occurs a short time after read, the output pulse will have passed.   The usual procedure is to store the information read in a flip-flop register.   This allows writing back information stored in the flip-flop so that the information in core storage is maintained.   It also provides a buffer register from which the computer can obtain information it had previously called for. Because of the buffer register the computer can be reading information from memory while doing some other operation or can call for a read operation and then do another operation before taking the memory data.   Since the write operation is required after each read, control and timing circuits are wired to carry out both operations automatically whenever a read is called for.   In this way a read operation is nondestructive.   A write operation, however, places new data in the memory cells and the old data is lost.

Figure 11–9 shows a simplified word-organized core memory. Each plane may be a 1024-bit plane similar to that shown in Figure 11–7. A coincident current will select a single bit on the plane. With forty planes as shown in Figure 11–9 the read operation selects a single core in each of the forty planes. Since each contains a stored bit, a forty-bit word results. All forty are read at once and appear on the forty select lines (one for each plane). A write command contains the address specifying which of the 1024 words is to be selected. The information to be written in is fed in on a third set of wires which may be called the z axis. A single wire is used for each plane which is logically the same as the sense wire. A separate wire is generally used for practical reasons. The individual core algebraically adds the component fluxes produced by the x select pulse, y select pulse, and z select pulse. These pulses may be of positive or negative polarity resulting in clockwise or counterclockwise flux components. Two positive half-select pulses result in an overall clockwise flux (Figure 11–10a) which remains after the

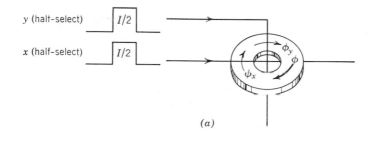

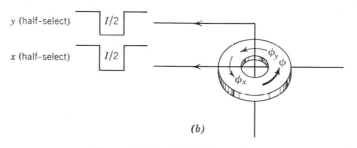

Figure 11–10.   Half-select pulses.

pulses have passed. If the two pulses are of negative polarity (Figure 11–10b), a counterclockwise flux will remain after the pulses have passed.

The third select wire, called "z" or often "inhibit" wire, also carries a pulse of half-select magnitude of negative polarity or of zero magnitude. If it is zero it of course does nothing. If, however, it is of half-select magnitude (negative polarity), it will oppose the positive polarity half-select pulses on the x or y lines. To see how this is used we must consider the full operation of reading and writing into a core of the memory. Defining clockwise flux as storage of a ONE (and counterclockwise a ZERO), read pulses must be of negative polarity so as to cause a flux reversal when a ONE is stored and none when a ZERO is stored. Coincident negative pulses, on the other hand, would cause counterclockwise flux, producing a large flux change if a ONE is present and little flux change if there is a ZERO (see Figure 11–11). The inhibit winding has no

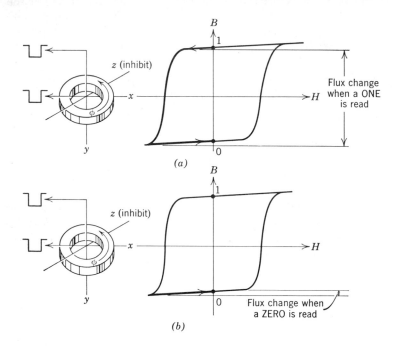

Figure 11–11.   Reading a core.

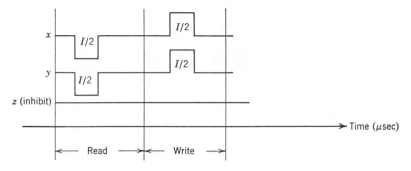

Figure 11–12.   Read/write cycle for storage of a ONE.

pulse applied during read time.   It is only operated during write time to provide for storage of the desired bit.

Before the write operation is considered, one more point must be made clear.   The operation of the memory is an established read-write cycle.   This cycle is necessary to provide for overall non-destructive readout of data.   Since we must always do a write after each read, we must also always do a read before each write operation. A read operation always results in resetting all cores of the word "read" to ZERO.   Thus, before each write we are assured that the cores to be considered are all in the ZERO state.   With this in mind we can now see how the inhibit properly provides for writing in a desired bit.   If no signal is applied to the inhibit winding, the x and y select pulses will cause the flux of the selected core to go clockwise, thereby storing a ONE.   Figure 11–12 shows the read/write cycle when a ONE is stored.

If the inhibit winding has a negative pulse present at write time (see Figure 11–13), it will oppose the flux of one half-select signal, thereby maintaining the core as it was, which was a ZERO because of the preceding read operation.   By inhibiting any change the z winding causes a ZERO to remain stored in the core.   A memory cycle, consisting of a separate read and write operation, takes in the order of a microsecond in most present-day computers.

Now that the details of the word-organized core memory have been considered, a complete memory operation might well be tied together (refer to Figure 11–9).   Consider the memory as operating separately but as part of a larger system.   When a memory operation

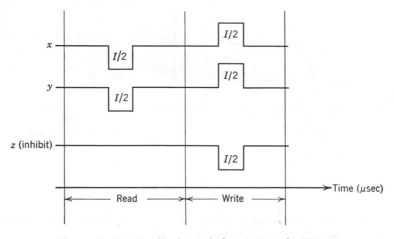

Figure 11–13.   Read/write cycle for storage of a ZERO.

is desired as indicated by a step in the program, the control unit takes the address of the word and feeds it to the x and y registers of the memory.   The two decode matrices (x and y) decode the address bits into single lines of x and y select.   Only one x and one y driver gate are thereby selected.   The control unit indicates that the memory operation should be carried out and also determines whether new data is being written in or stored data read out.   If read is desired, a single read pulse is applied to all driver gates.   Only the selected x and y driver gates on each plane provide the negative polarity read pulse, and the sense line of each plane indicates what the stored bit was.   To maintain this information until the write pulses appear they are stored in a buffer register.   During write time the same x and y driver gates are still selected, but now the input pulse is of positive polarity.   However, the inhibit line is also operated, and using the stored bit read out of that plane provides either no pulse or a negative pulse resulting in the writing of a ONE or ZERO, respectively.   The data read out now is stored in the buffer register and may be taken whenever the computer needs it.   It should be clear that although the word "read" is still stored in core memory, the buffer data will only be present until the next read or write operation.

In a write operation the x and y registers and matrices select the desired word of memory. During read the data in the word is placed into the buffer register, even though it will not be called for. On the write part of the cycle the inhibit input is taken from an out-side register of the computer and a new word is read into core storage. An alternate means of applying the new word to the inhibit windings would be to have it placed in the buffer register before write time and have the data read on the sense lines blocked from getting into the buffer registers. When the write operation occurs as usual, it puts a new word into core storage.

As a summary of the salient features of core memory, read-write speed is about 1 μsec, size is very small, but the cost high. Core memory can be operated random access allowing quickest selection of a word. The popular method of organizing the core array is coincident-current selection.

11–3.   Magnetic Drum Memory

A drum memory is quite different from a core memory. The core is very fast but the drum is slow; the core can be operated random access, the drum cyclically; the core is made of individual bit storage cells, the drum of a large storage surface; cost of core

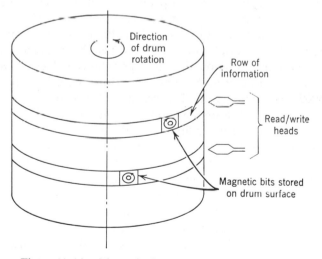

Figure 11–14.   Magnetic drum memory, simple sketch.

memory is high, for the same storage capacity the drum is cheaper; the core size is relatively small, the drum unit much larger. The drum memory is made of a cylinder whose surface is coated with a magnetic material. Data can be stored in rows around the circumference of the drum unit as in Figure 11–14. A special "head" is used to write or read information on the drum, the information being small magnetized areas as indicated. The drum is rotated at a fixed speed so that once around the drum is a specified time interval. A rotational speed of 12,000 revolutions per minute, for example, would produce a single cycle of rotation in

$$T = \frac{1}{\text{speed}} = \frac{1}{12,000} \frac{\text{min}}{\text{rev}} \times 60 \frac{\text{sec}}{\text{min}} = \frac{1}{200} \frac{\text{sec}}{\text{rev}}$$

$$T = 5 \frac{\text{msec}}{\text{rev}}$$

This is a realistic time for drum memories. Compare this to 5 μsec for a core memory and you see that there is a difference of a factor of 1000. This is an appreciably great difference. Actually, the data coming by the read head may appear immediately after it is desired or as long as 5 msec later. On the average it may take 2.5 msec using half a cycle as the average. This still is considerably different from the core access time. A computer using drum memory is therefore a slower-operating machine. This does not mean that the circuitry works at a slower clock rate. The bits may be coming off the drum at the rate of 1 million per second, but until the desired data comes by the read head may be milliseconds later so that the larger solution time is considerably reduced. With a 5-msec cycle time, storing 5000 bits on a row or track would mean that 5000 bits pass by every 5 msec, or $5000/5 \times 10^{-3} = 1 \times 10^6$, or 1 million bits per second, as previously indicated.

Drum rotational speed is limited by the mechanical drive system and the size and weight of the memory drum. Practical limits presently keep the cycle time to about 0.5 msec. In order to get a reasonable amount of data on the drum surface, the diameter must be fairly large. A 12-inch diameter might be considered average. Because the drum is useful for large memory storage, the cylinder height is around 8 inches to accommodate the large number of tracks desired. Figures of 20 tracks per inch and 200 bits per track inch (circumferential distance) are typical. A 100,000-bit drum memory is an average capacity.   Compare this to the complexity of 100,000 cores in many planes with all the operating circuitry. The drum requires only one read/write head per track, so that a few thousand bits need only one drive or pickup circuit.   The selector gating need only pick the one track out of a few dozen.   Simplicity of operation leading to a cost per bit much lower than that of the core system is a prime asset of the drum system.   Large capacity and cheap cost then are the main assets of the drum system, and these are the main points to consider.   Slow speed, though undesirable, is acceptable when capacity and cost are the main considerations.   When speed is too important to lose, the core must be used.   There are, as would be expected, some special systems using both drum memory for large storage and small "scratch pad" core memories for high operating speed.   The two work together, so that the computer is always operating at its highest speed and the core and drum aid each other.

A simplified picture of the read/write function is shown in Figure 11–15.   The read and write operation can be considered separately. To write a ONE or ZERO requires magnetizing a small segment of the track as it moves by.   By controlling the current polarity in the write head, the flux direction is fixed.   Clockwise could be a ONE and counterclockwise flux a ZERO.   The amount of flux induced on the drum depends on the strength of the current pulse (and fixed factors such as number of turns, core reluctance, surface-to-head

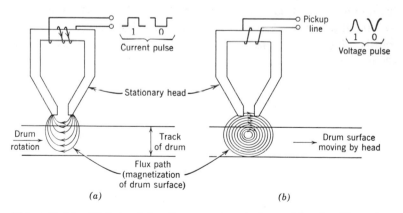

Figure 11–15.   Write/read function on magnetic drum: (a) write, (b) read.

spacing, etc.). The amount of voltage pickup depends on the strength of the magnetic field produced by the stored bit on the drum surface (and the fixed factors or rotating speed, air-gap, number of turns, head-surface spacing, etc.). The spacing (distance) of pickup or write head from the surface is very important. Distances of less than 5 mils (5/1000ths of an inch) are typical. Some high-speed machines use a technique of "floating heads" to try to achieve the minimum spacing. The heads are held off the surface by air pressure. As the surface expands from heating, the head spacing is kept constant by the air pressure. If the head were rigidly fixed 1 mil away and the surface expanded by a mil from heating, the two would touch, destroying that part of the drum. Floating heads provide improvement but also add mechanical complexity and cost.

Data is stored sequentially around the track and passes by the read/write head each cycle. To provide for simple addressing of the data, the information is laid out from a fixed starting point. Each word does not need an address number stored with it on the drum. Knowing that it is word 27 of track 6 is sufficient to allow reading it out. The outside circuitry must count the number of words coming by on the desired track and provide a start read command (and stop read command) at the correct time. Information is generally arranged bit serial, ten bits in a row representing a given word as an example. Since the tracks may be read out simultaneously, the data may be handled word parallel for expediency. Although a single head is able to read all the information by shifting it from track to track, such action further slows down operating speeds and provides poorer track resolution since mechanical accuracy will be reduced. It is usual to have a fixed head for each track.

Magnetic Drum Organization. A number of ways of organizing data on a drum are possible. Data could be stored in bit-serial format with words stored circumferentially in one track. As an example, consider a drum containing 32 tracks of 4096 bits per track. For a bit-serial machine (Figure 11–16a) with 32 bits per word each track will contain 128 words:

$$4096 \frac{\text{bits}}{\text{track}} \div 32 \frac{\text{bits}}{\text{word}} = 128 \frac{\text{words}}{\text{track}}$$

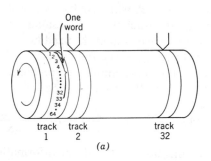

(a)

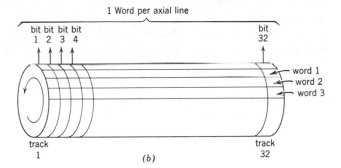

(b)

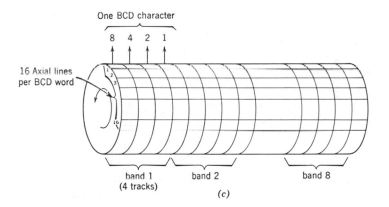

(c)

Figure 11–16.   Organization of data on a magnetic drum memory: (a) bit-serial organized memory, (b) bit-parallel organized memory, (c) bit-serial-parallel organized memory.

Track 1 will contain words 0–127, track 2 will contain words 128–255, etc.   Since each track will have its own read/write head, access time for a word of any track will be the same.   Once the beginning of the desired word appears under the fixed head of that track, it will take 32 bit-times to read out the full word.   If the drum rotational speed is 3600 revolutions per minute (60 revolutions per second) the transfer rate (to or from the drum) will be

$$128 \frac{\text{words}}{\text{rev}} \times 60 \frac{\text{rev}}{\text{sec}} = 7{,}680 \frac{\text{words}}{\text{sec}}.$$

A second organization of the drum information would be bit-parallel (or word-serial).   In this case the 32 bits of a single word are read at the same time (Figure 11–16*b*), each bit coming out of a different track head.   Access is still sequential but the word appears at one bit time.   The word transfer rate for this case will be

$$4096 \frac{\text{words}}{\text{rev}} \times 60 \frac{\text{rev}}{\text{sec}} = 245{,}760 \frac{\text{words}}{\text{sec}}.$$

This is much higher rate than the bit-serial operations and might be desirable in some applications.

Somewhere between the two extremes, bit-serial and bit-parallel, is bit-serial-parallel (Figure 11–16*c*).   This organization may be required for special coded forms of data.   For example, in using binary-coded decimal (BCD) data, four binary digits are needed to store a BCD character.   From this consideration the data might be organized in eight bands, four tracks to a band.   A character would be four bits of BCD.   If a word contained sixteen characters, each band would contain 256 words for a transfer rate of 15,360 words per second.   In all cases, the bit rate of any track would be

$$4096 \frac{\text{bits}}{\text{rev}} \times 60 \frac{\text{rev}}{\text{sec}} = 245{,}760 \frac{\text{bits}}{\text{sec}}$$

requiring circuitry to operate at a clock rate of about 250 kcps.

Maximum access time would be 1 revolution or about 16 msec ($\frac{1}{60}$ sec per revolution).   Average access would then be 8 msec.   It should be clear that although it takes a relatively long time to get to the information desired, the data comes off the drum at a high rate. Both the initial access time and the data transfer rate (words/second) are necessary to describe a magnetic drum memory system.

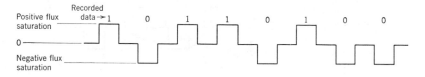

Figure 11–17.   Return-to-zero (RZ) recorded data.

Recording on Magnetic Surface.   Having considered the general organization of a magnetic drum memory, it might be well to look into some details of how data is stored on the magnetic drum surface and how it is read back.   Recording methods fall into two classes, return-to-zero (more generally return-to-reference) and nonreturn-to-zero.   In return-to-zero (RZ) recording the flux on the magnetic surface within a defined track always returns to a reference value between adjacent bits of stored information.   This reference value may be zero.   For the zero-flux reference value, binary storage might be flux saturation in one direction or the other.   Figure 11–17 shows the input recording data of an arbitrary group of bits for RZ operation.   Saturating the surface area where a bit is stored helps decrease voltage pickup variation produced by variations in the write current.   The recording head used for RZ recording might be that of Figure 11–18, where recordings of a ONE and of a ZERO are shown.

Circumferentially, the packing density depends on the head-to-

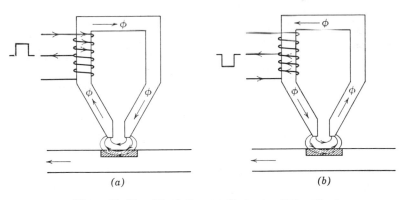

Figure 11–18.   Magnetic recording using RZ method.

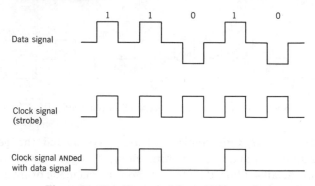

Figure 11–19.   Data read from RZ recording.

surface spacing, on the width of flux which penetrates the surface, etc.   It is also related to the recording method.   In RZ a guard position of zero flux exists between adjacent bits.   Furthermore, the negative voltage slope need not be considered when reading back the data.   Figure 11–19 shows a few arbitrary data pulses, a clock signal which is used as a strobe (used to set specific times when data is read), and the output data.

Notice that the same output would result if the negative data pulses were not present, since an output from an AND gate occurs only when both inputs are present.   This leads us to believe that more data could be stored in the same space.   Before considering this increased density recording method, it should be pointed out that return-to-bias or reference recording, although providing the same recording density as RZ, does have an important advantage.   If the bias level chosen is opposite saturation to that of the recorded ONE bit, the recovered signal is roughly twice that for RZ, and bipolar signals need not be handled by the read amplifiers.   Figure 11–20 shows the data read with a return-to-bias method.

A method of recording data at a higher density than that recorded by RZ is called nonreturn-to-zero (NRZ).   Figure 11–21 shows the same recorded data as in Figures 11–17 and 11–20 for RZ and return-to-bias recording.   Compare the three figures carefully to see the difference between them.   Note especially the difference between nonreturn-to-zero and return-to-reference recordings: these two appear the same to a casual glance but are quite different when observed carefully.   In nonreturn-to-zero recording the binary digit

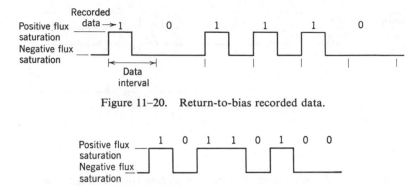

Figure 11–20.   Return-to-bias recorded data.

Figure 11–21.   Recorded data using nonreturn-to-zero (NRZ) recording.

is represented by a flux level (saturation level preferable).   If groups of similar digits are recorded in NRZ, the flux remains unchanged. In RZ or return-to-bias the flux always changes between adjacent bits, even if they are the same binary value.   The largest number of flux changes in NRZ recording occurs when alternate ONE and ZERO's are recorded, and even here the number of flux changes is half that of RZ recording.   By using NRZ recording, twice the packing density of RZ recording is obtainable.   In reading NRZ data, some means must be incorporated to indicate what the data read is when adjacent bits are the same, since the flux change occurs only when there is a data change and none occurs when bits are the same.   Figure 11–22 shows how a simple flip-flop circuit may be used to read data stored as NRZ.   The waveforms of the signals throughout the read circuitry are shown in Figure 11–23.

The flux waveform of the NRZ recorded data clearly shows the

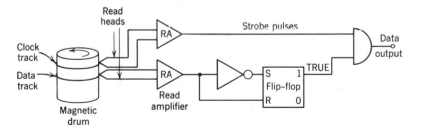

Figure 11–22.   Circuit for reading NRZ recorded data.

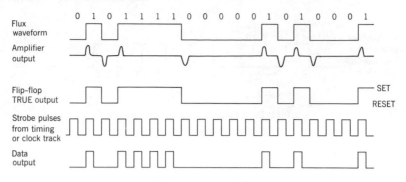

Figure 11–23.   Waveforms of signals for reading NRZ recorded data.

information stored.   Since only flux changes can be sensed, the constant-flux level of repeated ONE's and ZERO's is not directly evident in the amplifier output waveform.   If this output is used to SET and RESET a flip-flop, however, the recorded bits are clearly evident.   In the circuit shown the negative-going pulses trigger the flip-flop inputs.   By using strobe or timing pulses taken from a clock track on the drum, the data output is produced, providing bit-serial data which may be read into a buffer or storage register for use outside the memory unit.

Another NRZ recording method records only one of the binary signals.   Called NRZI ("I" meaning "invert"), the recording considers only, say, binary ONE's and records them as a single flux change (see Figure 11–24).   Because of this the one digit is sometimes a positive recorded signal and sometimes a negative recorded signal.   *Any* flux change is indicative of a ONE being stored and no

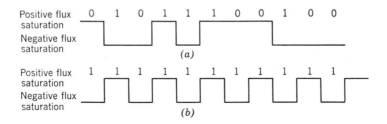

Figure 11–24.   Two binary digit waveforms using NRZI recording.

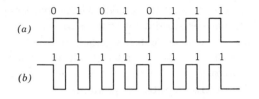

Figure 11-25.   Phase recording of data (an NRZ method).

flux change of a ZERO. Figure 11-24b shows that the pattern for successive ONE's have a flux change for every ONE recorded. Reading data is similar to that just described.

A third method of NRZ recording is called "phase recording" (or "Ferranti" or "Manchester"). Figure 11-25 shows two waveforms using this method. In recording a ONE, for example, the bit is recorded as a positive flux followed by a negative flux. A recorded ZERO would then be a negative followed by a positive flux. What is most important about this method is that from the highest frequency recording (all ONE's or all ZERO's) to the lowest, the frequency change is one-half. If the highest frequency the signal changes at is 200 kcps, the lowest is only 100 kcps. The lowest frequency occurs for alternating ONE's and ZERO's. With the two other NRZ recording methods the recording of a large number of ONE's and ZERO's would appear as a steady or quiescent level approaching dc operation. This is a restriction on the read-write amplifiers used since they must operate from direct current up to maximum frequency. With the phase-recording method indicated, the frequency range is quite limited and transformer-coupled amplifiers can be used. Reading the stored information is substantially that indicated in the first NRZ recording considered and need not be elaborated on here. It need only be noted that recording and reading of data must be carefully timed with this method, as with all others.

Having considered how data is both stored on a magnetic drum and organized on the drum, let us look at how the overall drum read and write operation is controlled. An origin (start) track containing only a single bit at the proper starting place circumferentially is provided. Another track called the "clock track" is also present for synchronizing purposes. This track contains alternate ONE's and ZERO's to provide an output clock whose frequency is fixed by the drum rotational speed (and bits per inch).   Because this speed may vary, and because an external clock may not occur at the recorded time of a bit passing under the head or may drift, this drum-controlled clock is the best for synchronization of read/write operation.   The external controller contains a bit or word counter which uses the track clock pulses and resets or starts over at the occurrence of the single origin pulse.   In this way the data is always timed according to the track layout.   Where the mechanical construction causes small alignment errors between tracks, the data is "strobed" or read out at a single favorable time for each bit.   Details of timing and strobbing are found in many books on drum memory design.   What is important here is that drum memory data must be handled cyclically and that external circuitry in conjunction with origin and clock tracks on the drum are used to operate the memory. Figure 11–26 shows the block diagram for cyclical readout.

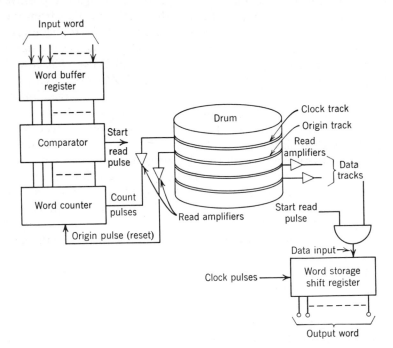

Figure 11–26.   Cyclical readout gating.

The word buffer register is the link between the computer and the memory, just as the A register was the connecting register for the arithmetic section. A word command tells the memory which word is desired. At the start of the data, as indicated by the origin track pulse, the counter is reset to zero and pulses from the drum clock track are counted. When the comparator "sees" the same number in the two registers, it puts out a start read pulse. This allows the data coming out of the read amplifiers to feed into a storage shift register. The clock pulses are used as shift pulses, since they are synchronized with the data. After the readout of ten pulses (word length for this case), the read operation is ended and the data is available for use in other computer circuits. Actually, the buffer register may have been used instead of another register, for the command word is not needed once read begins, and after shifting data into the buffer register it may be read in parallel (or serially) to another computer section.

11–4. Other Memory Devices

The two memory devices considered so far have erasable memory. That is, data can be erased and new data written in during operation. Some other memory devices do not have this desirable erasable feature. An optical memory is an example of a nonerasable memory. A drum made of optically clear material is coated with a photographic emulsion and exposed to a fixed code or data pattern. Once the data is imprinted on the drum it is permanent. Certain types of data are immediately useful with this type of memory. Tables of any kind that are referred to by the computer may be stored on such a memory. Being a drum memory, the access time is similarly restricted by mechanical speed considerations and access times of around 1 msec are good. Two main features of an optical memory are its large storage capacity and the fact that it costs less than the magnetic drum memory. The data is read by illuminating the track of data with a light source and using photo detectors to sense light. A ONE may be the absence of any coating on the optical drum so that light is received by the photo sensor, and a ZERO may be no light received because there is an opaque coating. Data is stored in tracks and read sequentially, as in the magnetic drum.

Timing tracks are printed on the drum surface for readout synchronization.

Ferrite sheet or thin-film memories operate basically like the core memory. Differences in construction allow higher operating speeds, less space, and lower cost. Because these are all good features, it is expected that this modified core memory device will grow in popularity. At present it is quite new and is used selectively. The memory is made either by threading thin copper wires on a form surface or, more recently, by depositing this conductor on a form surface. Construction is thus more compact than for individual core pieces, the smaller spacing allows operating at higher speeds, and the simplified technique of construction is far cheaper. Organization methods are exactly the same, and the memory is, of course, random access.

Another magnetic memory of recent consideration is the twistor memory. The twistor gets its name from the fact that it is constructed of a thin ribbon of magnetic wire wound around an insulated copper wire. The ribbon is very thin—about $\frac{1}{2}$ mil thick—and the wire is only a few thousandths of an inch thick. The winding of the ribbon on the wire is similar to the design on a barber pole. Another wire is wrapped circumferentially around a group of twistor sections. The coincidence of current pulses in the single wire and in the copper wire will magnetize a specific section of the ribbon. Using many of these single wires along the length of the twistor allows data to be stored along the length of the ribbon. Because there are a few other forms of twistor memories, the details will be left to outside literature. The twistor may be used for temporary storage in one form, or permanent in another. At present, twistor memory provides less storage capacity and less speed than core memory. Although any increase in the use of twistor devices is not immediately evident, time and research will decide its future applications.

A memory device which is the fastest available at present uses tunnel diodes as the storage element. The tunnel diode is a two-terminal semiconductor device which may be biased in a bistable state. A $V-I$ characteristic shown in Figure 11–27 has a load line superimposed with the two stable states indicated. The device may be operated ideally at kilomegacycle rates, so that memory access times of 1 nanosecond (10^{-9} second) are contemplated. It is the practical circuit connections, wiring stray capacitance, etc., which

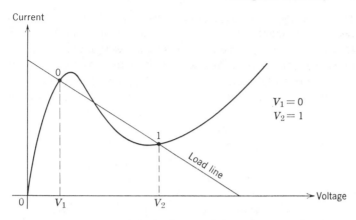

Figure 11–27.   Tunnel diode characteristic and memory function.

now limit the operating speed.   The tunnel diode memory has been used with experimental devices mainly because of its high cost and its low capacity (one bit per tunnel diode) and because there is need for continued research.   Time and research again will determine the extent to which this memory device is used.

Although many other devices exist and are also important, these mentioned give a good outline of the features to be found at present. Because no one type is adequate on all important accounts—size, cost, speed, operational simplicity, storage capacity, etc. the field is constantly being studied and changed.

Summary

A computer memory, as distinguished from input or output storage, must be small and relatively inexpensive, if possible, but most of all it must be very fast.   The magnetic core memory is now the most popular, and its applications continue to increase in number.   Core memories have become smaller and faster and are being used in larger and larger memory capacities.   Whereas 32,000 words of core storage was large a few years ago, capacities of hundreds of thousands are no longer rare.   Access times (time to read a word from the memory) are now in the tenths of microseconds for most new computers produced.

The core memory is organized as coincident-current random access. Coincident-current methods reduce the overall number of wires considerably. Random access indicates that calling for a word from one memory location takes as little time as from any other. Although the actual read operation with a core is destructive, use of a read/write cycle makes it possible to save the data stored when read. New data may, of course, be placed in a desired memory location during a write operation.

The magnetic drum memory was quickly replaced as an important computer memory unit not long after magnetic cores were developed. A magnetic drum memory is still used and is popular when speed is not essential and lower cost is desired.

An average access time of 1 msec is quite fast for a drum memory. However, the ability of a single head to handle many thousands of bits of data on a single track enables lower-cost storage, always an important factor.

A number of methods are used in recording data on a magnetic surface for drum, tape, or disk units. The return-to-zero (RZ) or return-to-bias method of recording is easy to read out, since a change occurs twice for every bit stored. Nonreturn-to-zero recording requires a little more care in reading at a proper time because there is no data change when consecutive bits are the same. It does allow twice the recording density so that the use of more complex circuitry is warranted. NRZI recording also achieves twice the recording density that RZ does. Phase recording is different in that the lowest data frequency is one-half the highest and allows using ac transformers and amplifiers for read/write operation.

The organization of a magnetic drum can be bit-serial, bit-parallel, etc. In all cases the drum contains a clock track for timing operations with the drum (and often other parts of the system) and an origin track with a single pulse indicating when to start counting so as to keep track of what data is at present coming through the read heads or when data should be fed through the write heads.

PROBLEMS

1. How many stages of storage are needed for the row address register (X) and for the column address register (Y) of a 4096-core plane.

2. How many stages of storage are needed for the row address register (X) and column address register (Y) and word register (Z) of a 10,240-core memory having a word length of twenty bits.

3. How many stages are needed for the X, Y, and Z registers (as in question 2) for a 20,480-core memory having ten bits per word.

4. (a) What is the average access time of a drum memory rotating at 18,000 revolutions per minute?

(b) What is the bit transfer rate (bits/second) if there are 1024 bits around a track of the drum.

(c) What is the time interval during which a single bit may be read.

5. A magnetic drum has sixteen tracks of 2048 bits per track.   If the drum is run at 12,000 revolutions per minute, what is its average access time.

6. (a) If the drum in question 5 is organized bit-serial, what is the data transfer rate (bits/second)?

(b) If the drum in question 5 is organized bit-parallel, what is the data transfer rate?

7. Show two ways the drum of question 5 may be organized for BCD characters.

8. Draw the flux waveform for return-to-zero recording of the following data: (a) 1 1 0 1 1 0 1 1 1 0 1 1 0, (b) 1 0 1 0 1 1 0 0 1 1 0 0 0.

9. (a) Draw the flux waveforms for nonreturn-to-zero recording for the data given in question 8.

(b) Repeat using NRZI recording.

10. Draw the flux waveforms for phase recording of the data of question 8.

1100

Input/output equipment

12-1. General Input/Output Techniques

Since most pieces of equipment used with computers are capable of providing data to the computer and also of reading it from the computer, input/output equipment will be considered one topic (see Figure 12–1). For the computer user the input/output pieces of equipment are the most important. They enable him to handle his data in the most efficient and expeditious manner. The computer proper is merely a high-speed calculator performing many solutions per second. It is the input/output equipment that is usually of most concern to the user. In the simplest terms, input equipment consists of pieces that provide binary or binary-coded data for use in the computer, and output equipment consists of those that accept binary (or binary-coded data) from the computer for outside handling or storage. The best-known units, such as punched card, magnetic tape, magnetic disk, paper tape, or high-speed printer, are used with general-purpose computers in varying types and combinations. Special-purpose computers use standard but less familiar equipment for analog-to-digital or digital-to-analog conversion operations. These will be discussed separately because they present different ideas and techniques.

Control of the input/output equipment may be in the central computer itself, in the specific piece of equipment, or in both. When only one or two units are operated, the central computer will probably control completely, providing signals that determine when to start feeding data, what data to use, and when to stop. Where larger numbers of units are controlled, the computer may send only a timing signal telling the specific outside unit to start, letting all other control be handled by the peripheral equipment. Since the input-output units are the slowest-operating of a computer system, the integration of many different pieces of equipment is necessary to provide the computer arithmetic unit with sufficient data to operate continuously. It is possible for one central computer unit to have a dozen magnetic tape and a few paper tape units providing input data to it while feeding data out to other magnetic tape and high-speed printer units. In fact, the problem of getting data fast enough and feeding it out to visual display equipment has required constant improvement in the fields of type printing, graphical presentation, visual oscilloscope, or cathode-ray display, etc., to provide the large amount of data processed to be presented in usable form for the operator.

Analog-to-digital (A/D), and digital-to-analog (D/A) equipment, on the other hand, generally provides data quickly enough to the computer but requires continued improvement in conversion accuracy. Direct current, alternating current, and rotation of mechanical shaft are examples of analog signals which must be converted into an equivalent digital form for use in the computer. For example, the dc voltage from 0 to $+10$ volts can be broken up into steps of 0.5 volt and represented for each 0.5-volt step by the binary numbers from 0 to 20. Two dc voltages can be added together in the computer by adding the binary numbers of these quantized voltages (remember that the computer proper can operate only with binary numbers) and the resultant number converted back to a voltage, if that is desired. Obviously, this procedure will not be necessary for such a simple operation. However, when many operations at high speed and high accuracy are desired, the computer becomes important. Specific conversions of current importance, such as dc voltage to digital (and digital to dc voltage) and shaft position A/D and D/A, are considered in some detail.

12–2. Punched Card

Punched card data processing provides a widely used method of feeding digital information to a computer. The card has a fixed layout and stores binary data in the form of punched-out holes or

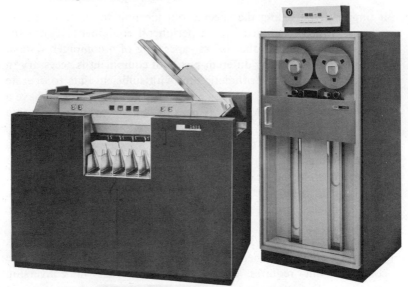

IBM 1402 Card Read Punch   IBM 2401 Magnetic Tape Unit

IBM 2201 Printer

Figure 12–1. Typical input/output units.

IBM 382 Paper Tape Reader   IBM 7550 Card Punch

IBM 1311 Disk Storage Drive

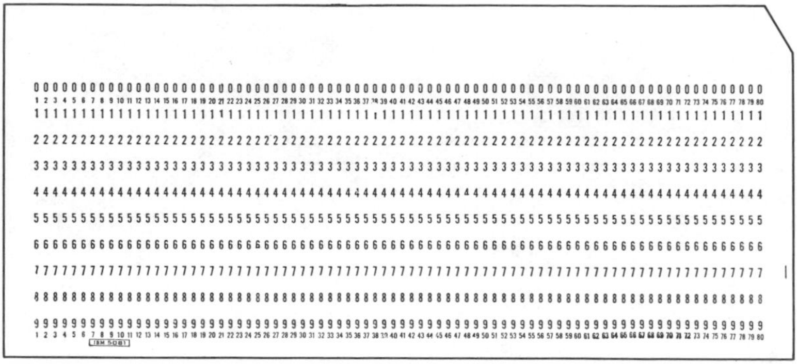

Figure 12–2.   Standard 80-column card.

none for 1 and 0, respectively. The data storage is, of course, permanent. However, for many operations this is a very desirable feature. A card can hold a small amount of data, usually on a specific item. Its direct relationship with one item (it could be an individual student in a school or a specific item of manufacture— such as a part for a car) is very useful when the ability to handle each card or each item separately is desirable, if not necessary. When items of data are stored on one card the cards can be separated by item using a card-sorting machine. For a set of cards representing each student in the school, the cards can be sorted by class section, degree program, or any other desirable breakdown for record purposes.

A card contains eighty columns and twelve rows (see Figure 12–2). Each column can be used to represent a character. The data is coded using a simple (not efficient) code so that the cards are easily read by an operator. Table 12–1 lists this code, and you will see that it can be applied and recognized quite easily and quickly. Refer to Table 12–1 and the card of Figure 12–3. The numbers are coded using the number of that row only. There are rows numbered 0 through 9 which then represent the decimal numbers 0 to 9 when a hole is punched there. Only one hole of twelve rows is punched for a number. To define a letter rows 12, 11, or 0 are punched out in addition to a numerical row (1–9). For example, a hole in row 12 and row 1 in the same column represents the letter A, row 11 and row 2 the latter K, and row 0 and row 9 the letter Z.

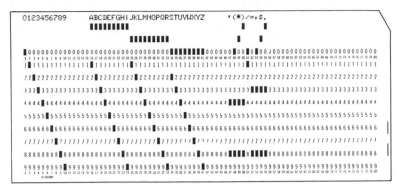

Figure 12–3. Punched card showing alphameric code.

Table 12–1. Punched Card Code

Numerical Zone (row) Only	Zone 12 Plus Numerical Row Below	Zone 11 Plus Numerical Row Below	Zone 0 Plus Numerical Row Below
0 = 0			
1 = 1	1 = A	1 = J	
2 = 2	2 = B	2 = K	2 = S
3 = 3	3 = C	3 = L	3 = T
4 = 4	4 = D	4 = M	4 = U
5 = 5	5 = E	5 = N	5 = V
6 = 6	6 = F	6 = O	6 = W
7 = 7	7 = G	7 = P	7 = X
8 = 8	8 = H	8 = Q	8 = Y
9 = 9	9 = I	9 = R	9 = Z

Punched cards are handled surprisingly fast. Reading rates of over 1000 cards per minute are currently available. Punching speeds are necessarily much slower. Punching rates vary from 120 cards per minute (2 per second) to 250 per minute. There are two popular types of card-reader units. The slower method uses wire brush sensors. If the brush goes over a hole it makes contact with a metal

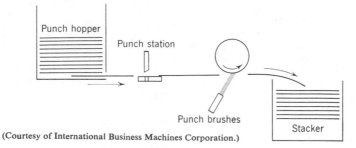

(Courtesy of International Business Machines Corporation.)

Figure 12–4. Wire brush punch and reader.

plate below and passes this on as a signal of a binary 1 being read. The brush-type readers only operate up to rates of about 200 cards per minute. The faster card-reading rates mentioned previously are obtained using optical readers. A light source on one side of the card will activate a photodetector (photodiode, photocell, etc.) if there is a hole to pass through (a binary 1) and does not activate the detector when the card face is present. Since the optical cell responds quickly, the reading rate can be increased considerably. Punching out the holes, however, requires taking material out of the card and is thus a slower operation. Figure 12–4 shows a wire brush punch and reader.

Control of the card reader or card punch is generally within the external unit; the computer only controls when to start reading in. The data stored on many cards might be used to fill up part of the core memory. Once filled, the computer operates at high speed from the internal memory. Punched cards may hold both program material and data for use in the computer. Recalling that the hardest part of the job may often be to provide data fast enough to keep the computer arithmetic section busy, you may find such combinations as punched cards feeding magnetic-tape units which are then used to fill up the core memory. Punched cards were necessary for easy handling of data on company products, magnetic tape for arranging the data in larger blocks of information (with faster read into the computer), and magnetic cores for handling smaller pieces of the large amount of data but handling it as fast as the computer can use it. Figure 12–5 shows a high-speed card reader and a high-speed card punch unit.

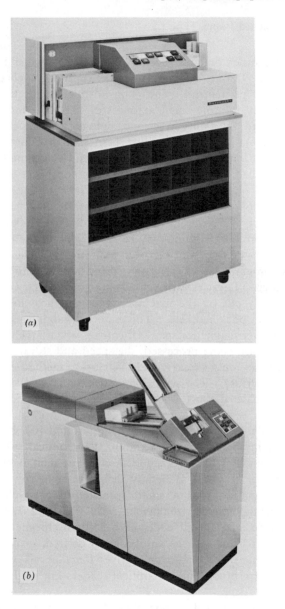

Figure 12–5. High-speed card reader and punch units: (*a*) card reader, (*b*) card punch.

12–3. Punched Paper Tape

Filling another practical need is the punched paper tape input/ output unit.   Data is again stored in the form of punched holes (or none) and is permanent.   The main advantages of punched tape are the ability to store small amounts of data in a more compact form than card, the ability to see what data is on the tape (not so with magnetic tape), the ease of handling these small amounts of information, and the low price of paper tape units.   A magnetic tape can only be handled in fairly large reels and is poorly set up to handle only a small amount of information.   When the individual piece requirement of punched cards is unnecessary, punched tape is a cheaper, more efficient method of handling the data.   As an example, a program routine may be stored on punched tape.   One program may be 5 feet of tape long, another 6 inches.   In either case each program can be separately stored and put into the machine when needed.   Large tape drive units are not necessary and the tape may be easily put on the machine, taken off, held in your hand, looked over, pocketed, etc.   This ease of handling is a distinct advantage over magnetic tape.   Of course, when large amounts of information are being processed, the speed and storage capacity of magnetic tapes are necessary, and this storage method does find the largest overall use.   The point here is that each of the three types considered have distinct operational advantages and find use in industry.

Tape readers (see Figure 12–6) operate around 100 characters per second for mechanical readers and 1000 for optical.   Tape punch units can punch as many as ten characters per inch at rates of fifty characters per second.   Generally there are eight rows of binary-coded information plus a small sprocket hole which serves to advance the tape through the machine (see Figure 12–7).   The eight rows provide an eight-bit code, each column storing a character. The tape can be as long as any program desired, or as short.   In reading the tape the reader unit drives the tape via the sprocket holes and wire brush pins, or optical readers are used (see Figure 12–7c).

The data is punched as one character per column.   Generally, three rows are on one side of the sprocket holes, and the rest are on the other.   These three are often the 1, 2, and 4-weighted positions as shown in Figure 12–7.   The next row (after the sprocket hole) is the eight-weighted position.   Since a five-position code can handle only 32 (2^5) characters, a special shift system is used to double the number of code characters possible.   One such shift system is that of preceding alphabetic characters with a code character indicating that all following characters are to be read as letters and a second code character which indicates that all following characters are to be read as figures or special characters.   No such problem exists with six-, seven-, or eight-channel codes since there are 64 (2^6) or more characters possible, and the number of numeric, alphabetic, and special characters usually found on a typewriter keyboard are less than 64.   Five-level (position) codes are popular in teletype equipment (although higher-level codes are readily used) for which the reduced number of bits per character transmitted is desired.

The check bit position contains a parity bit (usually odd parity, as discussed in Chapter 4) to provide a validity test when reading in data.   The sprocket holes on the tape serve two important purposes. First, it is used in the movement of the tape through the reader. The mechanical advance mechanism moves the tape a character at a time via the sprocket hole.   Second, the read pulse which tells the reader that the character is properly situated under the reading device (brush or photocell) is dependent on the sprocket hole.   Notice that the sprocket hole is smaller than the data holes and is located in the center of the data hole position.   Data is read only when a sprocket hole is in position under the read brush.   Since a signal pulse occurs during the time the hole is under the read brush, the sprocket pulse is a narrower pulse and is centered in the data pulse. The smaller sprocket hole aids reading accuracy and allows some margin of hole misalignment with proper operation still possible.

One popular use of paper tape in addition to computer use is in connection with a special electric typewriter.   To punch data onto a tape, the operator just types out the desired characters which are automatically punched out on a tape.   If this is a letter which is to be reproduced, for example, the tape can now be used to drive the typewriter automatically.   Since the tape may be used many times, the same message can be reproduced numerous times.

(a)

(Courtesy of International Business Machines Corporation.)

Figure 12–6.   Paper tape punch units: (a) Burroughs B341 paper tape punch, (b) IBM 962 paper tape punch.

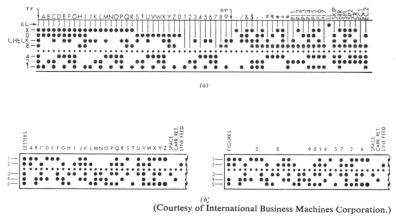

(Courtesy of International Business Machines Corporation.)

Figure 12–7a, b.   Paper tape showing (a) eight-channel code, (b) five-channel code.

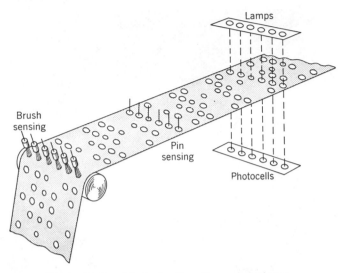

Figure 12–7c.   Methods of reading punched tape.

12–4. Magnetic Tape

Magnetic tape equipment (see Figure 12–8) provides one of the larger and most widely used data storage facilities.   As much as 20 million bits of information may be stored on a reel.   Although average access time (time from request of specific data until data is read) is in the order of seconds, mag tape (magnetic tape) is still one of the faster operating units.   The magnetic disk which operates in much shorter access time is considered separately in Section 12–5. The magnetic tape is of course a storage device, but because of its long access time it is not used directly with the arithmetic section. Improvements continue to increase the operating speed (reducing the access time), but the general access time is so long that its use remains outside that of a central computer memory.   Binary data is stored on magnetic tape as spots of opposite magnetic polarity. Seven rows (or tracks) of data are usual on $\frac{1}{2}$-inch-wide tape.   Total tape length may range from 50 to 2400 feet.   Data is stored in blocks, each block (group of words in prescribed order) being preceded by a label to identify the position on the tape.   Data is read out (or written in) sequentially and is erasable.   The ability to erase

Figure 12–8. Magnetic tape units: (a) General Electric, (b) Minneapolis-Honeywell, (c) Burroughs Corporation.

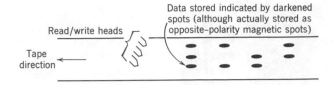

Figure 12–9. Magnetic tape data storage.

data and replace it with new data is a very important feature of magnetic tape. Bank records, as one example, can be continually updated when stored in this manner. Most other popular input/ output storage media are permanent and must be discarded when new data is accepted.

Figure 12–9 shows a magnetic tape section with read/write heads. It is similar to that used for home tape recording but has more tracks and stores the data in simple magnetized spots rather than complex wave patterns, as for music and voice. Figure 12–10 shows a piece of magnetic tape whose characters are stored as a seven-bit alphameric (alphabetic and numeric) code. Although the bits are written as magnetized spots of clockwise or counterclockwise polarity, they are shown here as the presence or absence of a magnetized spot for clarity. It should also be clear that although data may be erased, it is considered permanent in the sense that it can be retained indefinitely (with proper handling and storage of reel). Magnetic tape storage is nonvolatile in that the data will remain stored even if power to operate the unit is turned off.

The magnetic tape unit functions as both an input and output device. In the tape code shown (Figure 12–10) data is recorded in

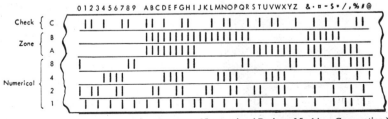

(Courtesy of International Business Machines Corporation.)
Figure 12–10.   Spots on magnetic tape showing alphameric code.

seven parallel channels or tracks, and each column (the width of the tape) contains a single character. The spacing between rows is fixed by the head spacing, and the spacing between characters is automatically established by the magnetic tape unit. Character density is around 200 to 600 characters per inch. The tape characters are stored with a check bit for even parity. In addition to this character parity check a track parity check may also be made on each record. At the time the data is recorded, the bits for each track are added and a check character is recorded at the end of the block. For each track with an odd bit count a check bit is recorded. Thus, when the record is read it should provide a satisfactory even parity check of each character and of the check word. Since all this data checking is being done by the magnetic tape unit, the computer need not be involved for the check character is not included as part of the record when it is passed on to the computer.

The magnetic tape drive mechanism (Figure 12–11) is far advanced of that used in a home recorder since high operating speed, fast start and stop, and greater reading and writing alignments are necessary. Drive motors are often kept running continuously, the capstan or pressure roller being controlled to move tape or not. This allows for faster response since the tape immediately takes off at high speed rather than being slowly accelerated as the motor speeds up. When the tape is to be moved, the drive capstan makes contact with the tape. When the tape is to be stopped, the drive capstan is removed and the stop capstan is immediately engaged to halt the tape fast. To allow for such high-speed start and stop operations without breaking the tape, a loop of tape may be held in a vacuum column, one for each reel. Since data may occur anywhere on the tape, the drive mechanism can backspace the tape or rewind it to the beginning of the reel. The reel is then driven until it reaches the desired place on the tape. On some tape drive units the tapes may even be read backward (opposite to the direction when data was written).

As the tape moves by the write head, pulses of flux magnetize spots on the surface of the tape. The seven heads of a character are operated simultaneously. Although the tape is moving by the head at speeds in the order of 100 inches per second or higher, the write time is so short that the tape appears to be virtually stationary. Two popular types of heads are the one-gap and two-gap heads. The one-gap head (Figure 12–12a) can be used for either read or

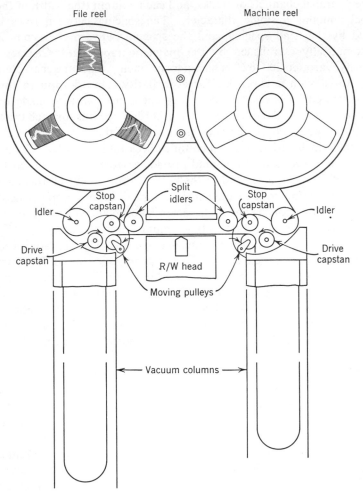

Figure 12–11.   Tape drive mechanism.

write but only one at any time.   The two-gap head (Figure 12–12*b*) can write a bit and read it back while the bit is still positioned under the head.   This is convenient for use with the tape-validity checking operations discussed.

The size of a record is generally not limited.   It may be only a few characters or a few thousand.   However, each record is preceded

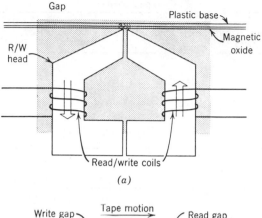

Gap

Plastic base

R/W head

Magnetic oxide

Read/write coils

(a)

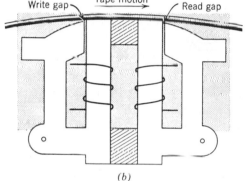

Write gap

Tape motion

Read gap

(b)

Figure 12-12. (a) One-gap read/write head, (b) two-gap read/write head.

by a gap (about $\frac{3}{4}$ inch) which allows for stopping and positioning of the tape before the desired data is read (see Figure 12-13).   During the write operation a fixed gap is left between or after every record recorded.   In this way every record is preceded and followed by an interrecord gap.   This blank section also allows for starting and stopping the tape between records.

As a summary, the magnetic tape can store from 200 to 600 characters per inch, or a few million characters on a 2400-foot reel of tape.   Storage is sequential, in blocks or records, and is erasable. It is cheap storage per bit but expensive for a few million characters. The magnetic tape unit has large storage capacity but long access time.

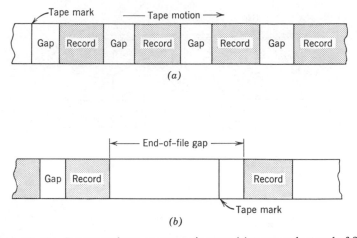

Figure 12–13.   Interrecord gap on magnetic tape: (*a*) tape mark at end of file, (*b*) end-of-file gap.

12–5. Magnetic Disk

Magnetic disk storage provides the largest data storage facility in a single unit of equipment (see Figure 12–14). A few million characters can be stored on a number of record or disk surfaces. The technique is similar to that used in recording for the phonograph, except that the recording is on a magnetic surface rather than cut grooves, and data is read back by a magnetic pickup mounted on a movable arm rather than by a needle.   A first apparent difference is that the data is generally contained on a number of disks and there are read heads for every disk.   Both upper and lower surfaces are available for read at all times (see Figure 12–15).

The data is stored in tracks (circumferentially on the disk) where each recording surface may contain typically 100 to 250 tracks. Disk diameters may vary from 1 to 5 feet.   The disk may be rotated at about 1500 revolutions per minute.   Considering the disk alone, the average access time would be about 50 msec.   However, there are many possible tracks and usually one head per surface.   Adding in the time needed to move the read arm to the desired track brings the overall average access time around 250 msec.   Though this may seem a long time compared to a magnetic drum, it is much shorter than the seconds to minutes with a magnetic tape.

Figure 12–14.   Magnetic disk drive unit, IBM 1301.

An NRZ recording method may be used to store data.   Access is considered random because you need only select the correct head and move it to the desired track.   You do not have to read all the data until that desired appears as with magnetic tape.   It should not, however, be compared to the random access speed of a magnetic core memory.   Data may be erased and storage is nonvolatile.   In fact, many disk drive units are set up so that a disk pack (containing a fixed number of record disks) may be easily removed and a new one replaced.

12–6.   High-Speed Printer

A high-speed printer providing typed data is one of the most popular permanent visual records used with computers (see Figure 12–16).   Whereas typewriters generate a character at a time, high-speed printers type a line at a time, thereby adding to its much higher

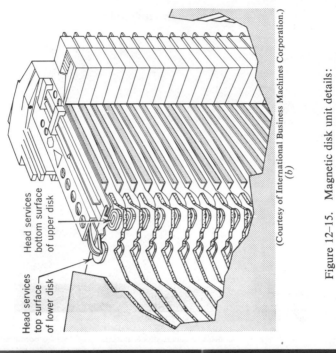

Head services
top surface
of lower disk

Head services
bottom surface
of upper disk

(Courtesy of International Business Machines Corporation.)
(b)

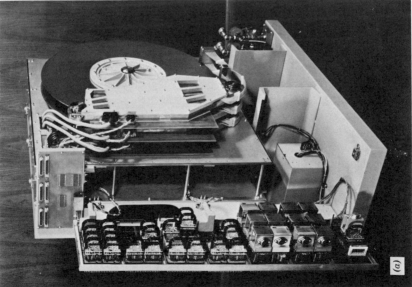

(a)

Figure 12–15.   Magnetic disk unit details:
(a) Burroughs Corporation, (b) IBM 1301 head arrangement.

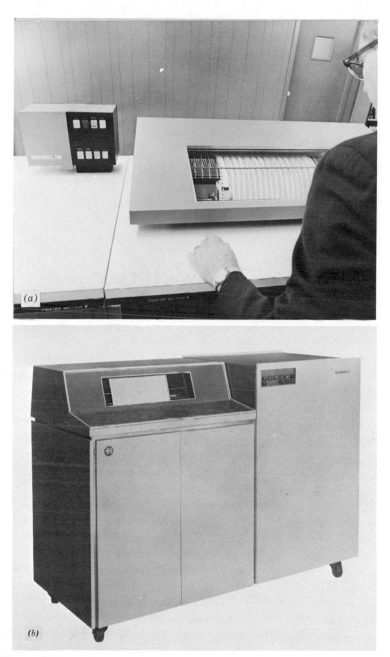

Figure 12–16. High-speed printer units: (*a*) Minneapolis-Honeywell, (*b*) Burroughs Corporation.

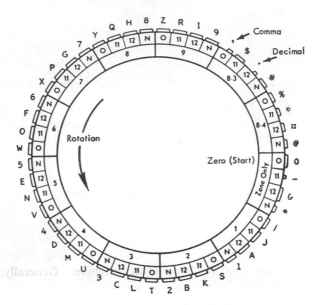

Figure 12–17.   Print wheel.

speed.   It also gains in speed of operation by sophisticated mechanical design.   Although there are both mechanical and electronic printers available, the former will be discussed in the most detail because it is at present the more popular type.

One form of printer has separate print wheels or print bars. There are as many print wheels as desired characters per line.   Each print wheel contains a complete set of alphanumeric characters and special characters (see Figure 12–17).   For the printing of each line, each wheel representing a character of the line must be rotated to the desired character.   When all print wheels are in position, mechanically driven hammers (one for each character) are activated and strike the ribbon, thereby printing all characters of the line at once. Since some wheels will rotate less than others for each line of print, the operation of the print wheels is a start-stop motion.   After the line has been printed the wheels again start spinning until they are each in the selected position.   For each line of print the computer feeds in new data to the printer unit.   Since the time to print a line is so slow compared to the computer data transfer rate, the line of information can be transferred either serially or in parallel, depending on how the computer is operated. After each line of print the paper and ribbon are moved slightly, the print wheels rotate to new positions, and the hammers, having moved off, strike again for the next line of print. A printing rate of 150 lines per minute is typical for such a printer unit.

Another form of a printer has a rotating drum with each character on a separate axial line. A drum may contain as many as 120 characters per line (see Figure 12–18). Commands for all 120 characters of a line are fed to the printer at one time. As each line of the drum passes by the fixed hammers, the individual hammers strike, thereby printing similar characters selectively over the entire line at one time. Within one revolution of drum all characters of a single line are printed. The paper, guided by pin feeds on each side, is provided in a continuous stack. It is perforated at regular intervals so that it may be taken off after a desired recording is complete, without stopping the operation of the machine. Generally, the

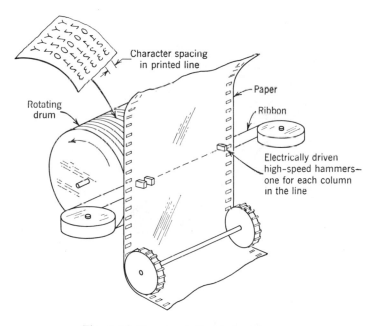

Figure 12–18.   A rotating-drum printer.

machine is designed to stop when no more paper is available. The machine also indicates this to the computer so that no new information is fed out at this time. Since the operation is continuous (the drum is always rotating), this type of printer operates much faster than the start-stop operation of the individual wheel printer. Printers of the drum type operate at speeds of a few hundred lines per minute to 1000 lines per minute. They can provide 64 different characters for up to 120 characters per line.

A third mechanical printer uses a continuously rotating character belt (Figure 12–19). The individual character hammers strike as the desired character on the belt passes underneath the hammer head. The belt may contain a number of sets of characters to cut down the time until the desired character lines up under a hammer. Printers now available can operate at speeds over 1200 lines per minute (20 lines per second). Synchronizing the operation is important because there is not a single hammer stroke and paper feed operation.

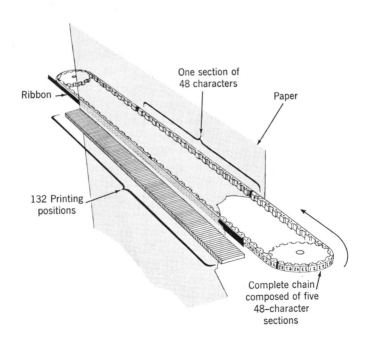

Ribbon

One section of
48 characters

Paper

132 Printing
positions

Complete chain
composed of five
48-character
sections

Figure 12–19.   A belt printer.

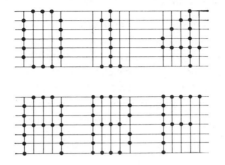

Figure 12–20.   Matrix character formation.

Each hammer strikes as the correct character passes under the head. After all hammers have struck once, the paper feed advances one line and the operation repeats. Although these speeds are seemingly very high (and they are), data is being generated hundreds of times faster in the computer.

Electrostatic printers do not require physical contact between paper and hammer surface. Instead, special paper exposed to an electrical discharge from a selected pattern creates the desired character. By using a grid matrix (as in electroluminescent displays), specific grid points are selected for a particular character and are energized to "print" the character (Figure 12–20).

Depending on the particular computer and the extent of the programs being run, one or more printers will be used, and these will be fed directly from the computer memory or via some other input/output unit—such as a magnetic tape unit. In smaller computers the unit is operated directly from the computer memory and no other operation can be done at this time. In larger-size computers the desire is to keep the computer continuously operating and data is fed only to magnetic tape, magnetic disk pack, or magnetic drum. From these higher-speed input/output units the data is fed out to punched card, punched tape, or in this case high-speed printers. Control of the printout is provided by the computer, but usually in the form of a few commands, after which the operation is taken over by the input/output unit and the computer is "free" to continue processing the program.

12–7. Analog-to-Digital (A/D) Conversion

Direct-current voltage can be converted into an equivalent digital count in a number of ways. Basically, these methods involve developing a changing voltage to be compared to the unknown dc voltage. As the known voltage changes, the digital count is advanced until a dc voltage comparator shows that the voltages are the same. This occurrence causes the count to be stopped so that the digital number is proportional to the unknown voltage. A simple representation of this operation is shown in Figure 12–21.

Two important factors of conversion are the accuracy and conversion time. The accuracy is determined primarily by that of the comparator circuit. Conversion time depends on the clock rate used and the maximum number of counts (or the number of counter stages). For example, at a 1.024-Mcps clock rate using ten stages the conversion time would be $1/1.024$ μsec × 1024 counts, or 1000 μsec. Since it takes 1000 μsec, or 1 msec, to do a conversion, there could be as many as 1000 conversions each second. At lower clock rates or for larger counts the number of conversions per second will be less. Another interesting factor is the resolution of the conversion. Whereas accuracy tells you how close you are to what the real voltage is, resolution tells you how closely you can discern between the two voltages. An accuracy of $+1\%$ means that 100 volts might really be 99 volts to 101 volts and you cannot distinguish any finer. Resolution of 100 mv means that you can distinguish between voltages more than 0.1 volt apart. A voltage

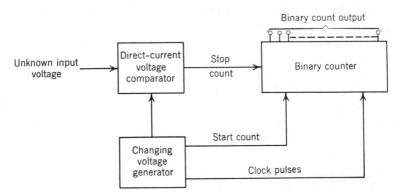

Figure 12–21.   Conversion from direct-current voltage to binary count.

of 10.6 volts and 10.65 volts (50 mv apart) would appear the same, since they differ by less than the resolution of the comparator. It is often not clear that an operation may be done with a greater resolution than the accuracy obtainable. You may distinguish between 10.1 and 10.2 volts, but the real voltage may have been 10.5 volts. The accuracy here was poorer than the resolution. It would seem to make sense to have the resolution only as good as the accuracy makes meaningful. On the other hand, a high accuracy and low resolution is also poor, since you may be very close to the real voltage but not able to discriminate in your operation between small differences. A resolution of 1 volt and accuracy of 1% with a 10-volt signal would mean that you cannot distinguish between 9.2 and 9.8, for example, whereas you are accurate to 0.1 volt. Bear in mind this distinction between accuracy and resolution in other areas of work as well, for it sometimes tends to be confusing.

The clock rate and voltage change have to be synchronized for the conversion. For example, a resolution of 10 mv would require for each 10 mv of voltage change a counter advance of one step. This would allow obtaining a different binary count for each 10-mv voltage difference. One popular method uses a "ladder network" to provide the changing dc voltage in step with the clock count change. The ladder is a voltage decoding network driven by a binary counter so that each step of the counter is decoded into a different voltage. Starting from 0 volts, the dc voltage increases in a stepwise manner as the count increases. Since the clock drives the counter, each step results in the count and voltage changing by one increment. A block diagram of the circuit used to implement this operation is shown in Figure 12–22.

The clock generator could be an astable multivibrator operating at a desired frequency. Until the dc voltage comparator indicates that the two voltages are the same (ladder network output voltage and unknown input voltage), the clock is qualified to advance the counter. The reference voltage is used to specify the maximum conversion voltage. As the counter advances, an increasing fraction of the reference voltage appears at the output of the ladder network. When the counter is at full count (all ONE's), the output voltage is the reference voltage value. The number of counter stages determines the resolution of conversion. For a ten-stage counter you can discern one part of 1024, or roughly a part in 1000 (0.1%). With

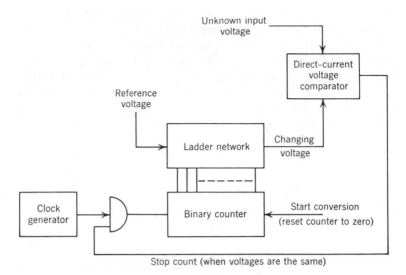

Figure 12–22.   Direct-current voltage conversion using ladder network.

a reference voltage of 10 volts this means a resolution of 1/1000 (10 volts), or 10 mv.   Higher resolution may be obtained using more stages.   In principle, the resolution can be made as small as desired by using more and more counter stages.   However, the conversion accuracy (dependent mainly on comparator) or the conversion time (dependent also on clock rate) are not taken into account.   Since the accuracy also depends on the changing voltage, the ladder network affects the accuracy as well.

Example 12–1.   What resolution (in %) is obtained using an eight-stage counter and ladder network?

Solution: For eight stages $2^8 = 256$.   One part in 256 is approximately $1/250 \times 100\%$ or 0.4%.

Example 12–2.   What resolution (in volts) is obtained using an eight-stage counter and ladder network reference voltage of 10 volts?

      Solution: Example 12–1 gave the resolution as 0.4% (approximately).

$$\text{Resolution} = 0.4\% \ (10 \text{ volts})$$

$$= \frac{0.4}{100} \ (10) = 0.04 \text{ volt}$$

$$= 40 \text{ mv}$$

Example 12–3.   For a clock rate of 10 kcps, what is the maximum conversion time using an eight-stage counter?

Solution: Since eight stages require 2^8, or 256, counts in total, and a 10-kcps clock takes $1/(10 \times 10^3) = 100$ μsec per count, the total time elapsed is 100 μsec × 256, or 25,600 μsec.   This is 25.6 msec per conversion (maximum).

Example 12–4.   How many conversions are possible using an eight-stage counter driven at 10-kcps clock rate.

Solution: At 25.6 msec per conversion, there could be about $1/(25 \times 10^{-3})$, or $1000/25 = 40$ conversions per second.

Problem 12–1.   What is the resolution (%) where the following number of counter stages are used.

(a) 12   (b) 6   (c) 9   (d) 11

Problem 12–2.   For each part of Problem 12–1 calculate the resolution (in volts) for each of the following reference voltages.

(a) 10 volts   (b) 1.6 volts   (c) 220 mv

Problem 12–3.   For each part of Problem 12–1 calculate the conversion time and solutions per second for each of the following clock rates.

(a) 150 kcps   (b) 820 kcps   (c) 1.6 Mcps

Problem 12–4.   How many counter stages are needed to get a resolution of about 10 mv using a reference voltage of 41 volts?   What clock rate is needed to obtain around 250 solutions per second?

Problem 12–5.   With a clock rate of 100 kcps and resolution of about 0.2%, how many conversions per second are possible?

The ladder network is made of resistors of two different values wired as shown in Figure 12–23.   The values R and $2R$ might be 1 kohm and 2 kohm, for example.   As indicated, the TRUE output

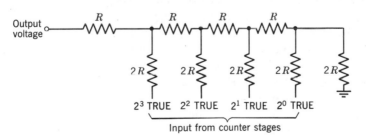

Figure 12–23.   Ladder network.

of each counter stage is connected to a specific resistor in the net-work. The voltage at these input points could be $+10$ volts and 0 volts (for 1 and 0), and the output voltage depends on where these are applied to the ladder circuit. Let us consider some simple cases first to see how the ladder output voltage is obtained.

For all inputs at 0 volts (no input voltage) the output is 0 volts. A count of 0 0 0 0 has an output voltage of 0 volts. Consider $+16$ volts as the input voltage representing logical ONE for ease of numerical designation. When the input of the 2^3 stage *only* is $+16$ volts, let us see what the output voltage is. With all inputs at 0 volts except the 2^3 which is at $+16$ volts, the circuit for this specific input combination is shown in Figure 12–24.

Working from right side over, the $2R$ parallel with $2R$ is the same as an R resistor (see Figure 12–25). This R is in series with another R resistor and can be combined into a single $2R$ resistor (see Figure 12–26).

Again there are two $2R$ resistors in parallel, giving a single equiva-lent R resistor. Adding this R to the series R resistor connected to it gives $2R$ again looking to the right from point 3. Repeating, we find that there is also $2R$ looking to the right from point 4 (not con-sidering the initial resistor connected vertically at point 4). This reduced circuit is shown in Figure 12–27. As a general rule it can be stated that looking to the right of a node such as 1, 2, 3, 4, the resistance seen is always $2R$.

Calculating the voltage at node 4 we find that it is the resultant of 16 volts through a voltage divider $2R$ and $2R$ or $E_{\text{out}} = 8$ volts. When the count is 8 for a maximum count of $16(2^4)$, the voltage is $\frac{8}{16}$, or half the full-scale value. One-half of 16 volts is 8 volts, as obtained. Let us repeat for an input count of 0 1 0 0. The network for this specific input is shown in Figure 12–28. Since the resistance seen looking to the right is always $2R$, the circuit can be reduced to that of Figure 12–29.

Calculating the voltage at node 3 using Thevenin's theorem gives $+8$ volts in series with R as in Figure 12–29b. Figure 12–29c shows that this can be further simplified adding the two series resistors. The voltage at node 4 can be calculated to be $+4$ volts using the voltage divider rule. The resultant output voltage is then 4 volts so that a count of 0 1 0 0 or 4 out of 16 possible counts $[\frac{4}{16} = \frac{1}{4}]$ gives one-fourth the output voltage $[\frac{1}{4}(16 \text{ volts}) = 4 \text{ volts}]$. So far the

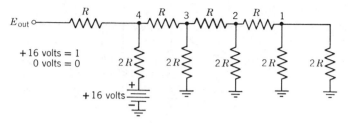

Figure 12–24.   Ladder network for 1000 input.

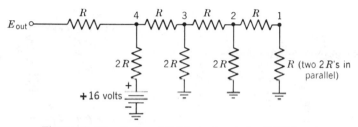

Figure 12-25.   Reduced ladder network for 1000 input.

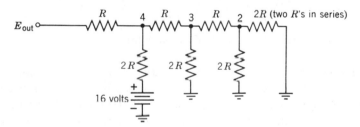

Figure 12–26.   Reduced network for 1000 input.

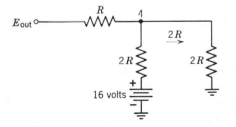

Figure 12–27.   Reduced network for 1000 input.

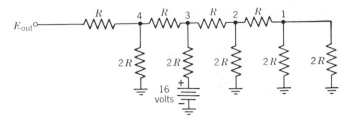

Figure 12–28.   Ladder network for 0 1 0 0 input.

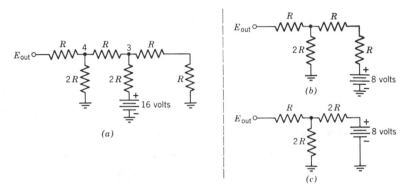

Figure 12–29.   Reduced network for 0 1 0 0 input.

output voltage developed by the network was the same proportion of the full voltage as the binary count of the full count.   Further consideration would show that a count of 0 0 1 0 would result in 2 volts output and a count of 0 0 0 1 in an output voltage of 1 volt. Since the rule of superposition allows us to calculate the voltage produced by more than one source in a network (more than one 1 in this case), we can find the output voltage for all sixteen combinations of input.   These are listed in Table 12–2 for input count and output voltage using a four-stage counter and $+16$ volts as logical 1 and 0 volts as logical 0.

Looking at the circuit more generally, we see the input voltage furthest from the output has the weight of 2^0/total count.   This continues in steps of 2 until the closest to the output has the weight of $\frac{1}{2}$.   For example, using ten stages, the lowest-value stage is $2^0/2^{10}$, or 1/1024.   The largest is $2^9/2^{10}$, or 512/1024 = $\frac{1}{2}$.

Table 12–2.   *Count versus Voltage Output for Four-Stage Ladder Network*

Input Count	Output Voltage (volts)
0000	0
0001	1
0010	2
0011	3
0100	4
0101	5
0110	6
0111	7
1000	8
1001	9
1010	10
1011	11
1100	12
1101	13
1110	14
1111	15

With logical 1 defined as 10.24 volts, the output voltage for 0 0 0 0 0 0 0 0 0 1 would be $1/1024(10.24) = 10$mv, for 1 0 0 0 0 0 0 0 0 0 $- 512/1024(10.24) = 5.12$ volts and for 1 0 0 0 0 0 0 0 0 1, $5.120 + 0.010$ or 5.13 volts.

Example 12–5.   What is the output voltage of a five-stage ladder network using $+6.4$ volts $= 1$ and 0 volts $- 0$ for the following binary counts.

(a) 1 0 0 0 0   (b) 0 0 0 0 1   (c) 0 1 0 0 0
(d) 0 1 1 0 1   (e) 1 0 0 1 0

Solution: (a) $2^5 = 32$; 1 0 0 0 0 is 16; thus, 1 0 0 0 0 gives $\frac{16}{32}$ (6.4 volts) or 3.2 volts.

(b) 0 0 0 0 1 $= 1$, so that $\frac{1}{32}$ (6.4) $= 0.2$ volt.

(c) 0 1 0 0 0 $= 8$ and $\frac{8}{32}$ is $\frac{1}{4}$ (6.4 volts) $= 1.6$ volts.

(d) Adding, $(\frac{0}{32} + \frac{8}{32} + \frac{4}{32} + \frac{0}{32} + \frac{1}{32}) \times 6.4$ volts gives $\frac{13}{32}$ (6.4 volts) $= 2.6$ volts.

(e) 1 0 0 1 0 gives $(\frac{16}{32} + \frac{0}{32} + \frac{0}{32} + \frac{2}{32} + \frac{0}{32})$ (6.4 volts) or $\frac{18}{32}$ (6.4 volts) $= 3.6$ volts.

Example 12–6. What is the output voltage using an eight-stage ladder network for the following counts. Use a reference voltage of 51.2 volts.

(a) 1 0 1 1 0 1 0 0   (b) 1 0 0 1 1 1 0 1   (c) 0 0 0 1 1 1 0 0

Solution:

(a) $E_{\text{out}} = \dfrac{2^7 + 2^5 + 2^4 + 2^2}{2^8}$ (51.2 volts)

$= \dfrac{128 + 32 + 16 + 4}{256}$ (51.2) volts

$= \dfrac{180}{256}$ (51.2) volts

$= 180 \, (0.2) = 36$ volts

(b) $E_{\text{out}} = \dfrac{2^7 + 2^4 + 2^3 + 2^2 + 2^0}{2^8}$ (51.2 volts)

$= \dfrac{128 + 16 + 8 + 4 + 1}{256}$ (51.2) volts

$= 157 \, (0.2) = 31.4$

(c) $E_{\text{out}} = \dfrac{2^4 + 2^3 + 2^2}{2^8}$ (51.2) $= \dfrac{16 + 8 + 4}{256}$ (51.2)

$= 28 \, (0.2)$ volts

$= 5.6$ volts

Problem 12–6. Calculate the output voltage of a six-stage ladder network with a reference voltage of 12.8 volts for the following binary numbers?

(a) 1 0 1 0 1 0   (b) 1 1 1 1 1 1   (c) 0 1 0 1 0 1
(d) 1 0 1 1 0 1   (e) 1 0 0 0 0 1

Problem 12–7. What output voltage is obtained for the conditions shown in the given ladder network (Figure 12–30)?

A drawing of the ladder network output voltage and the clock signal of the counter indicates the stepwise increase of the voltage (see Figure 12–31). The output voltage is often called a staircase waveform for obvious reasons.

Figure 12–32 shows that when the ladder staircase voltage

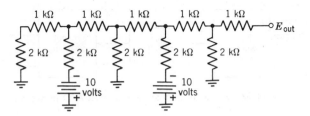

Figure 12–30.   Ladder network of Problem 12-7.

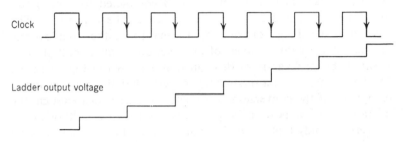

Figure 12 31.   Ladder output voltage (staircase waveform) and counter clock signal.

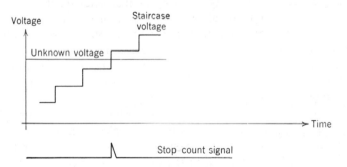

Figure 12–32.   Voltage comparison and stop-count signal.

becomes greater than the unknown voltage, a stop count signal is produced by the comparator to end counting.   The count now in the counter register is the digital equivalent of the unknown voltage. When the counter is reset to zero for a new conversion, the staircase voltage returns to zero volts and will cross the unknown voltage at a different time if the unknown voltage has changed.   Quite often a

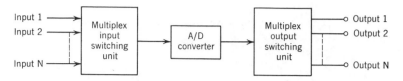

Figure 12–33.   Multiplex switching with A/D converter.

single A/D converter unit is used to handle a number of different analog inputs.   Then the conversion is completed for one input, the circuit reset, and a new input applied to the converter.   The method of switching from one input signal to another to allow one unit to handle many channels of information is called multiplexing. A simple block diagram of this function is shown in Figure 12–33. The figure shows that a single A/D converter handles many channels of signal.   If the conversion and multiplex time is fast enough, the operation may appear to be on a real time basis.   Although the converter is only looking at the signal of a particular channel for a short amount of time and then working on the other channel information, it is still getting back to the one channel often enough per second to appear as if it is always looking at that one signal.   The converter will appear to be always looking at one signal if the signal changes slowly compared to the rate of sampling (discrete interval operation on channel).   For example, a converter capable of 1000 conversions per second operating with ten channels can appear at each channel 100 times per second.   If the signal is changing at a slow rate of 2 cps, the amount of change in 1/100 of a second is so small as to be negligible and the converter appears to always be looking at the signal.   The study of sampled data systems is too complex to go into here, but basically it considers the operation of sampling varying signals, as in the example just given, and the relation of the sampled output signal in the system used.   Multiplexing itself is the method of switching many inputs into one channel, and the multiplexer is the sampler unit.   Since a computer can operate very quickly, this ability to sample many channels with one computer makes it a more useful device in a control setting.   One computer per channel would be uneconomical, but one computer for a whole aircraft system or spacecraft system operating many channels becomes a practical reality.

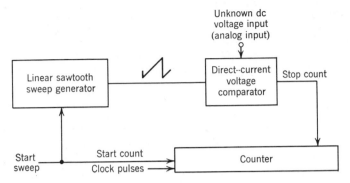

Figure 12-34.   Sawtooth sweep A/D conversion method.

Another technique of dc voltage to digital number conversion uses a constant varying voltage sweep to compare against the unknown voltage.   Figure 12-34 shows a block diagram of this circuit. A linear sawtooth sweep is a constantly increasing dc voltage.   When this voltage becomes equal to or slightly larger than the unknown dc voltage, a stop count signal is produced by the dc voltage comparator.   Start of a count and sweep start are synchronized to begin together.   An important feature (and a difficult one to implement) is that the full sweep interval and clock rate be properly adjusted so that a full count is obtained in that time.   The developed count is then available as the digital equivalent of the analog input voltage. Figure 12 35 shows a few cycles of sawtooth signal superimposed on an unknown dc voltage and the resulting count time interval.

Another popular conversion develops a digital count equivalent to a shaft rotational position.   Consider a single-turn potentiometer whose position can be adjusted 360°.   If the amount of rotation is taken as a variable signal, the computer needs the digital equivalent of the amount of rotation or the exact rotational position.   On an airplane this might represent the degrees of wing flap rotation, the amount a shaft was rotated to open a control valve, etc.   The computer needs this information in its calculations but needs it as a digital number.   Where space and design allow its use, an optical encoder is often chosen.   The encoder is an optical disk with clear areas and darkened areas and is coded so that each fixed fraction of a degree another combination is decoded.   Figure 12-36 shows a three-bit encoder using binary code.   By using a photocell to detect the

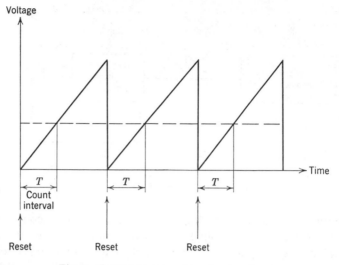

Figure 12–35.   Input and sawtooth voltages.

presence or absence of light, the eight different sectors around the disk can be distinguished.   By using three bits the 360° circumference can be divided into eight parts, so that the nearest 360°/8, or 45°, section can be known.   Usually an optical disk containing 10 to 15 bits is employed, allowing resolution as high as $360°/2^{15}$ or $360°/32,768 \cong 1$ minute of arc.   This high degree of resolution

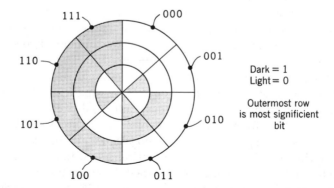

Figure 12–36.   Three-bit optical disk.

requires precise manufacture of the optical disk and a high degree of mechanical precision.

Example 12–7.   What degree of resolution is obtained using a ten-bit optical encoder disk?

Solution: Ten bits allow $360°/2^{10}$ resolution $= 360°/1024 = 0.36°$ or about $1/3°$.

Problem 12–8.   What resolution (in degrees) is obtained using a twelve-bit optical encoder disk?

Problem 12–9.   What minimum size (number of bits) optical encoder disk is needed to obtain a resolution of better than $1°$.

A major practical problem encountered using an optical disk is that of ambiguity or overlap in reading a code position. For example, 0 0 0 is next to 0 0 1 using the binary code disk. If mechanical tolerance is poor or there is some misalignment, the reading photocells may pick up the bits from both sectors, i.e., 2^0 bit from the 0 0 0 sector and 2^1 and 2^2 bits from the 0 0 1 sector. This does not seem such a problem for a three-bit code, but where the disk is made for sixteen-bit resolution using as small a disk as possible, the mechanical tolerances (for less than 1-minute resolution) become critical. The overlap is a problem when the code word from one sector to an adjacent sector changes by more than one bit. Going from 1 1 1 to 0 0 0 might give the following erroneous words if a single bit is off. Thus, reading the 2^0 and 2^1 from 1 1 1 and 2^2 from 0 0 0 would give 0 1 1 as the position, which is the position about halfway around the disk. An error of one bit may indicate a position on the other side of the disk (180° away). In many uses the reading of a position 180° away would cause havoc. One way of correcting this problem is to choose a code that changes by *only* one bit from one sector to the next. There are many different codes of this type for a set-size disk. Of these many, one particular code is used almost exclusively. For reading purposes the one-bit change code is desirable. For arithmetic purposes, however, the binary code is still the best. Remember that in the binary code more than one bit changes going from one word to the next so it is not the most desirable code to use on the disk. This means that a conversion from the disk code to the binary code would be necessary, and the particular disk code used is the one of the one-bit change codes that is most easily converted into binary. This particular disk code is called Gray code, and the required conversion is Gray code to binary code.   Recalling that the overall operation is conversion of mechanical rotational position into a digital number, the Gray-to-binary conversion is the main part of this A/D conversion.   A description of Gray-to-binary conversion follows.

The Gray code is a cyclic code having only one bit change at a time.   Cyclic codes are those in which the code words proceed in a set order, and after all possible code words have been used, the next code word is the one used first.   In this way the code form can cycle through all words back to the first, completing a cycle.   Although all one-bit change codes are not cyclic, the Gray code is.   As an example, the Gray and binary code words for decimal 0–15 are given in Table 12–3.

Table 12–3.   Gray and Binary Code for Decimal 0–15

Decimal	Gray Code	Binary Code
0	0000	0000
1	0001	0001
2	0011	0010
3	0010	0011
4	0110	0100
5	0111	0101
6	0101	0110
7	0100	0111
8	1100	1000
9	1101	1001
10	1111	1010
11	1110	1011
12	1010	1100
13	1011	1101
14	1001	1110
15	1000	1111

Look through the table to see that the Gray code only changes by one bit at a time whereas the binary code may change by all four bits (as from 7 to 8).

A description of how to convert Gray code to binary code and vice versa is given in Chapter 4, which should now be reread.   Here

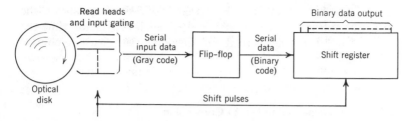

Figure 12–37.   Gray-to-binary code converter.

we shall discuss the circuit implementation.   As mentioned earlier, the Gray code is the most desirable because of the ease of implementing the conversion.   Actually, all that is needed is a single flip-flop.   However, a shift register is used to handle the data (Figure 12–37).

Data in the form of light and dark areas on the disk are read by picking up the illumination from a source light with the photocells or read heads.   When the light passes through a clear area it excites the reader head, and when it hits a dark area no light gets through. The read pulses are developed from a ring counter so that each bit of word is read into the flip-flop serially, most significant bit first. The serial Gray data is fed into the trigger or complementing input of the flip-flop and only complements the flip-flop state on a set direction change, e.g., when the pulse goes from high to lower voltage with *NPN* circuitry.   Considering positive logic for the discussion, a change from 1 to 0 would cause the flip-flop to change. If the input then stays at 0 or if it goes to 1 and stays, the output remains the same.   In effect, it does precisely what is required to change the Gray code data into binary code data, and on each shift pulse (or read pulse) the serial binary data out of the flip-flop is read into the shift register.   After the proper number of read steps (and shift steps) the number in the shift register is the binary code word indicating the position of the disk (or rotational position of the shaft). If the shift register is considered a buffer register or part of the conversion equipment, the circuit of Figure 12–37 comprises the entire A/D converter (including the logic gating needed to generate the read pulses).   When many optical encoding disks are used, the same converter circuit can handle all inputs if the data is multiplexed. After converting the input from one disk, the multiplexer can switch the read pulses to another disk so that conversion is done on the word read out of this second disk.   After each conversion time the word in the shift register is read into the computer for use in control or calculation.

12–8.   Digital-to-Analog (D/A) Conversion

After a computer has processed its data, which is in digital form, it must use it in the outside system being handled.   In general-purpose machines this may be typed data or data stored on punched card, punched tape, or magnetic tape.   In the special-purpose machine it is often necessary to use the digital answer to control or move a part of the external system.   To obtain such signal form requires converting the digital data into analog form using a D/A converter. Going back to the first type of analog signal discussed, the dc voltage, we find the conversion must take a digital number or word and develop an equivalent dc voltage.   Not surprisingly, the method uses much the same circuitry and technique as for the A/D conversion.   Often the same units can be used.   Figure 12–38 shows the simplified circuitry needed to accomplish the D/A conversion.

The circuitry is actually the simpler part of the A/D circuits. When developed by the computer, the digital number is fed into the digital buffer register which feeds the ladder network.   For the given number the ladder network, as described in the A/D section, provides an output dc voltage equivalent to the digital number. Data can also be multiplexed to handle many channels with a single

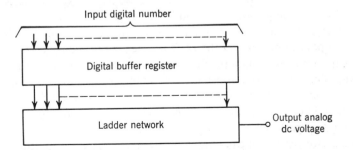

Figure 12–38.   Direct-current voltage, digital-to-analog converter.

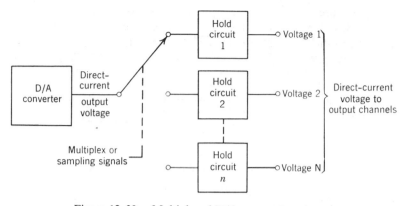

Figure 12–39.   Multiplexed D/A output dc voltage.

converter unit.   An added circuit is needed with the output to maintain the dc voltage after the ladder input is removed.   The circuit is descriptively called a "hold circuit" and may be simply described as a large capacitor.   If the developed ladder voltage is used to charge up a large capacitor, the voltage is held after the signal is removed.   Using a capacitor for each channel, we find the ladder output can be employed to develop the many different voltages which are then held for a time period by the capacitor.   As long as the voltage for that channel is developed enough times per second (conversions per second), it will appear as a steady dc voltage to the output.   Figure 12–39 shows the multiplexing and hold circuitry.

To drive an optical encoder to a specific digital position requires more circuitry.   First of all, a drive unit (motor) is needed to move the disk shaft around.   Second, a comparison must be made to determine when the disk has reached the desired position.   Figure 12–40 shows a typical circuit used for D/A conversion for shaft positioning.   The digital number is converted to pulses used to drive a stepper motor.   For each pulse the motor moves one position of the disk.   By counting down the given digital number, the disk is moved by the desired number of steps.   To know where the disk is, a Gray-to-binary conversion is necessary.   When the binary position is available, it is compared to the desired binary position (desired by the computer), and the difference is used for count down to drive the stepper motor connected to the disk shaft.

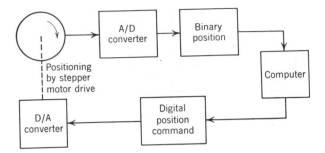

Figure 12–40.   D/A conversion and positioning of shaft encoder.

Summary

Input/output equipment plays an important role in the effectiveness of a computer system, for it provides the capacity to handle large amounts of data for a large variety of problems.   Each type of unit has advantages and disadvantages so that no one type predominates.   Punched card is widely used for input.   Handling pieces of information about an item on a card is convenient and the most practical method at present.   If the card represents a student in a school, the addition of a few more students will require the preparation of only a few separate cards.   Putting a computer program first on cards and adding only a few cards or changing others to rework the program have the same advantage.   Punched tape, on the other hand, is more troublesome to update or change, for a new tape must be run off.   Some advantages of punched tape are low cost and convenience in handling the various lengths of tape.

Magnetic tape and magnetic disk are proving very popular for large data storage.   Both allow large programs or amounts of data to be stored and quickly retrieved by the computer.   Installations such as banks and insurance companies store all customer accounts on these magnetic units.   Although the data is originally put on cards, it is placed on tape or disk before being used by the computer, and the results of computer operations are put back on tape or disk.

Data output may be on punched card, paper tape, magnetic tape, or disk.   Where printed output is desired high-speed printers are very popular.   Because it operates at rates as high as 1800 lines per minute, the volume of written material from a computer is large. Typewriters are used mostly for running the computer or trouble-shooting it.

With special-purpose computers conversion equipment for analog-to-digital or digital-to-analog is important.   Conversions of dc voltage or ac voltage and shaft position are very popular and make it possible to use the computer to control operations in such systems as aircraft, rocket, manufacturing plant, and others.

PROBLEMS

__1.__ Use the punched card code table (Table 12–1) and code in Figure 12–3 to read the card in Figure 12–41.

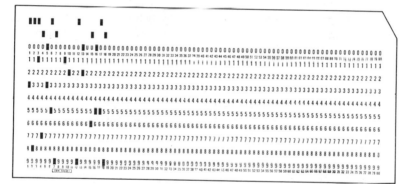

Figure 12–41.   Punched card for Problem 1.

__2.__ Use the five-level tape code shown in Figure 12–7 to read the punched tape in Figure 12–42.

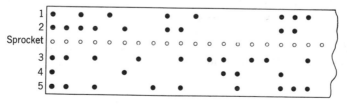

Figure 12–42.   Paper tape for Problem 2.

314   *Computer Units*

3. Use the eight-channel ASCII code shown in Chapter 4 to read the magnetic tape in Figure 12–43.

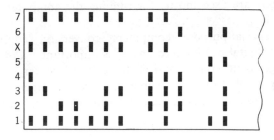

Figure 12–43.   ASCII code message for Problem 3.

4. A magnetic disk has 100 tracks of 16, 384 bits per track on seven disks.   What is the total storage capacity of the disk pack?   (Remember that both sides of a disk are used.)

5. A high-speed printer using a character belt printer has four sets of characters around the belt.   If the belt is driven at 100 revolutions per second, what is the approximate number of lines per minute that may be printed?

6. What is the maximum conversion time of an A/D converter using a clock rate of 512 kcps and a twelve-stage counter.

7. A dc voltage-to-digital converter using a ladder network has a reference voltage of 20 volts.   What resolution can be obtained if a twelve-stage binary counter is used.

8. How many counter stages are needed to get a resolution of 1 mv using a reference voltage of 10 volts.   What clock rate is needed to obtain around 100 solutions per second?

9. (a) Draw the circuit diagram of a four-stage ladder network using 2-kohm and 4-kohm resistors.

(b) Show the same network for an input of 1 0 1 1 (written with least significant digit on right).   Use 12 volts to represent the 1 state and 0 volts for the 0 state.

(c) Calculate the output voltage for this condition by circuit analysis.

(d) Compare the answer in (c) with that of the digital count (1 0 1 1 out of 1 0 0 0 0 counts).

10. Repeat problem 9 for a six-stage ladder network for an input of 1 0 1 0 1 1 and reference voltage of 6.4 volts.

Answers to selected problems

CHAPTER 3

1. (a) 55   (b) 56   (c) 21   (d) 42   (e) 126

2. (a) 11001   (b) 1000011   (c) 1100011
(d) 10000111   (e) 100010100

3. (a) 0.625   (b) 0.75   (c) 0.125   (d) 0.375   (e) 0.71825

4. (a) 0.111   (b) 0.0001011111 . . .   (c) 0.01010001 . . .
(d) 0.10001   (e) 0.0111

5. (a) $(37)_{10}$ (b) $(77)_8$ (c) $(175.375)_{10}$ (d) $(167)_8$ (e) $(1161.625)_8$

6. (a) $(155)_2$ (b) $(011111010)_2$ (c) $(56.7)_8$
(d) $(010111101011)_2$ (e) $(010101.101111)_2$

7. (a) $(1000001)_2$ (b) $(1000110000)_2$ (c) $(410)_8$
(d) $(4217)_8$ (e) $(1001001)_2$

8. (a) $(1011)_2$ (b) $(2611)_8$ (c) $(246)_8$
(d) $(10011110)_2$ (e) $(00110100101)_2$

9. (a) $(100001)_2$ (b) $(55717)_8$ (c) $(10100010)_2$
(d) $(1010)_2$ (e) $(30)_8$

CHAPTER 4

1. 0010   0101   0111   0011
3. 0011   1001   0010   1000   0111
4. 0101   1010   0100   1011
5. 10 00010   01 00100   10 00001   10 10000
6. 10 10000   10 01000   10 00001

7. 1011011011
8. 100100110
9. 0011 0   0101 0   0111 1   0010 1
10. 0101 1   1000 0   1100 1   1011 0
11. 01010010   01010111
12. 10100001   01001011   10100010   01011101   10100011

CHAPTER 5

1. A
3. V + UW
4. B
9. U′Y + V′Y′

CHAPTER 6

3. (1) For A = 1, B = 0, D = 1,   output is 11.3 volts.
     (2) For A = 1, B = 0, D = 0,   output is 0 volts.
     (3) For A = 1, B = 1, D = 0,   output is 8 volts.
     (4) For A = 1, B = 1, D = 1,   output is +11.3 volts.

6. Circuit $\beta = 39$ which is greater than h_{FE} of 20.   The transistor will not saturate at full load.

7. $(V_{BE})_{\text{off}} = -1.72$ volts

CHAPTER 7

6. $f = 1.52$ Mcps

CHAPTER 10

1. (a) 00011011   (b) 11011011
2. (a) 001001000   (b) 111000111
3. (a) 0100110   (b) 0001010
4. (a) 1001011   (b) 1111100

5. (a) 0001010   (b) 0101001

6. (a) 11001101   (b) 11110011

7. 11011

8. 10000010

9. 1010

10. 10

CHAPTER 11

1. 6 stages for X (row address)
6 stages for Y (column address)

2. Four and five stages for X and Y in either order, twenty stages for Z

3. Ten stages for Z, five and six stages for X and Y in either order

4. (a) 1.67 msec
(b) 307,200 bits/second
(c) 3.25 μsec

5. 2.5 msec

6. (a) 409,600 bits/second
(b) 409,600 bits/second

CHAPTER 12

1. CHAPTER 12 IS OVER

2. PAPER TAPE NO. 26

3. MESSAGE NO. 97

4. 22,917,600 bits

5. Approximately 400 lines per minute

6. 8 msec

7. Approximately 5 mv

8. 1 Mcps

9. (c) 8.25 volts   (d) 8.25 volts

10. (c) 4.3 volts   (d) 4.3 volts

Index